THE TREASURES AND
PLEASURES OF CHINA

Books & CD-ROMs by Drs. Ron and Caryl Krannich

101 Dynamite Answers to Interview Questions
101 Secrets of Highly Effective Speakers
201 Dynamite Job Search Letters
Best Jobs for the 21st Century
Change Your Job, Change Your Life
The Complete Guide to International Jobs and Careers
The Complete Guide to Public Employment
The Directory of Federal Jobs and Employers
Discover the Best Jobs for You!
Dynamite Cover Letters
Dynamite Networking for Dynamite Jobs
Dynamite Resumes
Dynamite Salary Negotiations
Dynamite Tele-Search
The Educator's Guide to Alternative Jobs and Careers
Find a Federal Job Fast!
From Air Force Blue to Corporate Gray
From Army Green to Corporate Gray
From Navy Blue to Corporate Gray
Get a Raise in Seven Days
High Impact Resumes and Letters
International Jobs Directory
Interview for Success
Job-Power Source CD-ROM
Jobs and Careers With Nonprofit Organizations
Jobs for People Who Love Travel
Mayors and Managers
Moving Out of Education
Moving Out of Government
The Politics of Family Planning Policy
Re-Careering in Turbulent Times
Resumes & Job Search Letters for Transitioning Military Personnel
Shopping and Traveling in Exotic Asia
Shopping in Exotic Places
Shopping the Exotic South Pacific
Treasures and Pleasures of Australia
Treasures and Pleasures of China
Treasures and Pleasures of Hong Kong
Treasures and Pleasures of India
Treasures and Pleasures of Indonesia
Treasures and Pleasures of Italy
Treasures and Pleasures of Paris and the French Riviera
Treasures and Pleasures of Singapore and Malaysia
Treasures and Pleasures of Thailand
Ultimate Job Source CD-ROM

IMPACT GUIDES

THE TREASURES
AND PLEASURES OF

China

BEST OF THE BEST

RON AND CARYL KRANNICH, PH.DS

IMPACT PUBLICATIONS
MANASSAS PARK, VA

THE TREASURES AND PLEASURES OF CHINA: BEST OF THE BEST

Library of Congress Cataloging-in-Publication Data

Krannich, Ronald L.
    The treasures and pleasures of China: best of the best / Ronald L. Krannich, Caryl Rae Krannich.
        p. cm.—(Impact guides)
    Includes bibliographical references and index.
    ISBN 1-57023-077-3 (alk. paper)
    I. Shopping—China—Guidebooks. 2. China—Guidebooks. I. Krannich, Caryl Rae. II. Title.

TX337.C6K73   1998
380.1'45'0002551—dc21   98-22829
                                                         CIP

For information on distribution or quantity discount rates, call (703/361-7300), fax (703/335-9486), e-mail (*china@impactpub-lications.com*) or write to: Sales Department, Impact Publications, 9104-N Manassas Drive, Manassas Park, VA 20111-5211. Distributed to the trade by National Book Network, 15200 NBN Way, Blue Ridge Summit, PA 17214, Tel. 1-800-462-6420.

Contents

PART III
The China Connections

Liabilities and Warranties

While the authors have attempted to provide accurate and up-to-date information in this book, please be advised that names, addresses, and phone numbers do change and shops, restaurants, and hotels do move, go out of business, or change ownership and management. Such changes are a constant fact of life in China. We regret any inconvenience such changes may cause to your travel plans.

Inclusion of shops, restaurants, hotels, and other hospitality providers in this book in no way implies guarantees nor endorsements by either the authors or publisher. The information and recommendations appearing in this book are provided solely for your reference. The honesty and reliability of shops is best ensured by **you**—always ask the right questions and request proper receipts and documents. Chapters 6 and 7 provide useful tips on how to best do this in China and especially in Beijing.

The Treasures and Pleasures of China provides numerous tips on how you can best experience a trouble-free adventure. As in any unfamiliar place or situation, or regardless of how trusting strangers may appear, the watch-words are always the same—*"watch your wallet!"* If it's too good to be true, it probably is. Any *"unbelievable deals"* should be treated as such. In China, as well as in Hong Kong and Macau, there simply is no such thing as a free lunch. Everything has a cost.

Preface

E xotic China offers wonderful treasures and pleasures for those who know what to look for, where to go, and how to best enjoy this fascinating country. Since first visiting China 15 years ago, we've witnessed the virtual transformation of its rather drab and gloomy cities into colorful and bustling places in the midst of rapid economic development driven by China's increased participation in the global economy. Today these cities are quickly shedding their socialist past as they prepare to enter the 21st century with a renewed sense of entrepreneurism and power. Today's rapidly developing China comes complete with new high-rise commercial buildings, five-star hotels, air conditioned shopping centers, international restaurants, and Western entertainment venues.

The economic changes in China during the past 10 years have been nothing short of revolutionary. They are based in part on a post-Mao vision of what China can and should be—the world's largest and greatest economy. As the old gives way to the new, traveling in China also has become more convenient and comfortable. Gone are the days when all visitors were herded into shoddy tours arranged by the national tourist authority. Today the tourism industry has become very entrepreneurial, offering visitors many different choices from independent travel to customized and group tours. However, because of language barriers, you are well advised to use local travel services that can make a significant difference between truly enjoying or being disappointed with your China venture.

If you try to do China completely on your own, you may find yourself frustrated in handling the basics of traveling in China.

The chapters that follow represent a particular perspective on travel to China. We purposefully decided to write more than just another travel guide with a few pages on shopping. While other shopping books primarily focus on the "whats" and "wheres" of shopping, we saw a need to also explain the "how-tos" of shopping in China. Such a book would both educate and guide you through China's slippery shopping maze as well as put you in contact with the best of the best in accommodations, restaurants, and sightseeing. Accordingly, this book focuses primarily on the shopping **process** as well as provides the necessary details for making excellent shopping **choices** in specific shopping areas, arcades, centers, department stores, markets, and shops.

Rather than just describe the "what" and "where" of travel and shopping, we include the critical "how"—what to do before you depart on your trip and when you are in China. We believe you are best served with a book which leads to both **understanding and action**. Therefore, you'll find little in these pages about the history, culture, economics, and politics of China; these topics are covered well in other types of books. Instead, we focus on the whole shopping process in reference to China's major shopping strengths.

The perspective we develop throughout this book is based on our belief that traveling should be more than just another adventure in eating, sleeping, sightseeing, and taking pictures of unfamiliar places. Whenever possible, we attempt to bring to life the fact that China has real people and interesting products that you, the visitor, will find exciting. This is a country of talented designers, craftspeople, traders, and entrepreneurs who offer you some wonderful opportunities to participate in their society through their shopping process. When you leave China, you will take with you not only some unique experiences and memories but also quality products that you will certainly appreciate for years to come.

Our focus on **the shopping process** is important for several reasons. The most important one is the fact that few non-Asians are prepared for Asian shopping cultures. Shops may be filled with familiar looking goods, but when there are no price tags on items, the process of acquiring them can be difficult if you do not understand such basic processes as bargaining, communicating, and shipping. What, for example, should you do when you find a lovely painting, antique, or piece of jewelry but no price tag is displayed? How do you know you are paying a "fair" price? More important, how do you know you are getting exactly what you bargained for in terms of quality and authenticity? And if you buy large items, how will you get them back home? These "how" questions go beyond the basic "what" and "where" of shopping to ensure that you have a successful and rewarding trip to China.

We have not hesitated to make qualitative judgments about the best of the best in China. If we just presented you with shopping and traveling information, we would do you a disservice by not sharing our discoveries, both good and bad. While we know that our judgments may not be valid for everyone, we offer them as **reference points** from which you can make your own decisions. Our major emphasis is on quality shopping, accommodations, dining, and sightseeing, and in that order. We look for shops which offer excellent quality and styles. If you share our concern for quality shopping, as well as fine restaurants and hotels, you will find many of our recommendations useful to your China adventure.

Buying items of quality does not mean you must spend a great deal of money on shopping. It means that you have taste, you are selective, you buy what fits into your wardrobe and home. If you shop in the right places, you will find quality products. If you understand the shopping process, you will get good value for your money. Shopping for quality may not be cheap but neither need it be expensive. But most important, shopping for quality in China is fun and it results in lovely items which can be enjoyed for years to come!

Throughout this book we have included "tried and tested" shopping information. We make judgments based upon our experience—not on judgments or sales pitches from others. Our research was quite simple: we did a great deal of shopping and we looked for quality products. We acquired some fabulous items, and gained valuable knowledge in the process. However, we could not make purchases in every shop nor do we have any guarantee that your experiences will be the same as ours. Shops close, ownership or management changes, and the shop you visit may not be the same as the one we shopped. So use this information as a starting point, but ask questions and make your own judgments before you buy.

We wish to thank the National Tourism Administration and the many provincial and municipal tourist offices for their hospitality during our stay in China. They are justly proud and enthusiastic about the New China and what it has to offer visitors who still know so little about their country. We also want to thank the many public relations managers and concierges who shared their insights into travel and shopping in China as well as Northwest Airlines who took us safely to and from China in record time and with exceptional service and comfort.

We wish you well with your China adventure. The book is designed to be used prior to and during your stay in China. If you **plan** your journey according to the first five chapters, **handle the shopping process** according to the next two chapters, and **navigate** the streets and waterways of China based on the six destination chapters, you should have a marvelous time. You'll discover some exciting places, acquire some choice items, and return home with fond memories. If you put this book to use, it will become your passport to the unique treasures and pleasures of China!

Ron and Caryl Krannich

THE TREASURES AND
PLEASURES OF CHINA

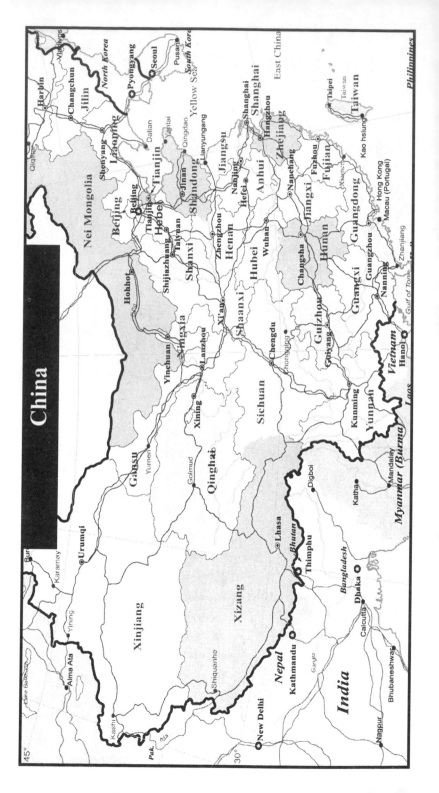

Welcome to
Surprising China

Welcome to the treasures and pleasures of fabulous China! You're in for a real treat as you travel the world's largest country of over a billion people. Boasting a 6,000 year old history, China is a state of mind, a people sharing a distinct culture with an ancient and tumultuous past. It's people and history everywhere. Forget all the stereotypes and negative stories about this place, its people, and its politics. They probably aren't accurate. And even if they are, they won't give you much currency in navigating China and enjoying its many treasures and pleasures. As you will quickly discover, it's best to be open-minded about this place.

If this is your first trip to China, you'll be experiencing the "New China" which boasts a rapidly developing economy offering numerous shopping treasures and travel pleasures. If you've been here before—perhaps 10 or 15 years ago—you're in for a real shock. You probably won't recognize this place, especially its new high-rise urban landscapes, bustling streets, grand hotels, and in-your-face shopping culture. That's okay because the New China has a lot more to offer visitors these days. It actually has a tourist infrastructure that works relatively well, despite occasional glitches. And if you return in another five years, expect to encounter another dramatically transformed China that may be equally difficult to recognize.

Welcome to one of the world's grandest theaters, a place where the stage, scenery, and parts are always changing. It's an exotic and unpredictable place that will forever impress you with its many interesting and talented people.

DISCOVER THE NEW CHINA

While this is an ancient, proud, and powerful country symbolized by the Great Wall, the terracotta soldiers of Xi'an, the Forbidden City, Summer Palace, and Tiananmen Square, it's also a country of 1.2 billion people. That's big, actually the biggest, by any standard. Only recently opened to the outside world, China's rapidly developing middle-class of cash-flush urban residents have quickly discovered the joys of consumerism and the pleasures of shopping. They fuel a newly emerging consumer-driven economy.

China has changed dramatically since Deng Xiaoping initiated radical economic reforms in the late 1970s that fundamentally moved this huge country towards a Chinese form of capitalism termed *"socialism with Chinese characteristics,"* or perhaps more accurately, *"communism with a capitalist face."* At least in the places you'll visit with us, this hybrid form of capitalism/communism/socialism has literally meant the near death of doctrinaire communism and the complete transformation of many major cities. New high-rise office buildings, shopping complexes, hotels, and expressways compete with each other in redefining the ever-changing chaotic urban landscapes of the rapidly developing cities of Beijing, Shanghai, Guangzhou, and Shenzhen. Nowhere is this so dramatic as in Shanghai which has pretensions of becoming the new Hong Kong of Greater China. Here you'll discover a bustling city seemingly preoccupied with making money, shopping, and pursuing the good life associated with spending money. Even some of the traditional evils of capitalism and Old China, such as scams and rip-offs, are now part of this new *"socialism with Chinese characteristics"* landscape. This is not what you might expect to see and experience in a stereotyped China of the 1970s and 1980s.

You can easily get lost in today's China if you approach it like the Old China. Armed with this book, we'll show you how to find your way around major parts of this New China, and avoid many of its old communist habits and renewed capitalist evils, as you acquire its unique treasures and experience its many pleasures. We expect you to have a wonderful time navigating China's many cities, streets, and waterways and acquiring its many unique treasures.

A TRIP WELL WORTH TAKING

We and many others have been somewhat ambivalent about traveling to China, a kind of love-hate relationship we sometimes quickly develop with a country we know so little about and find somewhat unsettling. Despite the glossy travel brochures touting a fabulous travel destination, for many people travel to China appears problematic, even though it is one of the best travel values found anywhere in the world; indeed, it remains a relatively inexpensive destination. This is still a huge and unpredictable country, one filled with contradictions, distortions, pride, and achievements. It's most noted in this century for its Long March, Cultural Revolution, Great Leap Forward, 1989 Tiananmen Square incident, and other assorted, and sometimes sordid, affairs. Just when you think you know it, you discover you really don't. It's still an exotic place that retains a certain aura of mystery. It's a place not to be either dismissed or missed.

❑ If you've visited China 10 or 15 years ago, chances are you won't recognize the place.

❑ China's hybrid form of capitalism has literally meant the near complete transformation of many major cities.

❑ Despite the glossy brochures and hype, this is still a huge country of great unpredictability, contradictions, distortions, pride, and achievements.

❑ Most of China's cities are frankly ugly, chaotic, congested, and heavily polluted, a kind of "East meets West" urban nightmare overlaid with some Third World charm and beauty.

❑ This is a country of enormous beauty, talent, and energy.

Known for being big, crowded, drab, chauvinistic, overwhelming, uncomfortable, polluted, and difficult to get around in, China always appealed to us more as a forbidden challenge than an object of great desire and impending fun. It has many faces, none which are completely satisfying. Like so many other countries transformed by communism, China experienced a great deal of social and economic upheaval and leveling along with international isolationism which are clearly reflected in its urban architecture and chauvinistic personality. Obsessed with being in control and projecting an image of greatness, while shackled with an exuberant yet unpredictable Third World economy, China exudes numerous contradictions which make it such an intriguing place to visit. Except for some of its well-preserved temples, palaces, gardens, monuments, and archeological sites and a few scenic spots, this is not an exceptionally attractive nor charming place to visit if you are looking for the treasures and pleasures of travel normally associated with Europe or North America. Most of China's cities are frankly ugly, chaotic, congested, and heavily polluted, a kind of "East meets West" urban nightmare overlaid with some Third World charm and beauty. Except for a few places, the much praised Chinese cuisine remains somewhat overrated and hard to find within China. Its people are interesting and often friendly but many are naive about the outside world. Except for noisy, smiling, friendly, and unruly children (what the locals call the *"spoiled little empresses and emperors"* produced under China's one-child family policy), the people often lack the friendliness, spontaneity, and charm readily found amongst their neighbors in Southeast Asia. Young people, however, tend to be more westernized and out-going.

Yet, the allure of a big, historical, mystical, exotic, and ever surprising China, and the promise of experiencing a new China-in-the-making, make this place very attractive and appealing to today's travelers in search of China's many treasures and pleasures. Despite one's past ambivalence, China is well worth visiting. And now is the time to go. After all, this is a very important country historically, the world's longest continuous civilization dating back more than 6,000 years. It's the country of the Great Wall, the Ming Tombs, the Forbidden City, the Summer Palace, the Silk Road, the terracotta soldiers of Xi'an, and mysterious, somewhat forbidden, Tibet—unforgettable sites reflecting the greatness of Chinese civilization. From the endangered Three Gorges of the Yangtze River to the colorful and exotic cultural performances in Beijing, Xi'an, and Shenzhen, this is a country of enormous beauty, talent, energy, and promise. It's also the country of several internationally important cities such as Beijing, Shanghai, and Guangzhou which house some great museums, especially the new world-class Shanghai Museum, and shopping.

Yes, shopping. China's new-found wealth coupled with tremendous over-production have contributed to a new shopping culture complete with modern escalator-laced air-conditioned shopping malls and fast food restaurants. While not exactly a shopper's paradise, China has a great deal to offer on the shopping front, from exotic street markets to chic boutiques. Indeed, you can even *"shop 'til you drop"* in Beijing and Shanghai and to a lesser extent in our other cities.

Whatever you do, decide to visit China soon. It's a country in great transition, one that will enter the 21st century with the world's largest population boasting also to have the world's largest economy. How "big" it becomes is anyone's guess. There's lots of hype, hope, and naivete here that can easily skew one's perspective. The symbols of the New China are cement, the construction crane, shoppers, and traffic. At least in terms of bricks-and-mortar building construction, the old is giving way to the new at a frantic pace as businesses take center stage in developing China's checkered Third World economy. If you want to experience this country's greatest transformation as it enters the 21st century with renewed pride and power, do so now. You won't be disappointed. China is such a large and diverse country that you may well have difficulty deciding where to go and what to do! But at least you should go soon.

TRAVELING IN TWO CHINAS

Yes, forget those stories you've heard about the Old China (pre-1994). For both the new and seasoned traveler, China's travel amenities have improved dramatically within the past few years stimulated by frenzied business investment activities. Even the service ethic is starting to take hold in a few hotels managed by major international hotel chains. This is now a country offering world-class hotels, international cuisine, increasingly convenient transportation, and a great variety of in-bound tour services. With the opening of China's economy to joint ventures—primarily driven by the wealth and investment initiatives of Overseas Chinese from Hong Kong, Taiwan, and Singapore—and greater international trade, China has had to accept new standards associated with international travel. And the results are a two-tiered hospitality industry that puts two different faces on travel in China.

❑ The symbols of the new China are cement, the construction crane, shoppers, and traffic.

❑ China has a two-tiered hospitality industry that puts two different faces on its travel industry—some service versus shoddy, lethargic service.

❑ The best hotels, restaurants, shopping, and service are found in the four- and five-star joint venture properties.

❑ Except in some joint venture hotels and restaurants managed by major international companies, the service ethic is nearly absent in China. Expect poor service in most Chinese establishments.

You'll need to make important travel choices here—whether you want to experience "China A" or "China B." "China A" consists of new four- and five-star joint venture hotels under management contracts with major international hotel companies (Shangri-La, Ritz-Carlton, Hyatt, Westin, Sheraton, Hilton, Holiday-Inn, Kempinski). The operation of such hotels has resulted in a whole new standard of accommodations, restaurants, and service. The difference in amenities and service between these hotels and the local one-, two-, and three-star Chinese hotels ("China B") is often the difference between night and day. Unless you want a cultural experience—complete with sub-standard and lethargic service—you are well advised to stay in the four- and five-star joint venture properties of "China A" where you will also find the best restaurants, and shopping. You'll even discover a budding service ethic, encouraged by an embryonic tipping culture, in these places!

As one might expect, "China A" is much more expensive than "China B." If you are on a shoestring budget, you can do China on the cheap by traveling in "China B." However, you'll basically get what you pay for—not much and potentially several headaches if you pay little. Don't expect much service; indeed, you'll quickly discover what service used to be like in the hospitality industry by the near total lack of service in China B! Nowhere else can you see such a direct relationship between travel value and costs.

ENCOUNTER A RICH HISTORY

Many Westerners have difficulty relating to China because of its unfamiliar history. Primarily versed in European history—with its Roman and Christian traditions yielding numerous stone ruins, castles, and cathedrals—these visitors suddenly encounter a very different history with a very different cast of characters and monuments to the past.

Representing the world's longest continuous civilization, Chinese history spans a period of more than 7,000 years. It's most noted for its many great monuments, such as the Great Wall, Ming Tombs, and the 6,000+ terracotta soldiers of Xi'an, which testify to the fact that China's history has often been on a grand and labor intensive scale dominated by major dynasties and numerous despotic rulers.

Wherever you go and whatever you do in China, chances are you will encounter some aspect of Chinese history. When the Chinese refer to their various historical periods, they do so in reference to specific dynastic periods. Here's a quick chronology of who ruled when and where during the past 4,000+ years:

Dynasties/Republics	Period	Capital
Xia Dynasty	21st-16th century BC	Yuncheng of Shanxi
Shang Dynasty	16th c. - 1066 BC	Erlitou, Zhengzhou & Anyang in Henan
Zhou Dynasty		
Western Zhou	1066-771 BC	Xian
Eastern Zhou	770-256 BC	
Luoyang		
Spring & Autumn Period	770-476 BC	
Warring States Period	476-221 BC	
Qin Dynasty	221-207 BC	Xianyang

Han Dynasty		
Western Han	206 BC-24 AD	Xian
Eastern Han	25-220 AD	Luoyang
Three Kingdoms Period		
Wei	220-265 AD	Xuchang
Shu Han	221-263 AD	Chengdu
Wu	222-280 AD	Nanjing
Jin Dynasty		
Western Jin	265-316 AD	Luoyang
Eastern Jin	317-420 AD	Nanjing
Southern Dynasties		
Song	420-479 AD	Nanjing
Qi	479-502 AD	Nanjing
Liang	502-557 AD	Nanjing
Chen	557-589 AD	Nanjing
Northern Dynasties		
Northern Wei	386-534 AD	Datong
Eastern Wei	534-550 AD	Linzhang of Hebei
Northern Qi	550-577 AD	Linzhang
Western Wei	535-556 AD	Xian
Northern Zhou	557-581 AD	Xian
Sui Dynasty	581-618 AD	Xian
Tang Dynasty	618-907 AD	Xian
Five Dynasties		
Later Liang	907-923 AD	Kaifeng
Later Tiang	923-936 AD	Luoyang
Later Jin	936-946 AD	Kaifeng
Later Han	947-950 AD	Kaifeng
Later Zhou	951-960 AD	Kaifeng
Song Dynasty		
Northern Song	960-1127 AD	Kaifeng
Southern Song	1127-1279 AD	Hangzhou
Liao Dynasty	916-1125AD	
Western Xia Dynasty	1038-1227 AD	
Jin Dynasty	1115-1234 AD	Beijing
Yuan Dynasty	1271-1368 AD	Beijing
Ming Dynasty	1368-1644 AD	Nanjing, Beijing
Qing Dynasty	1644-1911 AD	Shenyang, Beijing
Republic of China	1912-1949 AD	Beijing, Nanjing
People's Republic of China	1949-present	Beijing

You'll especially want to refer to this historical chronology if you plan to shop for Chinese antiques. You may be surprised how old you will be told an antique piece may be when, in fact, it was made during the Ping Dynasty, i.e., the PRC rule of Deng Xiaoping (1979-1996)!

MEET A DIVERSE PEOPLE

The Chinese are a diverse mixture of peoples and cultures. The Chinese consist of the dominant ethnic Han Chinese (93.3% of the total population) and 56 ethnic minorities. Most of the minorities live in the outer regions of West and Southwest China. They have historically posed numerous challenges to central authority. They also represent many different linguistic and cultural traditions. Even amongst the Han Chinese, significant cultural differences exist between the northern and southern Chinese. Northerners, especially those found in and around Beijing, tend to be more conservative and compliant to authority. Being politically dominant, northerners also like to exercise authority over southerners whom they view as somewhat radical, undisciplined, and entrepreneurial; they are potentially trouble-makers who occasionally need to be reigned in by Beijing. Not surprisingly, most Chinese entrepreneurs tend to be southerners from Shanghai, Guangzhou, and Hong Kong. In fact, much of China's most recent economic success has been due to the role of entrepreneurial southern Chinese who maintain vast networks of business relationships with Overseas Chinese who also tend to be southern Chinese. For now, Beijing has allowed these southerners to develop the Chinese economy under their watchful eyes.

In addition to millions of domestic tourists, over 50 million people visit China each year. Nearly 80 percent of these visitors are Overseas Chinese who return to visit relatives and engage in commerce.

❑ The Chinese consist of the dominant ethnic Han Chinese (93.3%) and 56 ethnic minorities.

❑ China's most recent economic success has been largely due to entrepreneurial southern Chinese who maintain vast networks of business relationships with Overseas Chinese who also tend to be southern Chinese.

❑ Northerners tend to be more conservative and compliant to authority. They also like to exercise authority over southerners.

❑ Tremendous distortions exist throughout the much hyped Chinese economy that has been financed primarily by Overseas Chinese monies.

THE NEW ECONOMY

During the past 20 years the Chinese economy has undergone a dramatic transformation that is evident everywhere. Bloated and inefficient state-owned enterprises have gradually given way to a diverse mixture of private sector participants—large foreign firms, local entrepreneurs, and street vendors. Today approximately 25 percent of the Chinese economy is in private hands. The collapse of the work unit, or *danwei*, that used to control people's lives via the workplace—housing, travel, and careers—has had a dramatic impact on how people orient themselves to the economy. The emerging private sector, driven by a new entrepreneurism, is expected to perform many of the former *danwei* functions, especially absorbing the more than 25 million who are looking for work in China's urban areas.

With continuing encouragement from the government, from Beijing to local governments, the private sector share of the economy should continue to expand in the coming decade. Today, the low-tech and low-wage village and township enterprises that contributed to China's remarkable economic growth during the past 15 years are being surpassed by a new urban entrepreneurism as more and more local residents start up their own businesses with the vision of joining China's new entrepreneurial elite. Indeed, by January 1998, 28.5 million people were registered as self-employed workers; 960,000 private enterprises employing 39 million people were registered. This represented one-third the number of state-owned enterprises. With the government's blessing, this budding private sector should continue to expand dramatically in the coming decade. It should create another New China that will look very different from today's New China.

ENCOUNTER SURPRISING COMMUNITIES

Our journey through China takes us into several surprising communities that have in recent years put on new faces for the outside world. Common to most of these cities is an ongoing building boom that is dramatically transforming the urban landscapes of each city. However, be careful how you interpret such frenzied construction activity. Despite Communist China's recent romance with capitalism, the building boom does not necessarily follow the capitalistic principles of supply and demand nor does it reflect an underlying healthy and booming economy nor a happy local population. On the contrary, poverty remains widespread throughout China, unemployment runs between 20 and 30 percent in many cities, and crowded commercial streets tend to have more window shoppers than spending shoppers. China may well be sitting on a classic boom and bust economy precipitated by an over-heated speculative real estate market.

Tremendous distortions exist throughout the much hyped Chinese economy that has been financed primarily by Overseas Chinese investment monies and bank loans funneled through the hands of powerful bureaucrats and relatives of high-ranking Chinese officials. Real estate speculation driven by an over-supply of investment capital has resulted in a tremendous glut of luxury office buildings, retail stores, shopping centers, and apartments. Over-estimating the size and purchasing power of

China's internal market, Overseas Chinese and foreign investors have over-invested in China's real estate market. The cities we visit have numerous physical monuments, especially luxurious shopping complexes, to this seemingly booming yet highly distorted economy.

Beijing, a city of over 10 million, is China's political and cultural center. A somewhat dry, dusty, and dreary city with pockets of grandeur expressing the wealth and power of recent Chinese dynasties and imperial courts, Beijing is all about the power of politics, government, and culture and the new consumerism. It offers an interesting mixture of the old and new. Except for a few major cultural and architectural attractions, such as the Forbidden City (Imperial Palace) and the Temple of Heaven, this is not a particularly attractive city for most visitors. Several major attractions tend to be found within a two to three hour drive of the city—Great Wall, Ming Tombs, and Summer Palace. But like other major cities in China, Beijing is undergoing a major transformation as old buildings are torn down to make way for new commercial buildings, hotels, and expressways. The traditional *hutongs* with their gates, temples, and neighborhoods tied together with mazes of alleys are gradually being replaced with steel and concrete buildings as Beijing continues to modernize. One of the real treats in Beijing is its shopping. This is a city of numerous markets, department stores, and shops offering a wide variety of arts, crafts, antiques, furniture, clothes, accessories, and jewelry. You can easily spend three days shopping this city.

Shanghai is China's largest and most important city for international trade and commerce. An energetic, bustling, and congested city of 12 million people, Shanghai is once again regaining its reputation as one of Asia's most important cities. This is China's main port and its major industrial center. Destined to rival Hong Kong as the country's major financial and trade city, Shanghai has undergone a dramatic physical transformation within the past few years. Indeed, for many visitors and residents alike, Shanghai reinvents itself every year with new high rise commercial buildings, hotels, and expressways. Shanghai's new sister city, the Pudong Economic Development Zone on the east side of the Huangpai River and opposite the famous Bund and anchored with the towering symbol of this city, the Oriental Pearl Broadcasting and TV Tower, epitomizes the new Shanghai, and the new China and Chinese pride. This is a city with a very ambitious future in mind, an extremely entrepreneurial city bent on expanding its growing wealth at a pace to eventually challenge Hong Kong's dominance in finance, trade, and commerce. It also may be a troubled city due to its tremendous overbuilding in the past few years. In fact, Shanghai is now building the world's tallest building, the 94-story, 1509-foot World Financial Center, while one-third of its existing office space remains vacant! Shanghai also is China's most famous shopping center for locals, the closest thing to a shopper's paradise. Department stores and shops offer the latest in fashionable clothing and accessories, electronics, and consumer goods as thousands of people jam the streets in pursuit of one of Shanghai's favorite past times— shopping. In Shanghai they do more than just window shop. They are into real shopping.

Xi'an, located 642 miles southwest of Beijing, is the capital of Shaanxi Province. It's an imposing and bustling ancient walled city most recently noted for its nearby archeological site—a fabulous collection of 6,000+ life-size ancient terracotta warriors and horses standing in battle formation. Most are still partially buried and undergoing reconstruction. Built as part of Emperor Qin Shihuang's Mausoleum in the third century BC, this awesome army of warriors and horses is one of the world's great archeological treasures. It's a powerful experience that brings to life an important period in Chinese history. Were it not for this terracotta army, Xi'an would see few of the many thousands of visitors who sojourn here each year to get a glimpse of some truly unusual archeological excavations. While Xi'an has few other attractions and limited shopping opportunities to justify a visit of more than one or two days, you will not be disappointed with this city; indeed, it may well be one of the highlights of your China adventure. For history buffs, Xi'an is one of China's great historical sites, the capital of 11 dynasties, including the Tang, and a major gateway to the famous Silk Road that more than 2,000 years ago connected China with Persia, Rome, and the world beyond. It has long served as an important economic and cultural crossroads between East and West.

❑ Beijing is China's political and cultural center. It's a city of numerous markets, department stores, and shops offering a wide variety of arts, crafts, antiques, furniture, clothes, accessories, and jewelry.

❑ Xi'an has long served as an important economic and cultural crossroads between East and West.

❑ Shanghai is regaining its reputation as one of Asia's most important and entrepreneurial cities. Outside of Hong Kong, this is China's major shopping center.

❑ Guangzhou remains one of China's most important industrial and trade centers. It offers good museums, shopping, and food.

❑ Shenzhen is where big bucks meet cheap labor in an economy primarily oriented toward exports abroad. But go to nearby OCT for education and entertainment.

❑ The Yangtze River experience includes the famous cities of Chongqing and Wuhan and the spectacular Three Gorges.

Guangzhou, also known as Canton, is one of China's major economic powerhouses and, until recently, the gateway city to southern China. Located in Southeast China north of the Pearl River Valley and within three hours driving distance from Hong Kong and Macau, this city also is the capital of the rapidly developing Guangdong Province and the Pearl River Delta. A city rich in economic and political history, because of its trade role vis-a-vis the outside world, and a city renowned for its beautiful flowers that bloom year-round, Guangzhou remains an important element in the overall development of southern China. While no longer China's major gateway city—a role it enjoyed for several decades but now superseded by direct international flights into Beijing, Shanghai, and even Xi'an—nonetheless, Guangzhou remains one of China's most important industrial and trading centers. The spring and autumn Guangzhou Trade Fairs continue to be Asia's most important trading events. A very busy, westernized, and working city primarily catering to the needs of businessmen, Guangzhou is not particularly noted for its beauty or tourist attractions. But it does offer good museums, shopping, and food, enough to justify a 2-3 day visit. It's a city in great transition.

Shenzhen, located adjacent to Hong Kong, is one of China's most interesting stories of how a newly planned city became an industrial giant in Asia. Until 1976 a sleepy town of nearly 20,000 people, Shenzhen today is a relatively new city of over 2 million inhabitants whose growth has been carefully planned and monitored in Beijing. This is where big bucks meet cheap labor in an economy primarily oriented toward exports abroad. One of China's most favored Special Economic Zones on the east coast, because of its close proximity to Hong Kong, Shenzhen has been literally built on Overseas Chinese and foreign investment monies. Numerous joint venture factories, producing everything from toys and electronics to footwear and garments, have located in and around this strategic city. Some outsiders consider this city to be an example of a well organized, high-tech "sweat shop" filled with dormitories of young factory workers who produce cheap electronics, toys, clothes, and footwear that find their way into the homes of millions of westerners. While Shenzhen is of little interest to tourists because of its industrial character, just three miles outside the city is another carefully planned settlement, the popular Overseas Chinese Town (OCT). This is where most tourists go for education and entertainment. OCT's population of 40,000 has hosted nearly 50 million visitors since 1989, 80 percent of whom are Overseas Chinese. This is China's Disneyland and Cultural Village all wrapped into one with three popular theme parks: Miniature of Splendid China, Folk Culture Villages, and Windows of the World. A fourth theme park, in collaboration with Disneyland, is on the drawing boards. If you have limited time in China, as well as extra time, be sure to visit the attractions at OCT. It may well become the highlight of your China adventure.

Yangtze River and its famous cities of Chongqing and Wuhan offer another exciting China adventure. Cruising China's largest river and experiencing its spectacular Three Gorges (Qutang, Wuxia, and Xiling) prior to the projected completion in 2009 of the world's largest and most controversial hydroelectric dam project (the gorges will be flooded, more than 1 million people will be displaced, and the environmental impact is expected to be tremendous) is a major highlight of any visit to China. You'll be witnessing the taming of a wild river along a picturesque route that will end forever in just a few years. You will see places that will soon disappear under the waters of the Yangtze. Start (or end) your adventure in the historically important city of Chongqing (previously known as Chungking, the World War II capital of Nationalist China), a surprisingly huge city located in the hills overlooking the Yangtze River. Discover its many artists and art galleries before boarding one of the many cruise ships that ply the muddy and heavily polluted waters of the river that eventually flow past Shanghai and into the sea. In three days you'll visit the beautiful gorges, stop in a few nondescript river towns, gawk at other cruise ships and working river boats, and eventually reach your destination, Wuhan, another historically important city made famous by Mao Zedong and the Long March and now noted for its steel mills and carpet factories.

Hong Kong is China's newest acquisition, a Special Administrative Zone (SAZ) returned to the People's Republic of China in rainy ceremonies on June 30, 1997 after nearly 100 years of British colonial rule. The world's most expensive and entrepreneurial city, and still a shopper's paradise, Hong Kong is in the process of being integrated into Greater China. While officially now part of China, this is a truly global community that looks and feels years apart from its Motherland. It's run by what used to be known as the Overseas Chinese who have bankrolled much of China's recent economic boom. Whatever you do, don't miss Hong Kong. It will give you a whole new perspective on China and the Chinese. We examine Hong Kong's major attractions in our separate volume, *The Treasures and Pleasures of Hong Kong: Best of the Best.*

SHOPPING SMART FOR TREASURES

Until recently, China's treasures were primarily found in its museums or presented as tourist attractions, such as the Great Wall, the Forbidden City, and the archeological sites in Xi'an—things you could see and perhaps touch, but not buy and take with you. But times are changing as more and more treasures appear in the urban markets, department stores, and shops in the form of arts, crafts, antiques, furniture, jewelry, clothes, and accessories. Today the treasures of China can be packed in your suitcase or shipped home with ease by air or sea. You'll have no problem finding lots of small inexpensive gift items and you'll discover many lovely collectibles approaching the status of fine art and antiques. If you love arts and crafts, you'll find a treasuretrove of unique items produced by talented artists and craftsmen who do exquisite handwork. China is especially well noted for its:

silk	furniture
clothes	antiques
paintings	pottery
embroidery	carpets
ceramics	carvings
porcelain	inkslabs
jewelry	tea
cloisonne	alcohol
lacquerware	traditional medicines

Within the arts and crafts, China also offers a great deal of tourist kitsch which you may or may not want to collect. While quality and prices tend to be good, you need to be a smart shopper who knows how to recognize quality and price accordingly.

China has a lot to offer international shoppers, with an overflow of goods available from traditional street markets to department stores and chic hotel shopping arcades. This is the New China where shopping is coming of age in major urban areas that have benefitted from the economics of joint ventures and local entrepreneurism. These places brim with goodies. Indeed, China has over-produced, from arts and crafts to apparel, much of what is offered for sale today. In fact, the over-supply problem is somewhat alarming for economists who report that China's factories produce 1 million men's shirts a day, but since most cannot be sold, they are placed in warehouses that already have stored more than 1.5 billion unsold shirts! As reported by the State Statistical Bureau in 1997, a similar situation is found with watches (10 million unsold), bicycles (20 million unsold), and autos and other motor vehicles (100,000 unsold). What this means for shoppers is that it's a buyer's market in many commodity areas. Street vendors, for example, offer lots of clothes and footwear at bargain basement prices.

China is a bargain hunter's paradise for many types of items. At the same time, outside the relatively trustworthy government operated Friendship Stores, China is a "buyer beware" country with many merchants engaged in some of the worst aspects of unregulated 19th century capitalism—misrepresentation of goods is common. And they do it so nicely, as if you were a long lost friend in need of special care. And special care you may well get as a clever merchant relieves you of your wealth! Contrary to what you may have heard about honesty and trustworthiness in this socialist paradise, *"socialism with Chinese characteristics"* also means you should trust no one when it comes to money transactions in China. If you don't know what you're doing and are too trusting of strangers who make claims of authenticity, you can easily get cheated in China. The shopper's watch-words in China are the same as in many other places of the world: *"If it's too good to be true, it probably is!"* Add to this these watch-words for shopping in the new China: *"Be wary of sales pitches by merchants."* So it's important that you really understand China's new shopping culture and how it may affect what you buy before you make any major purchases. If you don't, you may end up paying five to ten times more for what are ostensibly treasures but in fact are nothing more than recent copies.

- ❑ China is a bargain hunter's paradise for many types of items, which also have been over-produced.

- ❑ It's "buyer beware" when it comes to money transactions in China.

- ❑ The watch-words for shoppers are these: *"If it's too good to be true, it probably is!"* and *"Be wary of sales pitches by merchants."* You've got to be careful.

- ❑ Except for fabulous Hong Kong, great food and service are difficult to find in China.

SURPRISING PLEASURES

Try as it may, China is still a Third World country but one with a major difference: it has the world's longest continuous history. It also has the world's largest population attempting to shed its Third World past in favor of a First World economy with attendant work skills and ethics. The Chinese take great pride in their long history, and they remind you of it wherever you go. Despite nearly 50 years of Communist rule, a general socialist leveling of society, and a nonproductive work ethic, China still takes great pride in the monuments built during its feudal and rather decadent past. China's pleasures tend to center on its sightseeing which have a great deal of historical content. So if this is your first time to China, you will want to see the "basics," such as the Great Wall, the Forbidden City, the Summer Palace, the terracotta soldiers in Xi'an, and the Shanghai Museum. You also should take the unique Yangtze River Cruise where you will experience a combination of the old (Three Gorges) and the new (hydroelectric dam). And by all means treat yourself to an artistic and cultural feast by attending the cultural shows and performances in Beijing, Shanghai, Xi'an, and Shenzhen where you will witness some extremely talented performers and spectacular productions that truly rival the best of Disneyland and Las Vegas. If you enjoy evening entertainment in the form of bars, nightclubs, and discos, you'll have to go "light" on these in China; resign yourself to mainly doing karayoke bars and singing the "oldies but goodies" instead. Chinese opera and other cultural performances will have to "fill in" until you get to Hong Kong where such decadent pleasures are plentiful at night. However, this scene, too, is changing in Beijing, Shanghai, and Guangzhou as more and more Western forms of entertainment become available. In the meantime, take a couple of good books with you; they might make for some very satisfying evening entertainment on your own.

But don't expect to encounter other types of pleasures normally associated with international travel. In particular, great food or service is difficult to find outside the four- and five-star joint venture hotels. Despite what you've heard about Chinese food in general, China is not a gastronomic paradise. Fifty years of Communist rule has not been conducive to the development of the culinary arts normally associated with the kitchens of great restaurants patronized by upscale clientele. The great chefs long ago moved to Hong Kong or went off shore to restaurants in the great cities of other countries. In China you're likely to be presented with lots of food, but you probably won't eat it all and you'll have few memorable meals. When found, good food, service, and accommodations tend to be concentrated either in the four- and five-star joint venture hotels managed by international hoteliers or in China's new SAZ—Hong Kong. Really outstanding food, accommodations, and service are found in abundance in Hong Kong.

The hospitality industry in China has many years of hard

work ahead of itself to achieve the high international standards found in Hong Kong's hospitality industry. New management and work ethics are greatly needed before this can happen. In the meantime, China's tourist industry is struggling to become part of an international hospitality industry that gives good value by welcoming, pampering, and entertaining its visitors. China's current hospitality industry is run by a young and inexperienced workforce lacking an entrepreneurial work and service ethic. They work the clock rather than work the crowd!

For us, the real pleasures of China are more educational in nature—seeing the old and the new come together into a synthesis called the "New China." China fascinates us because it is so big, unpredictable, and filled with contrasts, many of which bridge centuries of human activity. It's a unique and colorful collage of diverse peoples, different generations, and contrasting levels of technology. China follows a different set of principles, many of which juxtapose the old and the new, for organizing the present and transcending its past. The human scenes and faces are striking, memorable, and instructive. For example, you may discover standing next to the newly arrived peasant farmer who window shops for cheap clothes in Shanghai a young well dressed businessman talking on his cellular phone. Barefoot and aging porters carry designer luggage down steep embankments and onto sleek cruise ships that ply the waters of the Yangtze River. Bicycles or human drawn carts haul televisions and computers across town. Walk through the narrow winding alleys of a traditional *hutong* with its distinctive sites and smells and emerge at the entrance of a new high-rise luxury office building with McDonald's located next door. Witness a huge broken down 150-passenger bus being pushed through an intersection by its passengers! These are contrasting peoples and sites you don't soon forget. They are all part of the New China.

China is a surprising country that challenges stereotypes and questions assumptions about the Third World and its people. After all, China is trying to quickly shed its Third World image as well as the many habits attendant with nearly 50 years of social leveling and socialist organization, management, and work habits as it attempts to realize Deng Xiaoping's pithy post-1979 fortune cookie platitude, *"to get rich is glorious."* Finding shortcuts on this new road to riches is the challenge facing many Chinese who have little or no experience in "doing business" the Western way. The people are a challenge simply because there are so many of them, everywhere. Stand at a major intersection or walk through Tiananmen Square in Beijing and you'll observe thousands of people plying the congested traffic on foot or on bicycle. Stroll along Shanghai's congested shopping street, Nanying Road, or along the famous Bund and you may be overwhelmed by the sheer number and energy of the people. Observe the worn river traffic and chaotic working towns along the Yangtze River. Or take in a cultural performance in Beijing, Xi'an, or Shenzhen.

Wherever you go, China is grand theater on a grand scale. While it's getting ready to enter the 21st century with great ambition, China also lives in many different decades and centuries. It has difficulty putting it all together for the 21st century since it has yet to master the 20th century. China's streets, sites, and shops yield a fascinating number and variety of people engaged in all types of human activity. At times you may think 300 years of history are simultaneously coming at you from many different directions. Today may be 1998, but it also could be 1970, 1950, 1930, 1900, or perhaps 1850, 1780, and 1650! At times you'll feel you are in a time warp spanning decades and even centuries. When you leave China and reminisce about its pleasures, you'll came back again and again to the sights and sounds of its people that bridge different time periods.

APPROACH IT RIGHT

To really enjoy your China adventure, you need to approach it right. This is not yet a do-it-yourself English-friendly country where you can just hop off a plane and get around on your own with ease. If you don't speak or read Chinese, China can be difficult to get around in. While many Chinese in the hospitality industry speak some basic English, you still face a formidable language barrier when you venture outside your hotel or leave an English-speaking tour guide. Try ordering food in a local restaurant, most of which have no English menus, and you'll quickly discover how difficult and inconvenient getting around China can be! Or try using public transportation when you don't know where the bus or subway train is heading or which crowded line you need to get in or out of at the railway station or airport.

This does not mean you must take a packaged tour to China. On the contrary, you have options here. The old days when all foreigners had to join a government-sponsored tour group (CITS) have all but ended. Today, you can travel on your own or join a variety of groups or do both. In fact, hundreds of government-sponsored travel agencies (these are entrepreneurial government corporations rather than private companies, examples of *"socialism with Chinese characteristics"*) now operate throughout China. These groups enable you to organize a relatively flexible travel experience in China by combining organized local tours with independent travel. In Shanghai alone, you will find more than 60 such companies competing with each other for tourists. Each offers different itineraries and rates tend to be very reasonable. Consequently, you can now arrange your transportation to Beijing, for example, and immediately join a three-day tour there and then leave two days in Beijing for on-your-own travel. If you want to visit Tibet for a few days, you can contact another tour group that can arrange a tour to Tibet either with a group or as an individual traveler complete with a car, driver, and English-speaking guide.

China also requires some attitude adjustment. Keep in mind that this is a huge country undergoing major economic, social, and political changes. Not everything works according to plan and many things may bother you. Schedules can go awry due to bad weather, canceled or overbooked flights, or just poor organization and management. Crowds can be massive and oppressive at major attractions, such as the Great Wall and the Forbidden City, and along major shopping streets and in department stores. In fact, the largest number of tourists (80%) visiting the major sites are local tourists who are first discovering the many treasures and pleasures of their own country! If you are used to greater personal space, the sea of humanity may be somewhat unsettling. Pollution, sanitation, smells, noise, chaos, lines, and eating and drinking behavior may at times appall you. And don't expect much service since this is not yet a service-oriented society. Service is often lethargic, brisk, rude, or just plain absent. But you will also welcome many of the tour services that make travel and communication in China both convenient and educational.

If you approach China with tolerance, an open mind, and a sense of adventure, China will surely reward you with its many treasures and pleasures. While you may at times feel "left out"

❑ Good food, service, and accommodations are concentrated in four and five-star joint venture hotels managed by international hoteliers.

❑ China fascinates us because it is so big, unpredictable, and filled with contrasts. The human scenes are striking, memorable, and instructive.

❑ Wherever you go, China is grand theater on a grand scale. At times you'll feel you are in a time warp spanning decades and even centuries.

❑ You can travel in China on your own or join a variety of groups, or do both.

❑ Pricing of goods is some of the most bizarre we have encountered anywhere.

❑ If you stay paranoid, chances are you will get good value for your money when shopping in China. *"To be paranoid is glorious"* should be your philosophy of smart shopping in China!

because the language barrier prevents you from communicating with many of the people, nonetheless, China will speak to you like no other country. It has many interesting stories to tell visitors, stories that make travel such a rewarding adventure.

ORGANIZE FOR CHINA

The following chapters are designed to give you a glimpse into some of the major treasures and pleasures of China. Our choice of destinations was purposeful: we sought those areas that offered some of the best shopping, sightseeing, and tourist facilities in all of China. Not surprising, the *"best of the best"* tends to be concentrated in and around the major cities of Beijing, Shanghai, Xi'an, Guangzhou, and Shenzhen, with the exception of the Yangtze River. These areas also are frequented the most by foreign visitors, be they businesspeople, officials, or tourists. Since the tourist infrastructure also tends to be best developed in these areas, you should have little difficulty getting around and moving on to your next travel-friendly destination.

GETTING VALUE, BEING PARANOID

While this is not a budget guide to China, neither is it designed to be an expensive guide to upscale China. If you share our passion for quality shopping, chances are you will spend a lot more in China than you originally budgeted. But then, you'll have some really nice things to show for your efforts. Like good shoppers anywhere, we look for excellent value wherever we travel. And we're usually successful in returning home with a treasuretrove of wonderful buys, lasting memories, and a desire to return again to extend our adventure further into a country.

We also may be able to save you a lot of money and headaches if you follow our advice in Chapter 6 on how to bargain and avoid scams and rip-offs aimed at people like you—a wealthy looking foreigner who is viewed as having unlimited resources. In fact, pricing of goods in China is some of the most bizarre we have encountered anywhere in the world. For example, the first quoted price of $3,000 for a painting drops below $200 within five minutes (and we thought from previous experience in other Third World countries that a 40-60% discount would be good!); and the price keeps dropping as we walk out of the shop saying *"not interested today"*! An ostensibly antique porcelain figure priced at $1,500 from what seemed to be a reputable art and antique shop appears to be a real steal when we bargain it down to $535, but then we discover several identical figures under a staircase in the same shop, and its identical "made yesterday" sister in a nearby flea market for $35! This is truly a bizarre shopping world where you can easily get cheated to the tune of hundreds or thousands of dollars if you don't know what you're doing or if you play by a different set of rules (*"I trust what you say is honest and true"* or *"a 50% discount is what you can expect from hard bargaining"*). In this neo-capitalist society, shopping and pricing rules seem to be made and remade in each situation. After all, as a class of transient people passing through an over-supply socialist economy where supply and demand has little relevance to pricing logic, you stand out for special pricing treatment by charming sellers who simply want as much money from you as they can get. We came to believe that many of the merchants who tried to dupe us did not view their behavior as "dishonest," but rather an exchange in which both buyer and seller attempted to see who was the more "clever." If he could pass off a recent reproduction as a Tang Dynasty original, we were simply ignorant foreigners with more money than we know what to do with. He was simply "more clever" and if he didn't relieve us of our money, another merchant would!

Put simply, this is a "buyer beware" shopping culture in many places of China. While *"to be rich is glorious"* may be a fitting philosophy for many upwardly mobile merchants who desire to taste the fruits of capitalism, *"to be paranoid is glorious"* should be your philosophy of smart shopping in China! However friendly merchants may be, you need to be cautious in how to deal with many of these people. If you stay paranoid, chances are you will get good value for your money when shopping in China.

Our primary emphasis on shopping is also purposeful. Like other volumes in our Impact Guides series, we take as our departure point an old saying attributed to Winston Churchill: *"My needs are very simple—I simply want the best of everything."* Long ago we discovered that one of the best ways to learn about a country and its people is to go shopping for the best of the best of what they produce, be it arts, crafts, jewelry, clothes, accessories, furniture, or antiques. Although we occasionally buy tourist kitsch, especially ubiquitous T-shirts, more often we go for quality products, especially art, antiques, and home decorative items, that eventually grace our home. In so doing, we get to meet a lot of very interesting, talented, and friendly people who are variously merchants, artists, and craftspeople; we learn about them as well as a whole new dimension of their society. We visit their workshops and studios and sometimes join their families for dinner. We also learn how to avoid shopping mistakes, including over-pricing and scams, and we share our warnings with our readers. Indeed, travelers using our guides report having a wonderful time discovering quality products and outstanding buys as well as meeting wonderful people they would not have otherwise met had they not gone shopping according to our advice. Whenever possible, we include travel tips, bargaining strategies, and recommended shops, hotels, and restaurants to make sure you are approaching China with the right knowledge and skills to truly enjoy your adventure. In the end, we hope this book will whet your appetite to further explore many other fascinating places in China, such as Fuzhou, Hangzhou, Nanjing, Tianjin, Urumqi, Lhasa, Quilin, Nanning, Xiamen, Chengdu, and Kunming.

EXPECT A REWARDING ADVENTURE

Whatever you do, enjoy your shopping and travel adventure to China. This is a very special country that offers many unique treasures and pleasures for discerning travelers.

So arrange your flights and accommodations, pack your credit cards and traveler's checks, take your sense of humor, wear a smile, and head for one of the world's most interesting shopping and travel destinations. You should return home with much more than a set of photos and travel brochures and a weight gain attendant with new eating habits. You will acquire some wonderful products and accumulate many interesting travel tales that can be enjoyed and relived for a lifetime.

Experiencing the treasures and pleasures of China only takes time, money, and a sense of adventure. Take the time, be willing to part with some of your money, and open yourself to a whole new world of treasures and pleasures. If you are like us, your shopping adventure will introduce you to an exciting world of quality products, friendly people, and interesting places that you might have otherwise missed had you passed through China only to eat, sleep, see sights, take pictures, and keep up with a tour group's hectic schedule. When you travel and shop in China, you learn about some exciting places by way of the people, products, and places that define this country's many treasures and pleasures.

Enjoy. May your treasures last a lifetime and forever enrich your life. For to be enriched in China is also glorious!

PART II

Traveling Smart

2

Know Before You Go

I f you are a first-time visitor to China, you should be aware of certain basic facts about this place before you arrive. This information should help you better plan how, when, and where you will arrive so you can literally hit the ground running!

POPULATION AND AREA

Anyway you look at it, China is a big country in terms of both population and area. It looks big, it feels big, and it is big. Its population of 1.2 million is the world's largest, representing 22 percent of all the people in the world. Its cities also are some of the world's largest and most congested. Wherever you travel in China, it seems there are people everywhere. Indeed, there are few places in China where you won't see people. After awhile, you begin understanding the rationale behind China's one-child family planning policy: too many people competing for too few resources.

China also is the world's third largest country in terms of area, ranking just behind Canada and Russia. Covering an area of 9.6 million square kilometers, China borders Korea in the northeast; Mongolia and Siberia in the north; Kazakhstan,

Kyrgyzstan, Tajikastan, Afghanistan, Pakistan, India, and Nepal in the west; and Bhutan, Bangladesh, Myanmar, Laos, and Vietnam in the south. It boasts one of the world's longest coastlines (14,500 kilometers) and an awesome 22,143 kilometer border that encompasses numerous nationalities, climates, and typographies, from deserts and snow capped mountains to pine forests, fertile valleys, and deltas. Only 10 percent of the land is arable. While much of China's climate approximates that of the United States, it is more extreme, ranging from subarctic in the north to tropical in the south. Beijing in the north often feels like New York or Philadelphia. Shanghai near the central east coast feels like Atlanta or Houston. And steamy Guangzhou and Hong Kong in the south approximate subtropical Miami or San Juan.

❑ China's population of 1.2 million represents 22 percent of the world's population.

❑ China is the world's third largest country in land area.

❑ China shares a 22,143 kilometer border with 16 countries.

❑ Only 10 percent of the land is arable.

❑ Nearly 90 percent of China's 55 million foreign each year are Overseas Chinese.

❑ China's tourist infrastructure primarily focuses on the needs of the Overseas Chinese and foreign business communities.

If you plan your visit to China around its seasons and climate, you should think in terms of traveling to various areas of the United States throughout the year. April and October tend to be the overall best months to visit China, especially if you plan to cover several areas that span from north to south China. But these also tend to the busiest months for tourism in China, times when major tourist attractions can become overcrowded.

TOURISTS AND OVERSEAS CHINESE

China also thinks big when it comes to reporting tourism figures. You'll need to put its official arrival figures into a "Greater China" political and cultural perspective.

China is big in terms of its total number of visitors. Its tourism figures are inflated to the point where China officially ranks as the fifth most popular tourist destination in the world. This ranking really is not true if you're concerned about comparing apples to apples. It's true that each year nearly 55 million people visit this country. However, this number includes a particular tourist phenomenon that is unique to China and explains much of its recent economic development. Nearly 90 percent of these visitors consist of Overseas Chinese—individuals who trace their ancestral homes to China, especially southern and coastal China. Most of them currently reside in Taiwan, Hong Kong, and Macau and regularly visit China for business, pleasure, and family obligations. Many also come from wealthy Chinese communities in Singapore, Thailand, Malaysia, and Indonesia, the groups that control much of their own country's economies. This same group is largely responsible for China's post-1979 economic development. In fact, the Chinese government has specifically targeted the Overseas Chinese for special treatment, appealing to their linguistic and cultural affinity and ancestral roots and providing them with economic incentives to invest in China. While some Western investment has gone into China during the past 15 years, such investment pales in comparison to that of the Overseas Chinese. Not surprising, this so-called foreign investment is disproportionately found in South China which is where most Overseas Chinese maintain important family ties as well as where they best understand the culture, speak the language, and enjoy the regional cuisine. And it is these ties that have increasingly played a central role in developing important business relationships that have contributed enormously to transforming China's economy during the past 15 years.

If you eliminate Overseas Chinese and business travelers (especially those from Hong Kong and Taiwan who ostensibly are part of China) from the total "arrivals" figures, tourism to China is very modest. Indeed, fewer than 5 million non-Chinese people visit China each year as foreign tourists. While the tourist infrastructure for these 5 million people is improving, it has a long way to go. Most of the tourist infrastructure currently remains focused on the Overseas Chinese and foreign business communities.

CLIMATE, SEASONS, WHEN TO GO

Given the vastness of China, its seasons and climates vary depending on when and where you visit China. In general, we like to compare China to the United States and much of Europe. It's hot, it's cold, it's rainy, it's dry, depending on where and when you visit the country. China experiences extreme cold and heat. Although there is no one ideal time to visit China, Spring and Fall, especially the months of April and October, are usually good times to visit. If you plan to primarily visit the subtropical south, the winter months of November to February are excellent times to visit this area. However, a cold spell in the South can be very chilling since no heating is found in buildings south of the Yangtze River. If you're primarily interested in visiting the Beijing and the north, do so in late spring or early fall. If you plan to visit the Yangtze River area, be forewarned that this area has long hot summers beginning as early as April and ending in October. Three cities in this area—Chongqing, Wuhan, and Nanjing—have long been known as China's "Three Furnaces"! Visit this area in July or August and you will most likely have a very uncomfortable stay.

Secrets Of Getting There— The Great Northwest Connection

Most visitors arrive in China by air via Beijing, Shanghai, or Hong Kong. Despite the opening of several cities to direct international flights, Hong Kong remains the major entry point for China. Hong Kong also is serviced by major passenger ships and freighters. Assuming your arrival choice is air, connections into China are frequent and convenient. Fifty airlines have regularly scheduled flights to Hong Kong and other parts of China. Several charter airlines also service Hong Kong. Airfares to Hong Kong from the United States, Canada, or Europe are some of the best airfare buys in the world.

On our most recent trip to China and Hong Kong, we chose **Northwest Airlines**. We found their schedules to be the most convenient, the flights very comfortable, the service attentive, and the food well prepared. We have often appreciated the good service we find as we travel in Asia. We found the attentive but not obtrusive service on Northwest compared very favorably with what we have experienced traveling overseas. The flight attendants went out of their way to make passengers comfortable and well cared for. In fact, when one flight attendant found out the date of our return flight, he told us he was scheduled to fly that route that day and he would see us then. When we boarded our return flight four weeks later, he broke into a wide grin upon seeing us. We felt as if we were encountering an old friend!

Best of all, we found Northwest Airlines' routes—especially from East Coast and Midwest cities in the United States—cut

- ❑ There's no one best time to visit China in terms of climate, although Spring and Fall may be good.

- ❑ Avoid the Yangtze River area during the summer—unless you enjoy extreme heat and humidity

- ❑ Northwest Airlines has the best direct flight to Beijing from Midwest U.S.—only 13 hours and 15 minutes!

- ❑ Over 150 tour groups operate within China.

- ❑ China is a relatively inexpensive distination for group travel.

flying time off the long journey by using polar routes. In fact, we traveled to Hong Kong by starting in Beijing, visiting several cities in China and then stopping in Hong Kong as our last destination. The routing from Washington Dulles International Airport to Beijing cut nearly ten hours off the time it usually takes us to travel to Asia. They cut travel time both by using the polar route and flying direct to Beijing without the usual stop at Narita, Japan. We flew from Detroit to Beijing in just 13 hours 15 minutes; add to that a 1½ hour flight from Washington Dulles to Detroit and including the time we took to change planes in Detroit, the whole trip took less than 16 hours—far better than the usual 24 hours. This special routing immediately sold us on Northwest Airlines!

But Northwest offers more than just a great routing to Hong Kong and China. We really enjoyed our Northwest flight and were impressed with several innovative programs that should appeal to anyone interested in ecology. Northwest has been cited for the second consecutive year as the most eco-friendly airline. Indeed, Northwest developed the first in-flight recycling program, and it pioneered a program to allow passengers to choose their food items from an a la carte service which both pleases passengers and has cut food waste by 20 percent.

If you fly frequently, consider membership in Northwest's WorldPerks℠ (frequent flyer) and WorldClubs℠ (airport lounges and special services) programs. For more information on the **WorldPerks℠** frequent flyer program which also is partnered with KLM, contact Northwest by phone (1-800-447-3757) or mail: Northwest Airlines Customer Service Center, 601 Oak Street, Chisholm, MN 55719. For information on the **WorldClubs℠** program, contact Northwest by phone (1-800-692-3788), fax (612-726-0988), or mail: Northwest Airlines, Inc., WorldClubs Service Center, 5101 Northwest Drive, Department A5301, St. Paul, MN 55111-3034. You may want to make these contacts before doing your ticketing.

For most tourists from America and Europe, the flight to Beijing or Hong Kong is a long one. Thus, you may wish to upgrade your ticket to "Business Class" for more room and comfort. You will pay more for this upgrade but the increased comfort may be well worth it.

TOURS AND INDIVIDUAL TRAVEL

Should you travel to China on your own or join a packaged tour? That's up to you, depending on how you normally travel and how much time you have available to organize your own itinerary. China can easily accommodate both styles of travel, although group travel is usually the cheapest and most convenient way to see the country.

If this is your first trip to China, you may want to join one of the more than 150 tour groups that operate in China from North America and Europe. Since China still remains an inexpensive destination, most of these groups offer good value and convenience. Fourteen-day trips that include stops in Beijing, Shanghai, Xi'an, and Hong Kong, use first-class hotels, and include most meals can cost as little at $1,700 per person, including round-trip airfare. It's virtually impossible to match that amount by traveling to China on your own, unless you are an extreme budget traveler who enjoys staying at the low end of the economic spectrum and utilizing the "workers" transportation system. This may be fun and enlightening, a very special cultural experience that puts you in close contact with locals, but it can also be very time consuming trying to figure out bus and train schedules and off-the-beaten path locations for accommodations. If your time is limited and you're not in search of a low-end cultural experience, you actually may end up paying less by joining an inexpensive first-class packaged tour than if you try to do China on your own as a budget traveler.

We highly recommend shopping around for a packaged tour to China. While many itineraries are similar, you may find some unique features that are well comparing tours. Your travel agent should have plenty of brochures on regularly scheduled tours to China and other parts of Asia. Some of the major tour operators include:

- **Orient Flex-Pax Tours:** 630 Third Avenue, New York, NY 10017, Tel. 1-800-545-5540 or Fax 212/661-1618

- **Pacific Delight Tours, Inc.:** 132 Madison Avenue, New York, NY 10016, Tel. 1-800-221-7179 or Fax 212/532-3406

- **China International Travel Service:** 138B World Trade Center, San Francisco, CA 94111, Tel. 1-800-362-3839 or Fax 415/989-3838

- **U.S. China Travel Service, Inc.:** 212 Sutter Street, 2nd Floor, San Francisco, CA 94108, Tel. 1-800-332-2831

- **Pacific Holidays:** 2 West 45th Street, Suite 1102, New York, NY 10036, Tel. 1-800-355-8025

- **Orient Odyssey:** 1482 Gulf Road, Suite 268, Point Roberts, WA 98281, Tel. 1-800-637-5778

- **Distant Horizons:** 350 Elm Avenue, Long Beach, CA 90802, Tel. 1-800-333-1240 (specializes in cultural tours to Asia with distinguished scholars/lecturers)

- **China Travel Consultants:** 18-20 Jordan Road, Fair Lawn, NJ 07410, Tel. 1-800-613-0721

- **China Focus:** 870 Market St., Suite 1215, San Francisco, CA 94102, Tel. 1-800-868-7244

- **World Value Tours:** 17220 Newhope St., #202, Fountain Valley, CA 92708, Tel. 1-800-795-1633. Web: *http://www.vwtours.com*

- **The China Connection:** 1051 Keolu Dr., #242, Kailua, HI 96734, Tel. 1-800-942-4462

- **Journey to the East, Inc.:** P.O. Box 1334, Flushing, NY 11352-1334, Tel. 1-800-366-4034 or Fax 718/358-4065

- **Elderhostel:** 75 Federal Street, Boston, MA 02110-1941, Tel. 617/426-8056

- **Asian Pacific Adventures:** 826 South Sierra Bonita Avenue, Los Angeles, CA 90036-4704, Tel. 1-800-825-1680 or Fax 213/935-2691

The "best of the best," which also means going in style with the "most expensive of the expensive," is the venerable **Abercrombie and Kent:** 1520 Kensington Road, Oak Brook, IL 60521-2141, Tel. 1-800-323-7308 or Fax 708-954-3324.

If you plan to cruise the Yangtze River, many tour companies include the cruise as part of their larger "Visit China" package. However, you may want to contact the two major river tour operators directly, especially if you are planning to put together your own China itinerary:

- **Regal China Cruises:** 57 West 38th Street, New York, NY 10018, Tel. 1-800-808-3388 or Fax 212/768-4939

- **Victoria Cruises, Inc.:** 57-08 39th Avenue, Woodside, NY 11377, Tel. 212/818-1680 or Fax 212/818-9889. Web: *http://www.victoriacruises.com*

If you are interested in specialty types of tours to China, including cruising the Yangtze River, we highly recommend surveying the many advertisements that appear in *International Travel News* or *ITN*. Each issue of this useful monthly newsletter runs over 150 pages and is filled with information on exotic travel destinations, including tips from travelers who frequent China. For a free sample issue, contact: ITN, P.O. Box 189490, Sacramento, CA 95818. Yearly subscriptions run only $18.00. To subscribe, call 1-800-366-9192.

Independent travelers increasingly find traveling to China on their own to be more and more convenient. Unlike 10 or 15 years ago when all foreign travel to China had to go through the highly centralized China International Travel Service, today you'll encounter a proliferation of entrepreneurial "public" travel agencies eager to assist you with you local travel plans. For example, in Shanghai alone you can choose from amongst 60 different travel agencies, many of which can make local arrangements for travel to other locations, including Tibet. If you prefer not being confined to a tour group throughout your stay in China, one of the best ways to travel is to contact local travel agencies in each place you visit.

During the past few years the travel industry in China has been increasingly decentralized to provincial travel agencies that function as public corporations and in competition wto each other. Many of these local travel agencies also can arrange travel itineraries to other places in China. Many of the travel services located in Beijing also have branch offices in other cities. Some of the major such travel services include:

- **China International Travel Service:** Head Office. 103 Fuxingmennei Ave., Beijing 100800. Tel. 86-10-7660111 or Fax 86-10-66059512

- **China Travel Service:** Head Office. 2 East Beisanhuan Road, Beijing 100028. Tel. 86-10-64622288 or Fax 86-10-64612556

- **CYTS Tours Corporation:** 23C Dongjiaominxiang, Beijing 100006. Tel. 86-10-65243388 or 86-10-65249809

- **China Merchants International Travel Co.:** 6th Floor, Huapeng Bldg., 19 North Dongsanhuan Rd., Chaoyang District, Beijing 100020. Tel. 86-10-65062228 or Fax 86-10-65011308

- **China Railexpress Travel Service:** Blk. 3, Multi-Service Building, Beifengwo Road, Haidian District, Beijing 100038. Tel. 86-10-63246645 or Fax 86-10-6326182

- **Beijing China Travel Service:** Beijing Tourism Tower, 28 Jianguomenwai Street, Beijing 100022. Tel. 86-10-65150624 or Fax 86-10-65158557

- **Shanghai CITS Company Limited:** 308 Zhonghua Road, Shanghai 200010. Tel. 86-21-63217200 or Fax 86-21-63291788

- **Shanghai China Travel Service:** 881 Yan'an Road (M), Shanghai 200040. Tel. 86-21-62478888 or Fax 86-21-62475878

- **Shanghai CYTS:** 2 Hengshan Road, Shanghai 200031. Tel. 86-21-64331826 or Fax 86-21-64330507

- **Shanghai Jinjiang Tours:** 191 Chang Le Road, Shanghai 2000230. Tel. 86-21-64720500 or Fax 86-21-64662297

- **Guangzhou Tourist Corporation:** 4-155, Huanshi Rd. (W), Guangzhou, Guangdong 510010. Tel. 86-20-8666-5182 or Fax 86-20-86677563

- **Guangdong China Travel Service:** 10 Qiaoguang Road, Guangzhou, Guangdong 510115. Tel. 86-20-83336888 or Fax 86-20-83336625

- **Guangdong China International Travel Service:** 179 Huanshi Road, Guangzhou, Guangdong 510010. Tel. 86-020-86666271 or Fax 86-020-86666284

- **Shenzhen China Travel Service:** 5th Fl., China Travel Service Bldg., 40 South Renmin Road, Shenzhen, Guangdong 518001. Tel. 86-755-2255888 or Fax 86-755-2227907

- **Shaanxi China Travel Service:** 45 Xingquing Road, Xi'an, Shaanxi 710048. Tel. 86-29-3244352 or Fax 86-29-3241070

- **Xi'an China International Travel Service:** 32 North Changan Road, Xi'an, Shaanxi 710061. Tel. 86-29-526-2066 or Fax 86-29-2561558

If you are Internet savvy, you can easily access information on travel to China through one of the major travel sites. Start with the first site (*http://www.travelfile.com/get?chinanto*), which is operated by the China National Tourist Office, and then explore the other sites. The final site (*http://www.hkta.org*) focuses on Hong Kong:

> *http://www.travelfile.com/get?chinanto*
> *http://www.travelocity.com*
> *http://www.expedia.com*
> *http://www.city.net/countries/china*
> *http://www.asiadragons.com/china*
> *http://www.asiatravel.com*
> *http://www.insidechina.com*
> *http://www.hkta.org*

Also, try searching for a particular city by using one of the major search engines, such as HotBot, Yaahoo, Infoseek, or Lycos. If you have the time and patience to search through all the information clutter on the Web, you might find some useful information as well as make contact with a travel group. However, your local travel agent will probably yield better quality results and save you a lot of time.

If your initial destination is Hong Kong, you may want to get a special package to Hong Kong and then arrange your China adventure in Hong Kong which is relatively easy to do. Consult your travel agent and survey the travel sections of the Sunday *New York Times, Washington Post, Los Angeles Times,* and other major city newspapers for special packages to Hong Kong. West coast newspapers, especially the *Los Angeles Times,* will often carry ads for special Hong Kong shopping tours, some of which may extend into Greater China.

DOCUMENTS YOU NEED

You will need a visa to enter China. Make sure you give yourself plenty of time to get this visa prior to departure. For a tourist visa, which is good for 30 days and can be renewed, you are required to complete an application and submit one recent 2x2 photo and a valid passport. The cost is US$30 for a single-entry visa; US$30 for a two-entry visa; and $50 or $80 for a multi-entry (6 or 12 months) or visa. Allow a minimum of 15 days for visa approval. If you do not apply in person, it's best to send a self-addressed prepaid Federal Express, UPS, DHL, or Airborne air bill with your application. Apply at a Chinese embassy or consulate nearest you. In New York City, the consulate is located as follows:

> Chinese Consulate
> 520 12th Avenue (at 42nd Street)
> New York, NY 10036
> Hours: 10am-12noon; 12:30pm-3pm
> Monday-Friday
> Tel. 212/330-7408 or Fax 212/502-0245

If you are traveling with a tour group, you will not need to get a visa because you will be traveling under a group visa. But be sure to check with the tour group before departing to make sure you will be covered accordingly.

You also can easily get a visa to China while visiting Hong Kong. Contact the CITS on the 6th floor, Tower 2, South Seas Center, 75 Mody Road, Tsimshatsui, Kowloon, or the visa office of the Foreign Ministry of the People's Republic of China which is located in the China Resources Building, Wench, Hong Kong Island.

If you plan to visit Tibet, check with a Chinese consulate before you depart for China. While special permission is no longer required, this can change, depending on the political situation in Tibet. For more information, contact the Tourist Bureau of Tibet (Fax 86-891-6334632).

If you only plan to visit Shenzhen which is adjacent to Hong Kong or Zhuhai which is next to Macau, you can get five-day visas at the border crossings. However these border visas are only good for visiting these special status cities.

CHINA NATIONAL TOURIST OFFICES

You may want to contact a China National Tourist Office for brochures and maps on China. If you use the Internet, start by visiting their Web site: *http://www.travelfile.com/get?chinanto*. Their offices can be contacted by mail, phone, or fax as follows:

UNITED STATES
China National Tourist Office, New York
350 Fifth Avenue, Suite 6413
Empire State Building
New York, NY 10118
Tel. 212-760-9700 (information)
Tel. 212/760-8218 (business)
Fax 212/760-8809

China National Tourist Office, Los Angeles
333 West Broadway, Suite 201
Glendale, CA 91204
Tel. 818/545-7504, 7505
Fax 818/545-7506

FRANCE
Office du Tourisme de Chine, Paris
116, Avenue des Champs–Elysees
75008 Paris, France
Tel. 33-144218282
Fax 33-144218100

UNITED KINGDOM
China National Tourist Office, London
4 Glentworth Street
London NW1, U.K.
Tel. 44-71-9359787
Fax 44-71-4875842

AUSTRALIA
China National Tourist Office, Sydney
19th Floor, 44 Market Street
Sydney, N.S.W. 2000 Australia
Tel. 61-2-2994057
Fax 61-2-290-1958

JAPAN
China National Tourism Administration
    Tokyo Office
6F Hamamatsu Cho Building, 1-27-13
Hamamatsu-cho, Minato-Ku,
Tokyo, Japan
Tel. 81-3-34331461
Fax 81-3-34338653

ISRAEL
Office of China International
    Travel Service, Tel-Aviv
P.O. Box 3281
Tel-Aviv 610303, Israel
Tel. 972-3-5226272, 3-5240891
Fax 972-3-5226281

SINGAPORE
China National Tourist Office, Singapore
1 Shenton Way, No. 17-05
Ribina House, Singapore 0106
Tel. 0065-2218681/82
Fax 0065-2219267

GERMANY
Fremdenverkehrsamt der VR China
Ilkenhansstrabe 6
D-60433 Frankfurt am Main, Deutschland
Tel. 49-69-520135
Fax 49-69-528490

SPAIN
China National Tourist Office, Madrid
Gran Via 88, Grupo 2, Planta 16-8
28013 Madrid, Espana
Tel. 0034-1-5480011
Fax 0034-1-5480597

HONG KONG
China International Travel Service, Hong Kong
6th Floor, Tower 2, South Seas Center
75, Mody Road, Tsimshatsui
Kowloon, Hong Kong
Tel. 852-27325852–American/Canadian Department
Fax 852-23676785–American/Canadian Department

China generally does not require health documents or vaccination certificates. If you are arriving from a cholera or other epidemic infected area (yellow fever in certain African and Latin American countries), you will probably need to present a health card certifying that you have been inoculated against such diseases. It's always best to check with your travel agent on current health requirements before departure.

Nor do you need to take any special shots before you go, unless you plan to go native and eat in local restaurants or along the streets where you are risking hepatitis because of poor food handling and dish washing practices as well as the habit of reusing unsanitary wood chopsticks (carry your own or go for the familiar fork and spoon). Contrary to what others may tell you about cleanliness in China, cleanliness is often a form of window dressing that does not translate into Western standards for restaurant and food stall hygiene. Be careful where and what you eat and drink.

ORDERING YOUR ITINERARY

If you visit all of the locations covered in this book, including Hong Kong, you may want to start in Hong Kong and work your way north and west via Shenzhen, Guangzhou, Shanghai, Wuhan, the Yangtze River, Chongqing, Xi'an, and Beijing. Alternatively, you may want to start in Beijing and proceed west and south by way of Xi'an, Chongqing, the Yangtze River, Wuhan, Shanghai, Guangzhou, Shenzhen, and Hong Kong.

❏ No health documents or vaccination certificates are required unless you come from an epidemic infected area.

❏ If you travel with a tour group, you do not need a visa since you'll be covered by a group visa.

❏ Special permission is no longer required for visiting Tibet, although this may change depending on Tibet's political situation.

❏ We recommend starting your China adventure in Beijing and then working your way west and south to Hong Kong.

❏ Most major hotels have English news programs as well as major international English-language newspapers and magazines.

We've gone both directions and much prefer the Beijing to Hong Kong routing. Part of the reason for this preference is the wonderful Northwest Airline connection to China via Beijing. Taking only 13 hours and 15 minutes from Detroit, this is the quickest way to enter China. We also prefer this route because Hong Kong is a wonderful place to end a trip. It's a great place to celebrate your trip with fabulous hotels, restaurants, shops, and entertainment. If you are a shopper, you can always do your last minute shopping and arrange any shipping in Hong Kong after you've had a chance to shop the major cities in China. You might find some terrific bargains in Beijing and Shanghai, for example, that are one-fifth the price of what you might pay in Hong Kong. If you start your adventure in Hong Kong, you may make purchases that you later regret once you get to Shanghai and Beijing.

We prefer celebrating the end of our trip in Hong Kong. At the end, Hong Kong, along with perhaps a short visit to Macau, pulls everything together as a terrific trip to China. After having visited Greater China first and experienced many of its rough edges, we enjoy Hong Kong and its services more than ever!

RECOMMENDED READING

You'll find lots of good reading on China. Some books you may want to read in preparation for your China adventure. Other books you may want to take with you, especially for the lengthy Yangtze River cruise, flights between cities, and evenings in your hotel room.

If you enjoy history, politics, and society, you should read Jung Chang's *Wild Swans*; Nien Cheng's *Life and Death in Shanghai*; Edgar Snow's *Red Star Over China*; Arnold Brackman's *The Last Emperor*; Sterling Seagrave's *Soong Dynasty*; Zhisui Li's *The Private Life of Chairman Mao*; Harrison Salisbury's *The New Emperors*; Jonathan Spence's *The Search For Modern China*; Witold Rodzinsky's *The Walled Kingdom*; Jacques Gernet's *A History of Chinese Civilisation*; Orville Schell's *Discos and Democracy*; John King Fairbank's *The Great Chinese Revolution 1800-1986*; Lu Xun's *The True Story of Ah Q*; and the classics *Journey to the West* and *Romance of Three Kingdoms*.

If you're looking for interesting travel writing and novels related to China, both fiction and nonfiction, we recommend any of Pearl S. Buck's books on China, especially *The Good Earth*, *Children of the Pearl*, and *Pavilion of Women*; Gu Hua's *A Small Town Called Hibiscus*; Tsao Hsueh-Chin's *The Dream of the Red Chamber*; Amy Tan's *Joy Luck Club* and *The Kitchen God's Wife*; James Clavell's *Taipan* and *Noble House*; Peter Jenkins' *Across China*; Paul Theroux's *Riding the Iron Rooster*; Colin Thubron's *Behind the Wall*; and Mark Salzman's *Iron and Silk*.

NEWSPAPERS, MAGAZINES, AND TELEVISION

You'll find English-language newspapers in most major cities. The local English-language newspapers, such as the *China Daily* (nationwide distribution) and the *Shanghai Star*, have a decided government tone to them, and their international news tends to be very bland and self-serving. Most five-star hotels in Beijing, Shanghai, and Guangzhou have copies of the *International Herald-Tribune*, *The Asian Wall Street Journal*, and *USA Today*. International magazines, such as *Time*, *Newsweek*, *The Economist*, and *The Far Eastern Economic Review* also are available in these hotels.

Many of the major hotels will have local English-language news programs as well as CNN and/or STAR-TV. Hotels in Guangzhou and Shenzhen also have access to English-language broadcasts originating in nearby Hong Kong.

As might be expected, availability of foreign publications and television programs depends on the prevailing political winds blowing out of Beijing. Censorship, which can be both subtle and quite obvious, is still well and alive in China, and it occasionally affects such publications and broadcasts.

Prepare For a Unique Adventure

C hina is not like just any other country you have traveled to. It's different. It has attitude about tourism. The tourist infrastructure is still going through growing pains as is the concept of tourism. The government wants to encourage tourism while, at the same time, make sure guests see and do the right things that will reflect positively on China. They are proud of their country, people, and attractions, and they try hard to put their best foot forward to ensure that you enjoy your stay. As a guest of China, they want you to travel in a convenient and comfortable manner. Accordingly, they want your visit to be well planned. They do not encourage spontaneous travel where guests come into their country and wander aimlessly to satisfy their curiosity and possibly get into trouble seeing and doing the wrong things. Anyway you approach China, it involves planning.

Preparation is the key to experiencing a successful China adventure. But it involves more than just examining maps, reading travel literature, and making airline and hotel reservations. Preparation, at the very least, is a process of minimizing uncertainty by learning how to develop a travel and shopping plan, manage your money, handle Customs, and pack for the occasion. Preparation helps organize all the aspects of your trip and focuses your attention on what is important to see and do.

DEVELOP AN ACTION PLAN

Time is money when traveling abroad. This is especially true in the case of China where traveling on your own can be very difficult. If you are traveling with a tour group, chances are you have an all-inclusive travel package; most of your schedule will be planned in detail for you, from sightseeing tours and entertainment to three meals a day. However, if you are traveling on your own or have lots of free time during or between tours, the planning you do will be important to the overall success of your trip. The better you plan, the more time you will have to enjoy your stay.

If you want to use your time wisely and literally hit the ground running, you should plan a detailed, yet tentative, schedule for each day. Start by getting a good map of each city you visit. Unfortunately, you may have difficulty getting useful, detailed city maps until you arrive in the particular city. Your hotel concierge should have one; ask the concierge to mark the places you wish to visit as well as give you some ideas as to how much time you'll need to get to and from each area. You especially want someone knowledgeable about the city to mark key shopping areas on the map since we have yet to find a map that includes important shopping information. This initial map exercise should be the basis for planning your schedule.

❑ China does not encourage spontaneous travel where travelers wander around aimlessly to satisfy their curiosity and possibly get into trouble.

❑ You may have difficulty getting useful, detailed city maps. Contact your hotel concierge for assistance in getting and reading a map.

❑ Check the Web site of the China National Tourist Office for travel information on China or contact one of their offices for maps, brochures, and other information.

Next, **list** in order of priority the five to ten things you most hope to accomplish in the time you have. At the end of each day **summarize** what you actually accomplished in relation to your priorities and set your priorities for the following day.

Planning is fine but it will not ensure a successful trip, especially in a country such as China where serendipity, or chance occurrences, affects much of what you see and do. People who engage in excessive planning often overdo it and thus ruin their trip by accumulating a list of unfulfilled expectations. Planning needs to be adapted to those unexpected events which may well become the major highlights of your travel and shopping experiences.

CONDUCT RESEARCH AND NETWORK

Do as much research as possible before you depart on your China adventure. As we noted on page 34, individuals with access to the Internet should begin by visiting the Web site of the China National Tourist Office:

http://www.travelfile.com/get?chinanto

Also try various online search engines, such a HotBot, Yahoo, WebCrawler, Infoseek, Excite, and Megallen, to find information on China. Several travel magazines, such as *Travel & Leisure* and *Conde Nast Traveler,* are now on the World Wide Web. If you belong to one of the commercial online services, such as America Online, CompuServe, or Prodigy, check out their travel sites for useful information on China.

You next may want to visit the periodical section of your local library. Here you will find numerous magazine and newspaper articles on travel and shopping in China. Indeed, China is one of the most popular subjects for travel writers, especially Beijing, Shanghai, and the Yangtze River. When you find references to shops, add these names to your growing list of places to visit.

You should also **network for information and advice**. You'll find many people, including relatives, friends, and acquaintances, who have recently traveled to China. Many of these people are eager to talk about their trip as well as share their particular China shopping secrets with you. They may direct you to some great shops where they found art, antiques, cloisonne, cashmere, pearls, or jade of good quality or at exceptional prices. Ask basic who, what, where, why, and how questions:

- **What** shops did you particularly like?
- **What** do they sell?
- **How** much discount should I expect?
- **Whom** should I talk to?
- **Where** is the shop located?
- **How** do I get what I want?
- **Is** bargaining expected?
- **When** were you there?

This final question is particularly significant. Prices and shops do change. Information gleaned from people's experiences over the past two years will be most relevant.

Be sure to record all the information that you receive in an orderly manner. Use, for example, an ordinary address book to list the names, addresses, telephone numbers, and products of shops; list them alphabetically by types of merchandise.

Don't neglect to contact the China National Tourist Office nearest you (see pages 35-37). Call, fax, or write them for maps, brochures, and any information on travel and shopping in China that would assist you in planning your trip. This is a free service.

CHECK CUSTOMS REGULATIONS

It's always good to know customs regulations before you leave home. If you are a U.S. citizen planning to return to the U.S. from China and Hong Kong, the United States Customs Service provides several helpful publications which are available free of charge from your nearest U.S. Customs Office, or write P.O. Box 7407, Washington, DC 20044.

- *Know Before You Go* (Publication #512) outlines facts about your basic exemptions, mailing gifts, duty-free articles, and prohibited and restricted articles.

- *Trademark Information For Travelers* (Publication #508) deals with unauthorized importation of trademarked goods. Since you will find many copies of trademarked items in China—the ubiquitous "knock-offs"— this publication will alert you to potential problems with custom inspectors prior to returning home.

- *International Mail Imports* answers many travelers' questions regarding mailing items from foreign countries back to the U.S. The U.S. Postal Service sends all packages to customs for examination and assessment of duty before it is delivered to the addressee. Some items are free of duty and some are dutiable. The rules have recently changed on mail imports, so do check on this before you leave the U.S.

- *GSP and the Traveler* itemizes goods from particular countries that can enter the United States duty-free. GSP regulations, which are designed to promote the economic development of certain Third World countries, permit many products, especially arts and handicrafts, to enter the United States duty-free. China currently does not have GSP status, but its status could change in the future. At the same time, Hong Kong no longer enjoys GSP status. Therefore, it is unlikely that items you purchase in China or Hong Kong will be exempted from duty. Antiques, defined by U.S. Customs as over 100 years old, are free of duty. Be sure this is noted on your sales receipt.

If you are in Beijing or Shanghai and are uncertain about U.S. duties on particular items, contact the U.S. Embassy in Beijing or the U.S. Consulate in Shanghai. In Hong Kong, phone 523-9011 for local U.S. Customs assistance.

MANAGE YOUR MONEY WELL

It's best to carry traveler's checks, two or more major credit cards with sufficient credit limits, U.S. dollars, or a few personal checks. Our basic money rule is to take enough money and sufficient credit limits so you don't run short. How much you take is entirely up to you, but it's better to have too much than not enough when you're shopping in China and probably also in Hong Kong.

We increasingly find **credit cards** to be very convenient for managing our money in China. We prefer using credit cards to pay for major purchases as well as for those unanticipated expenses incurred when shopping. Most major hotels and stores honor MasterCard, Visa, American Express, and Diner's cards —and in that order of preference.

If you decide to use **traveler's checks**, take US$100 checks only. Smaller denomination checks are more trouble than they are worth. And once you get to Hong Kong, you will be charged a transaction fee on every traveler's check regardless of its denomination. You should receive a slightly better exchange rate for traveler's checks than for cash. It's best to carry the following traveler's checks: American Express, Thomas Cook, or Bank of America.

The days of the old and inconvenient Foreign Exchange Certificates (FECs), which were responsible for creating a black market for currency, ended in 1994. Now foreigners exchange their money for the local currency. While a black market still functions in a few cities, it's best to avoid it altogether (you may be approached in a market about "change money") since you may get cheated in the process by being given old discontinued notes or even a lower rate than the bank in exchange for your cash.

It's very easy to exchange money in China. Most major hotels, Friendship Stores, and large department stores have a Bank of China exchange booth that gives local currency in exchange for cash or traveler's checks. Since the exchange rates are all the same, you need not shop around for the best rate. The local currency is called the *Renminbi* or *yuan*. The yuan is divided into 10 *jiao* which, in turn, is divided into 10 *fen*. The currency is issued in bills of 2, 5, 10, 50, and 100 yuan and coins of 1 yuan, 5 jiao, and 1, 2, and 5 fen. The yuan is currently exchanged at the rate of 8.27 yuan per U.S. dollar.

Use your own judgment concerning how much **cash** you should carry with you. Contrary to some fearful ads, cash is awfully nice to have in moderate amounts to supplement your traveler's checks and credit cards. But of course you must be very careful where and how you carry cash. Consider carrying an "emergency cash reserve" primarily in $50 and $100 denominations, but also a few $20's. Cash can be used instead of your larger denomination traveler's checks when you want to change a small amount of money to local currency.

While ATM machines are widely available and used in Hong Kong, don't expect to use them in China at present. If you're only traveling to China, leave your ATM card at home. If you're planning to visit Hong Kong, you're home free with your ATM card.

USE CREDIT CARDS WISELY

Credit cards can be a traveler's blessing if used in the right manner. They are your tickets to serendipity, convenience, good exchange rates, and a useful form of insurance. Accepted in many places throughout China, they enable you to draw on credit reserves for purchasing many wonderful items you did not anticipate finding when you initially planned your adventure. In addition to being convenient, you usually will get good exchange rates once the local currency amount appearing on your credit slip is converted by the bank at the official rate into your home currency. Credit cards also allow you to float your expenses into the following month without paying interest charges and may even add miles to your frequent flyer account. Most important, should you have a problem with a purchase— such as buying a piece of jewelry which you later discover was misrepresented or has fake stones, or electronic goods which are incompatible with your systems back home—your credit card company may assist you in recovering your money and returning the goods. Once you discover your problem, contact the credit card company with your complaint and refuse to pay the amount while the matter is in dispute. Although your credit card company is not obligated to do so, many times they will assist you in resolving a problem. Businesses accepting these cards must maintain a certain standard of honesty and integrity. In this sense, credit cards may be an excellent and inexpensive form of insurance against possible fraud and damaged goods when shopping abroad. If you rely only on cash or traveler's checks, you have no such institutional recourse for recovering your money.

□ Use credit cards to pay for hotels and restaurants and for major purchases.

□ Carry one or two bank cards and an American Express card.

The down-side for credit cards in China is that they are primarily accepted in major hotels, Friendship Stores, and large department stores. That leaves a lot of places, from restaurants and small shops to some airline offices, that only accept cash. And once you arrive in Hong Kong, many shops will want to charge you a "commission" for using your card, or simply not go as low in the bargaining process as they would for cash or traveler's checks. Commissions in Hong Kong will range from 2 to 6 percent. This practice is discouraged by credit card companies; nonetheless, shops do this because they

□ Consider requesting a higher credit limit on your bank cards.

□ Take plenty of $100 traveler's checks.

□ Carry an "emergency cash reserve" primarily in $50 and $100 denominations.

□ Keep a good record of all charges in local currency— and at official exchange rates.

□ It's a good idea to write the local currency symbol before the total amount on your credit card slip.

must pay a 4-5 percent commission to the credit card companies. They merely pass this charge on to you.

A few other tips on the use and abuse of credit cards may be useful in planning your trip. Use your credit cards for the things that will cost you the same amount no matter how you pay, such as lodging and meals in the better hotels and restaurants or purchases in Friendship Stores and large department stores. Consider requesting a higher credit limit on your bank cards if you think you'll be charging more than the current limit allows.

Be extremely careful with your credit cards. Be sure those who do a credit card transaction write the correct amount and indicate clearly whether this is U.S. dollars or yuan on the credit card slip you sign. It is always a good practice to write the local currency symbol before the total amount so that additional figures cannot be added or the amount mistaken for your own currency. For example, 200 yuan is approximately equivalent to $24.15 U.S. dollars. It should appear as "¥200" on your credit slip. And keep a good record of all charges in local currency—and at official exchange rates—so you don't have any surprises once you return home!

Secure Your Valuables

Be sure to keep your traveler's checks, credit cards, and cash in a safe place along with your travel documents and other valuables. Consider wearing a money belt or a similar safety cache. While the money belt may be the safest approach, the typical 4" x 8" nylon belts can be uncomfortable in hot and humid weather. Women may want to make a money pouch which can fasten inside their clothing. Another approach for women is to carry money and documents in a leather shoulder bag which should be kept with you at all times, however inconvenient, even when passing through buffet lines. Choose a purse with a strap long enough to sling around your neck bandolier style. Secure the purse with a strong grip and always keep it between you and the person accompanying you. Pick pockets and purse snatchers, which are found in crowded market areas and in and around busy train stations, can quickly ruin your vacation if you are not careful.

Men should carry their wallet in a front pocket. If you keep it in a rear pocket, as you may do at home, you invite pickpockets to demonstrate their varied talents in relieving you of your money, and possibly venting your trousers in the process. If your front pocket is an uncomfortable location, you probably need to clean out your wallet so it will fit better.

You may also want to use the free hotel safety deposit boxes for your cash and other valuables. If one is not provided in your room, ask the cashier to assign you a private box in their vault. Under no circumstances should you leave your money and valuables unattended in your hotel room or at restaurant tables. While theft other than pickpocketing is usually not a problem in China, it's always best to be safe than sorry. You may want to leave your expensive jewelry at home so as not to be as likely a target of theft. If you get robbed, chances are it will be in part your own fault, because you invited someone to take advantage of your weaknesses by not being more cautious in securing your valuables. In our many years of traveling we have not been robbed. But we try to be careful not to encourage someone to take advantage of us. We know people who have had problems, but invariably they were easy and predictable targets, because they failed to take elementary precautions.

TAKE KEY SHOPPING INFORMATION

Depending on what you plan to buy, you should take all the necessary information you need to make those important shopping decisions. Put this information in a separate envelope. If you are looking for home furnishings, along with your "wish list" you should include room measurements to help you determine if particular items will fit into your home. You might take photographs with you of particular rooms you hope to furnish. Be sure to include measurements of dining tables and beds since you may find table linens and bedspreads in China.

If you plan to shop for clothes, your homework should include taking an inventory of your closets and identifying particular colors, fabrics, and designs you wish to acquire to complement and enlarge your present wardrobe. If you have been color-charted, be sure to take your chart with you. While we do not recommend having tailoring work done in China, except at the very top hotels, chances are you may want to have tailoring done in Hong Kong. Since Hong Kong tailors are particularly talented at copying designs from pictures or models, we strongly recommend that you assemble a file of pictures with styles you wish to have copied. If you have a favorite blouse or suit you wish to have copied, take the actual article with you. It is not necessary to take patterns, because Hong Kong tailors do not use these devices for measuring, cutting, and assembling clothes. All they need is to take your measurements and have a clear idea of your style and fit preferences. For details on how to communicate effectively with tailors, see our companion Hong Kong volume, especially Appendix A, "Custom Tailoring Tips."

KEEP TRACK OF ALL RECEIPTS

It's important to keep track of all of your purchases for making an accurate Customs declaration. Since it's so easy to misplace receipts, you might want to organize your receipts using a form similar to the one on page 50. Staple a sheet or two of notebook or accountant's paper to the front of a large manila envelope and number down the left side of the page. Draw one or two vertical columns down the right side. Each evening sort through that day's purchases, write a description including style and color of the purchase on the accompanying receipt, and enter that item on our receipt record. Record the receipt so later you'll know exactly which item belongs to the receipt. Put the receipts in the envelope and pack the purchases away. If you're missing a receipt, make a note beside the appropriate entry. In fact, you may have difficulty getting receipts from many shops in China.

Customs Declaration Record Form

	RECEIPT #	ITEM	PRICE (¥)	PRICE (US$)
1.	14	painting	¥800	$96.63
2.				
3.				
4.				

PACK RIGHT FOR CHINA

Packing is one of the great travel challenges for many people. Trying to get everything you think you need into one or two bags can be frustrating, especially if you are visiting areas of a country that have different climates. You'll either take too much, and carry more than is necessary, or you'll take too little, thinking you'll buy what you need there, only to find that just the right items are ever so elusive.

☐ Take an extra piece of luggage for your shopping treasures.

☐ Shops tend to wrap to disguise rather than wrap to protect.

☐ Include a repacking kit of bubble wrap, tape, scissors, cord, business cards, and "Fragile" stickers.

☐ Throw in a comfortable pair of shoes for all the walking you will be doing.

☐ Pack a battery calculator which should come in handy when bargaining.

We've learned over the years to err on the side of taking too little. If we start with less, we'll have room for more. Our ultimate goal is to make do with three changes of very versatile outfits, packed into the lightest and largest checked bag the airlines will allow. Good hotels provide efficient laundry and dry-cleaning services, and you can always hand wash your "undies" yourself if you choose. Since extremely inexpensive luggage is readily available in China, there's really no need to take any extra luggage for purchases you may make along the way. However, if you know you're going to buy a lot, you might decide to take a second empty suitcase with you. We have done this by nesting one inside the other with our trip clothing packed in the inside piece of luggage or by stuffing a second piece of luggage with the bubble wrap and other packing materials we will need later to protect our purchases. While soft-sided luggage is lighter weight, it may not provide as much protection as a good hardsided piece for either your clothing or your shopping treasures.

We always travel with a basic repacking kit since shops invariably do a poor job of packing delicate items. Shops tend to wrap to disguise an item rather than wrap to protect it against damage. At the very minumum, we include at least 15 feet of bubble wrap (2-3 foot wide), both scotch tape and straping tape, a black magic marker, scissors, nylon cord, business cards, and airline "Fragile" stickers.

We include our business cards for three purposes: (1) give them to shopkeepers to introduce ourselves and develop a relationship that may result in a better bargained price; (2) give them for correct addressing information to shopkeepers or shippers who will be shipping our items; and (3) affix them as name and address tags to all purchases we take with us.

Your goal should be to avoid lugging an extensive wardrobe, cosmetics, library, and household goods around the world. Above all, you want to return home loaded down with wonderful new purchases without paying extra weight charges. Hence, pack for the future rather than load yourself down with the past. Our guiding principle for packing is this: *"When in doubt, leave it out."*

TAKE COMFORTABLE SHOES

Since you can expect to do a lot of walking in China, be sure to take a good pair of shoes to navigate many miles of very hard concrete sidewalks and asphalt streets. Please don't buy new shoes for your trip unless you have several weeks to break them in. We prefer to clean up and polish two very comfortable pair of shoes which we've worn for a year or more.

We recommend taking at least one pair of comfortable walking shoes and one pair of dress shoes. Several major manufacturers of sport shoes make attractive shoes designed just for walking. Take only essential shoes which will coordinate with all of your outfits. Should your shoes become damaged, they can be repaired inexpensively and quickly in China.

THROW IN A CALCULATOR

Since you will be doing a great deal of shopping, take a small battery operated calculator for adding your purchases and converting currency equivalents. Using a calculator when bargaining also impresses upon shopkeepers and market vendors that you are a serious shopper who seems to know what you are doing. Solar calculators may be convenient to carry, but you may have difficulty operating them in dimly lit shops. Several brands of "conversion calculators" are now available, usually found at your local luggage shop. Once you enter the conversion factors for the foreign currency its easier to calculate the equivalents. These conversion calculators also aid you in converting meters to yards and celsius to fahrenheit.

A currency conversion chart also can be a time-saver for figuring currency equivalents. You can make your own by listing the equivalent amounts for several standard US$ amounts ($5, $25, $60) on a small piece of heavy paper or on a business card; keep a copy in your pocket for quick reference.

Navigating Your Way
Through China

You should now be well prepared to begin your travel and shopping adventure in earnest as soon as you arrive in China. Assuming you will arrive and depart China by air, it's useful to examine how to best orient yourself to the arrival and departure processes so that you can truly enjoy China from the very moment you arrive.

ARRIVING AND GETTING AROUND

As we noted in Chapter 2, we prefer starting in Beijing and traveling west and south to Xi'an, Chongqing, the Yangtze River, Wuhan, Shanghai, Guangzhou, and Shenzhen and then exit by way of Hong Kong. We've found this routing to be the best for several reasons. We also prefer flying to most of our destinations. After all, this is a big country where distances can be great and travel very time consuming. The domestic airlines, which consist of regional carriers, have improved their service and equipment considerably in recent years. Most airlines now fly Boeing and McDonnell Douglas aircraft.

The train is interesting, but such travel in China takes a great deal of time and loses its romantic appeal after a few hours of relatively bland travel. We prefer a two-hour flight to an exhausting 32-hour train ride. Taking the express train between Guangzhou and Hong Kong, however, may make a lot of sense given the close proximity of these two cities (25-minute flight versus a 2-hour train ride).

Be sure to book your domestic flights well in advance of your arrival in China. Many flights to China's most popular destinations tend to be fully booked weeks in advance. If you wait until the last minute to book these flights, especially during high season, you are likely to be disappointed and your travel plans for all of China may quickly go awry. Ask your travel agent to book all of your domestic flights at the same time you do your international ticketing. Once in China, be sure to *always* reconfirm your on-going flight as soon as you arrive in a city. If you fail to do so, your reservation is likely to be automatically canceled. You'll arrive at the airport without a reservation. Your hotel concierge will take care of this reconfirmation. In fact, the first thing you should do upon checking in to a hotel is to ask the front desk or concierge to reconfirm your airline ticket.

> ❑ Most domestic airlines now fly Boeing and McDonnel Douglas aircraft.
>
> ❑ Book your domestic flights well in advance since flights to the most popular destinations tend to be fully booked weeks in advance.
>
> ❑ Always reconfirm your on-going flights. If you don't, you will most likely lose your seat.
>
> ❑ All of China is on a single time zone—Beijing Time or GMT+8.
>
> ❑ Taxis are plentiful and relatively inexpensive in most cities.

The airports in most of China's major cities are relatively new and modern facilities or they are being renovated in response to the increased air traffic impacting on most of China's airports. In some airports baggage retrieval areas are too small to easily handle international flights. Most airports are well organized in terms of Immigration, Customs, information services, and airport to city transportation. The major problem tends to be very crowded facilities and long and chaotic lines when waiting to check in for flights to popular destinations. If you are with a tour group, you will be able to avoid many of the hassles involved in handling your own tickets and check-in. If not, just get in line and push your way to the front.

Given the crowded conditions of many airports, plan to arrive at least one hour before departure time. Flights generally leave on time. But expect to occasionally experience delays due to a combination of weather conditions and mechanical problems. Overall, we found most airports to be relatively efficient despite the crowded conditions.

DEPARTURE TAX

All airports have a departure tax which is what they call a "Construction Fee." It costs from US$5 to US$10. This fee literally goes toward the ongoing construction of the airport which is often in a state of reconstruction. You'll need to go to a separate desk, which is well marked in both Chinese and English, to pay this fee and get a receipt. You must show this receipt when you go through security.

CUSTOMS

Be sure to complete the Customs declaration form upon arrival which requires you to itemize valuables and declare the amount of foreign currency you are bringing into China. You'll need to present a copy of this form when you leave China. You can bring in computers, tape recorders, radios, and 8mm and ½" video cameras without special permission as long as you are not planning to use them for commercial purposes. Photographers working with 16mm and ¾" video cameras need special permission. While China does prohibit the import of printed matter, films, or tapes that are deemed detrimental to China, chances are Customs will not take away any politically sensitive reading material. Neither should you advertise your library to encourage confiscation.

TIME ZONES

It's real easy to keep track of time in China since all of China is on a single time zone—Beijing Time or GMT+8. China does go on daylight savings time during the summer. When it's noon in China, it's 2pm in Sydney and Guam; 6pm in Hawaii and Anchorage; 8pm in Los Angeles and Vancouver; 9pm in Denver; 10pm in Chicago; 11pm in New York and Montreal; 4am in London; 5am in Paris, 6am in Cape Town; and 7am in Moscow.

INTERCITY TRANSPORTATION

You should have little difficulty getting around in most cities and outlying areas. **Taxis** are plentiful and relatively inexpensive in most cities. They can be found at hotels and outside major department stores or they can be called by telephone.

While taxis have meters, drivers don't like to use them. Consequently, bargaining is often in order when taking a taxi. Be sure to agree to the fare before departing since drivers have a habit of "miscommunicating" and overcharging; it's best to write down the agreed upon fare in *yuan* in front of the driver. Fares vary and drivers will give receipts. Since most drivers do not speak English, make sure you have directions written in Chinese before you get into a cab. It's most convenient to hire a taxi for a half day or full day and have the driver wait for you at each stop.

Subways operate in Beijing and Shanghai and are on the drawing boards for other cities.

Buses and trolley services operate in all major cities, although it may be difficult to figure out where they go. They also tend to be very crowded and uncomfortable.

You also will find other forms of transportation in most cities, from **motorcycle taxis** and **motor-tricyles** to **pedicabs** and **bicycles**. You can usually arrange a bicycle rental through your hotel. However, keep in mind that traffic can be dangerous for bicyclists and you will need to observe bicycle parking areas which can be maddening for the uninitiated.

CURRENCY AND EXCHANGE RATES

China's currency is called the *renminbi* which is abbreviated and referred to as RMB. The basic unit of *renminbi* (RMB) is the *yuan* (¥) which is subdivided into *jiao* and *fen*: 10 *jiao* = 1 *yuan*; 10 *fen* = 1 *jiao*.

The current exchange rate is 8.27 *yuan* to US$1 or 1 *yuan* equals US$.121. The Bank of China has exchange desks at all hotels, airports, and Friendship Stores. You will receive a slightly higher exchange rate on traveler's checks than on cash.

Credit cards are accepted in most hotels and state-run shops of major cities. The accepted ones include Visa, MasterCard, American Express, Diner's Club, Federal Card, Million Card, and JCB Card. Many locally operated hotels, restaurants, and shops only accept cash.

WATER AND DRINKS

Tap water in China is not potable even though it is chemically treated in most cities. Bottled water is readily available and can be purchased in many shops. Hotels provide bottled and/or boiled water in rooms for drinking purposes.

There's plenty to drink in China, from teas, coffees, and

local beers and wines to locally bottled Coca Cola, Pepsi, and fruit juices.

ELECTRICITY

Electricity throughout China is supplied at 220 volts and 50 cycles AC. Electrical outlets are configured in four different patterns: three-prong angled pins (Australian style); three-prong round pins (Hong Kong style); two flat pins (American style); and two round pins (European style). If you're traveling with appliances, such as a hair dryer, or a computer, be sure it converts to 220 volts. Also, take a set of conversion plugs to handle the different electrical configurations, although the Australian and American style plugs should handle 90 percent of the situations you encounter. Otherwise, ask hotel housekeeping for an adaptor.

We always travel with our handy and much used little 15-foot extension cord. Invariably we find electrical outlets for using our computer and hair dryer to be inconveniently located behind furniture or far from good lighting or a mirror. In many hotels we would be better off with 25 feet of extension cord or two 15-foot lengths!

- ❏ Since most drivers do not speak English, have someone write directions in Chinese before getting into a cab.

- ❏ Agree on the cab fare in writing before starting out since drivers have a habit of overcharging tourists.

- ❏ Credit cards are accepted in most major hotels and state-run shops.

- ❏ Tap water is not potable. It's best to buy bottled water.

- ❏ Dinner is usually served between 6 and 7pm. Most restaurants shop serving after 8:30pm.

BUSINESS HOURS

Banks, government offices, and business offices are open Monday through Saturday and generally open at 8 or 9am, close for two hours during the day, and then close for good at 5 or 6pm.

Shops are generally open seven days a week, from 8 or 8:30am to 7:30 or 8pm.

Hotel restaurants maintain similar hours as their Western counterparts. However, restaurants outside the hotels tend to both serve and close early, although you can usually find a restaurant that stays open later. Dinner is usually served between 6 and 7pm. If you'll looking for a relaxing evening of dining outside your hotel, forget it. Most restaurants stop serving after 8:30pm. Plan such dining in a hotel restaurant.

China observes nine public holidays: New Year's Day (January 1); Spring Festival (in February); International Working Women's Day (March 8); International Labour Day (May 1); Youth Day (May 4); Children's Day (June 1); Founding of the Communist Party Day (July 1); Founding of the PLA Day (August 1); and National Day (October 1). Government offices, businesses, and most shops close on these holidays.

LANGUAGE

The first spoken language for nearly 70 percent of the population is Mandarin. Most of the literate population read the same language. If you don't speak or read Chinese, expect to encounter frequent communication problems outside your hotel. Most major hotels have English-speaking staffs. When venturing outside your hotel, ask the concierge or other staff members to write your destination in Chinese. Be sure to take a hotel card with you that has your hotel name and address in Chinese.

❑ If you don't speak Chinese, be sure take a hotel card with you that has your hotel name and address in Chinese.

❑ Local travel agents tend to be full-service operations that can arrange most of your travel needs.

❑ Tipping is officially prohibited, and it shows in many places that exude lethargic service. Tip when you feel it is appropriate. Good service needs to be recognized and rewarded.

❑ This is a safe country to travel in. However, watch your wallet and purse in markets and at train stations where pickpockets occasionally target tourists.

When shopping, you will encounter many people who speak some basic English, or at least enough English to carry on a transaction. The best English will be spoken in hotel shops and Friendship Stores. But even many vendors in the market speak some English. So communication should not be a serious problem unless you frequent shops or markets used primarily by locals. However, since many signs are in Chinese, wandering the streets on your own looking for a particular address can present difficulties. Even when accompanied by a Chinese-speaking guide, finding addresses can be challenging and thus may have little to due with language problems.

If you decide to dine in local restaurants, expect major language problems. If a menu exists, it's usually in Chinese. Few, if any, restaurant personnel speak even basic English. As a result, you will probably have great difficulty ordering anything in such restaurants, including a drink.

In certain cities, such a Shanghai, you may be approached

on the street by students who want to practice their English with you, the foreigner. This may be a good opportunity for you to converse with a local about life in their community.

TOURS AND TRAVEL AGENTS

If you arrive on your own, you'll have no problem arranging local tours through a variety of travel agents who offer a wide range of travel services. As outlined in Chapter 2, numerous travel agents operate in each city. When in doubt about whom to contact, see your hotel concierge or the tour desk at your hotel. Unlike travel agents in many other countries that primarily book individuals and groups for prescheduled tours, local travel agents in China tend to be full-service operations that are very responsive to individual travel needs. For example, they can quickly arrange half-day to full-day tours, with or without groups. They also can arrange travel to other cities, including customized all-inclusive tours (includes guide, private car, transportation between cities, hotels, all meals, and all sightseeing). While you can do some travel on your own by hiring a taxi driver for a half or full-day, you will probably find it's more convenient, and perhaps less expensive in the long run, to go through a travel agency to hire a car and driver who speaks some English and understands the needs of tourists.

TIPPING

While tipping is officially prohibited, the practice is changing as China's hospitality industry becomes more and more service oriented. In fact, you can help improve this industry by tipping individuals who genuinely provide excellent service, especially hotel personnel. As you will quickly discover, the service ethic is not widespread in China's growing hospitality industry. One of the reasons for this is the lack of financial rewards. Many individuals just do their job without much sense of giving a service to customers. We encourage you to tip when you feel it is appropriate, but don't just routinely tip 10 or 15 percent like you might do back home. If you do, you will more often than not be sending the wrong message—poor service gets rewarded!

SAFETY AND SECURITY

China is a relatively safe country to travel in. Assaults, rapes, robberies, or murders are very rare and seldom directed against tourists. However, it's always best to be safe than sorry. Pickpockets are well and alive in China and they tend to congregate near train stations and crowded market areas. Be sure to secure your valuables and assume anything can happen when dealing with strangers.

ANNOYANCES

China has its shares of annoyances that can bother visitors after awhile. **Service**, or the lack thereof, is a persistent problem which you'll initially notice upon arrival, from the airport to your hotel and with your tour guides. Don't expect things to get done like back home. Work gets done but often not according to expectation. Hotel service in local hotels, and even in many joint-venture hotels, can be very irritating, especially if you are in a hurry. After awhile you will probably get use to this poor level of service and just tolerate it as "the way things get done."

Noise: Chinese cities tend to be very noisy because of the many loud vehicles and construction. At times it gets so noisy that you may have difficulty conducting conversations.

Pollution: Air pollution is especially bad in cities due to a combination of pollution-belching vehicles and factories. Water pollution is widespread because raw sewerage and factory wastes are pumped into rivers and lakes.

Crowds: It's people everywhere! Cities and attractions tend to be very crowded. City streets are especially congested during early morning and late afternoon rush hours. If you value private space, you may find the crowds to be very tiring.

Queues: The Chinese do not queue in the same manner as many Westerners. If you are a strict line observer, you may get irritated at the many people who push and shove their way in front of you at hotel front desks, ticket counters, entrances, and shops. However, this situation is getting better, especially at airports where lines often look like queues.

Restrooms: Public restrooms may shock you. They tend to be filthy and toilet paper may be non-existent. If you need to use restroom facilities, the cleanest will generally be found at the top hotels.

Beggars: You will occasionally encounter beggars, especially along popular tourist streets in Beijing. Some are professionals while others may be genuinely in need, although the former are more likely than the latter. We do not recommend supporting beggars since doing so further encourages this activity—especially professional beggars who are not as poor as they look.

Gross personal habits: Many people have habits that may appear gross in your culture—clearing throats and noses in public, spitting on sidewalks and streets, and shoveling food in mouths.

Overpricing: Foreigners tend to be officially charged more for everything, from airline tickets to entrance fees. The rationale for this two-tier price structure is simple: foreigners tend to be rich and locals should have access to local transportation and sites. You may feel ripped-off as a tourist because of such official discriminatory practices. Nothing you can do about it. You also may be unofficially over-charged for taxis and goods in markets and private shops. However, you can do something about this: bargain or just walk away.

Smoking: The Chinese are heavy smokers. Many public areas tend to be thick with noxious smoke.

Littered public areas: Many public areas are littered with trash. Many people litter public areas as is if they belong to no lone.

Pestering: While service may not be good, this does not mean you will be left alone with shopping. Since many shops are over-staffed, the personnel may closely follow you around and try to sell you everything. If you prefer being left alone to "just look," at times you will find these people very irritating to the point where you will want to flee the shop!

Limited communication: You often may feel uninformed, neglected, and subject to arbitrary decisions because you are not given enough information about decisions affecting you. If, for example, your flight is delayed or canceled, airport personnel may not tell you what's going on; they may say it's delayed but not tell you why or when your flight will be rescheduled. If you're informed by your tour guide about a change in travel plans, chances are you won't be told why or given other options; you'll be informed you're doing Plan B. The tradition of top-down communication, the inability or unwillingness to keep people informed, and the lack of good customer relations are well and alive in China's tourist industry. If you are used to being kept informed about what's happening, or having some input into decisions affecting your travel plans, you may feel left out and subject to arbitrary decisions. You also may get angry when this happens.

Acquiring
Treasures
With Ease

5

China's Shopping Treasures

I f you like to shop for arts and crafts as well as browse for antiques, collectibles, and home decorative items, you're going to love China. This place is a unique shopper's paradise, one big arts and crafts emporium offering a wide range of fine handcrafted items. While it's not the same as *"shop 'til you drop"* Hong Kong, with it's profusion of European designer name clothes and accessories, Greater China does offer many shopping opportunities for acquiring excellent quality arts and crafts at reasonable prices. In fact, one of the major highlights of visiting China is discovering its many shopping treasures. In so doing, you should have several opportunities to meet artists and craftspeople who often demonstrate their work as well as sell directly to visitors.

Rich in history and cultural traditions, China is a country of talented artists and craftspeople who produce a sometimes bewildering array of arts and crafts in traditional designs. Indeed, the sheer volume of such shopping can be overwhelming, especially when visiting the multi-storey Friendship Stores that house a representative sample of China's many shopping treasures. It's also a country of talented merchants who may or may not become your favorite people. Many practice the post-1979 philosophy of *"to be rich is glorious"* on unsuspecting and naive tourists!

WORKSHOP TO THE WORLD

In many respects, China is one big workshop producing everything from ceramics, carvings, papercuts, fans, and furniture to embroidered silk, paintings, and calligraphy. While many of the arts and crafts have a decided ethnic look—ornate and dowdy—others integrate well with Western homes and wardrobes. Department stores, shops, and markets are packed with goods produced for China's growing number of tourists, both domestic and foreign, as well as for its large Western-oriented export market.

Consider for a moment what you will be encountering on your China adventure: a country of 1.2 million people with a 6,000 year old history centered around imperial court traditions that supported the profusion of visual arts and crafts; it's a country that continues, under government sponsorship, to promote both the production and distribution of arts and crafts. Not surprising, you encounter an incredible number of arts and crafts, as well as lots of fake antiques, wherever you visit in China, in hotels, museums, palaces, temple complexes, popular historical sites, and ubiquitous bus stop shops that include everything from Friendship Stores and factories to private arts and crafts emporiums. Indeed, you will on more than one occasion wonder where all of this stuff came from and where it will eventually go since so much of it seems over-produced in relation to market demand. Like so many other things produced in China, including its many factories manufacturing clothes and consumer goods, over-production characterizes much of what appears on the local markets. The new capitalism does not operate according to a good market-driven supply and demand model—just a top-down supply model. China may be the ultimate "field of dreams" when it comes to arts and crafts. It could become your field of dreams for acquiring many of China's treasures.

CAPITALISM WITH AN OLD FACE

China also is a country of very talented and aggressive merchants who, despite nearly 50 years of communist leveling and social upheaval, have not lost their entrepreneurial touch; they are eager to make money the old fashioned way. And the old fashion way sometimes includes taking advantage of buyers who are often naive about quality and value and susceptible to charming salespeople. This is especially true in private shops and markets, some of which are found in such public places as museums, where you are often targeted as a rich tourist who is ripe for plucking. Welcome to China's tiger streets and commerce!

There is a high probability you will encounter such charming yet ruthless capitalism. Like supply and demand, market forces tend to play an insignificant role in determining prices. Many of these merchants put on a friendly yet exploitive face of capitalism. As you will probably quickly discover, this is not the Mom and Pop shop nor shopping mall-variety capitalism you may be used to navigating and trusting back home. It's closer to carnival-variety capitalism. Merchant logic is simple: you're here today and gone tomorrow, so let's get what we can before you're gone forever! It is also a game of who is the more clever: the merchant or the customer.

Welcome to the new capitalist face of China where you definitely need to watch your wallet and be quick on your feet. Except in the government's fixed-priced Friendship Stores, you should be wary of merchants and entrepreneurs in China; this is not the time to be sympathetic nor to romanticize China's new capitalism since it's not the shopping mall-variety capitalism you may expect. In today's new shopping China, only paranoid shoppers survive and prosper in such an environment.

❑ This is a country of talented artists and craftspeople who produce a sometimes bewildering array of arts and crafts in traditional designs.

❑ Over-production characterizes much of what appears on the local markets. Indeed, you'll see tons of arts and crafts throughout China.

❑ Be very careful when dealing with dealing with local merchants and entrepreneurs— this is carnival-variety capitalism.

❑ The first rule to shopping in China is *"Whenever and wherever I shop, it's best to be paranoid."*

Indeed, the first rule to shopping in China, one you need to repeat over and over, is this: *"Whenever and wherever I shop, it's best to be paranoid."*

THREE SHOPPING CULTURES

You are likely to encounter at least three different shopping cultures in China, as well as a fourth shopping culture in some cities, each with its own characteristics and set of shopping rules:

1. Government fixed-priced shops
2. Private shops and markets with negotiable prices
3. Shopping arcades with upscale shops offering designer goods at fixed prices

The first shopping culture grew up with nearly 50 years of communism: central government control of production and distribution. Today most **government fixed-priced shops** are the Friendship Stores. These are huge multi-storey, product-rich department stores offering everything from food and clothes to arts, crafts, furniture, and antiques. Navigating one of these shops is like walking through a well organized bazaar; it can easily take an hour or more. Most of these places are over-staffed with personnel who often seem to have little to do. While many of these stores are aging and somewhat worn in comparison to newer and more modern joint venture depart-ment stores and private emporiums, others are being modern-ized to compete with the more appealing joint venture depart-ment stores; most still have a reputation for quality, honesty, reliability, and convenience (they in-clude money exchanges, taxi stands, and handle shipping). Selections are often excellent and prices appear reasonable compared to what you may pay for similar items in joint venture department stores and pri-vate emporiums. If you want to do comparative shopping, a Friendship Store should be the first place you visit in any city before venturing into the other shopping cultures.

❑ The government's Friendship Stores are known for quality, honesty, reliability, and con-venience. Visit these shops first to do comparative shop-ping.

❑ Pricing in private shops and markets tend to be all over the place and subject to sig-nificant negotiations.

❑ Don't be timid in going for 50, 60, 70, 80, and even 90 percent discounts, because you will often get them for the asking!

❑ Shopping arcades and design-er boutiques are primarily found in and around 5-star joint venture hotels. They represent a new shopping culture.

Private shops and markets have proliferated throughout China within the past decade. This is what we call the "slippery shopping culture"—it's fun but you can easily fall down and lose your wallet! This is where only the paranoid survive—if it seems too good to be true, it probably is. Aren't you incredibly lucky, for example, to find a Tang Dynasty ceramic tomb figure for only US$800? Aren't you fortunate someone else didn't happen upon this "deal" before you? And isn't it great the merchant doesn't seem to know it should be worth much more? Watch your wallet in this culture and have a healthy sense of scepticism. Many of these shops are found in museums or major government tourist sites such as the Forbidden City or Temple of Heaven (look public but they are private concessions) or function as arts and crafts emporia. Many also are street shops specializing in particular consumer products. Some of the larger arts and crafts emporiums, where many tour buses stop, claim to be fixed-price

"Friendship Stores" or "government shops" which obviously, and purposefully, confuses them with the more reputable and reliable government-run operations. Except for joint venture department stores, where prices are both fixed and displayed, pricing in private shops and markets tend to be all over the place and subject to significant negotiations. Don't be surprised, for example, to be quoted an initial starting price of US$3,000 for a painting that may actually be worth no more than US$100. Or you may be told a US$30 ceramic figure may be a 500-year old antique worth US$800. The "buyer beware" scenarios go on and on in this rather slippery shopping culture where you should be justifiably paranoid and bargain very very hard for everything. Don't be timid in going for 50, 60, 70, 80, and even 90 percent discounts, because you will often get them for the asking! As we will see in Chapter 6, you need to approach this shopping culture with certain bargaining strategies and techniques that work well in this environment.

Shopping arcades and designer boutiques have increasingly proliferated in the major cities and in and around 5-star joint venture hotels. If you've been to Hong Kong recently, or even Singapore, Milan, Paris, and London, you'll instantly recognize this shopping culture for its fabulous designs, exquisite quality, and very high prices. Many of these places showcase a wide range of products, especially clothing and accessories, produced in China's joint venture factories. You'll probably recognize most of the Italian, French, British, and American labels that are produced under licensing arrangements in China, such as Valentino, Yves Saint Laurent, Polo Ralph Lauren, Christian Dior, Perry Ellis, and Charles Jourdan. Others offer imported clothes and accessories representing such famous labels as Givenchy, Versace, Escada, Gucci, Hugo Boss, Ferragamo, Prada, Louis Féraud, Fendi, Cartier, Kenzo, Alfred Dunhill, Louis Vuitton, Celine, Cerruti 1881, Mondi, Gieves and Hawkes, Ermenegildo Zegna, and Bally. Upscale department stores and shopping arcades, such as the Palace Hotel Shopping Arcade in Beijing; Nextage (Yaohan) Department Store, Maison Mode, and Jin Jiang Dickson Center in Shanghai; and the Guangzhou World Trade Centre Complex and the Garden Hotel Shopping Arcade in Guangzhou are good examples of this new shopping culture. Frequented by newly affluent young people who are employed by joint ventures, expatriates, and many Asian tourists interested in name brand products, this new shopping culture is just emerging in China, representing the fact that major international fashion houses are betting on the future of the Chinese economy. While they may not be profitable at present (few have paying customers but most have lots of window shoppers), they are establishing important foot-holds in a market that should prove lucrative in the long-run. They are branding their names through extensive advertising and fabulous displays. They seem to at least have the attention, if not the money, of this new market.

You will probably be most interested in navigating the first two shopping cultures since they especially appeal to foreign visitors in search of China's unique treasures. The imported European and American shopping culture of designer label products is an interesting commentary on where the future of shopping in China may be going for local consumers in the emerging middle and upper middle classes. However, you may find the selections and sizes too limited and the prices too high in these shops for your budget. If you love designer label clothes and accessories, you'll probably do better purchasing them back home or in Hong Kong, Singapore, Milan, Paris, London, and New York. At the same time, you may find some overruns and knock-offs of these products in China's second shopping culture, especially in the street markets of Beijing.

 ## WHAT TO BUY

You won't run out of things to buy in China. This is one big shopping emporium for arts, crafts, furniture, foods, clothes, and accessories. Once you arrive in China and visit a few Friendship Stores, department stores, museum shops, and markets, you will quickly get a good overview of what lies ahead. The product mix tends to be very similar wherever you go. Indeed, you may become tired of seeing so many of the same things wherever you go, especially the ubiquitous carpets, jade carvings, and traditional paintings that flood the arts and crafts markets and factory emporiums.

While you will encounter lots of shopping in China, chances are you will buy only a few things as you quickly learn to become a discriminating shopper. It's really not difficult to become a discriminating shopper in China because only certain items will appeal to your sense of taste and design. The reason for this is the fact that much of what appears on the local markets tends to be very ethnic, ornate, or dowdy in nature. The fascinating embroidery handwork, for example, which is very interesting to watch for its artistic and technical details, is something you may want to observe rather than buy in China; you may feel you really don't have a place to display such unique work back home. Indeed, unless you collect a lot of tourist kitsch, your home decor may not support the introduction of traditional Chinese designs and colors however interesting the handwork may be. Traditional local designs don't appeal to many visitors who prefer more modern and simple international designs. This observation goes beyond cultural preferences. China simply lacks good design talent that is oriented to an international market that demands an upper class look. This is probably one of the reasons why window shopping for Western name-brand fashion goods and accessories is so popular—the designs are gorgeous and they appeal cross-culturally to individuals with similar class preferences. Much of what you see in China's arts and crafts emporiums, for example, are more handicrafts than quality arts and antiques. While organized to appeal to foreigners, most of these places exhibit limited design talent that would appeal to the shopping tastes of foreign visitors.

In terms of sheer volume, China is a shopper's paradise. Its major shopping strengths include:

❏ **Antiques:** Defined as anything more than 100 years old. Includes lots of old porcelain, ceramics, cloisonne, carvings, chops, art, and furniture. Many antiques are available in government shops, especially municipal and provincial antique shops, museum shops, and the antique sections of Friendship Stores and joint venture department stores. Some antiques can be exported but they must have a red or brown wax seal (color varies with the province) indicating they are approved by the government for export. While many newer items may have this seal affixed, if you purchase an old item that may be more than 100 years old, you will need to get it approved for export. If a shop claims its item is antique but does not have a wax seal, insist that the shopkeeper get a seal as well as document the age of the item in an official receipt you will need to show Customs. It usually takes time to get an item approved for export. In some cities, the Arts Object Clearing Office may only be open one day each week. Be wary of any merchant who claims he can have an item approved for export later the same day. It could be possible if you are in his shop early in the day, if is the day of the week the Clearing Office is open, and if he is highly motivated to take the item to the Clearing Office and wait for approval. However, some merchants may try to cheat by creating their own wax seal and not providing paper the necessary paperwork declaring the age of an item. This is a good sign that you have not purchased an antique. Indeed, don't be surprised to discover enterprising shopkeepers putting fake red seals on copies of ostensible antiques that have real antique prices! If you are interested in buying truly old pieces, you must be wary. Will you know if the item is truly old? Will you know what the official government wax seal looks like in the province where you are making your purchase or will a similar "design" seal of the appropriate color fool you? It is illegal to take items that date prior to 1900 out of the country. You run the risk of being "taken" twice. You buy an object purported to be from an early dynasty and pay according and in reality you bought a nice reproduction. Or you purchase a truly old piece and then run the risk it is confiscated as you leave China. Be sure to record purchases of antiques on your currency declaration form and be prepared to present copies of receipts when leaving China. You may never be asked to show anything. We have not been asked to do so. But it is best to be prepared.

❑ Much of what appears in the arts and crafts emporiums are more handicrafts than quality arts and antiques.

❑ Most arts and crafts emporiums exhibit limited design talent that would appeal to the shopping tastes of foreign visitors.

❑ You'll find few genuine antiques in China—most are fakes and many of these are extremely good fakes. If an item is presented as an antique, make sure you get the proper seals and paper work for official export.

❑ Silk yardage is an excellent buy in China if you can find colors and designs that are right for you.

❑ **Silk:** China is especially famous for its fine silk. Relatively inexpensive (from US$7 to US$20 a meter), you'll find numerous shops selling silk by the meter. Friendship Stores and hotel shops tend to have some of the best selections. If you are used to exquisite Italian and French silks—many of which are actually Chinese silks dyed and printed to the specifications of talented Italian and French designers—you may not be impressed with the colors and designs of silks available in the shops of China. Many of the designs look very ethnic or the colors aren't quite right for your wardrobe. However, silk yardage is an excellent buy in China if you can find colors and designs that are right for you. Also, look for silk scarves and neckties that may make inexpensive gifts. But, again, you may or may not be like what you see in terms of colors and designs. But cheap, yes.

❑ **Cashmere products:** Fine cashmere sweaters, scarves, and other products are widely available in department stores. Prices are okay (around US$100-130 for a sweater) but not terrific for the type of colors and styles available. You may do just as well back home watching good sales in department stores on cashmere sweaters, many of which may be made in China anyway but may be more stylish.

❑ **Clothes and accessories:** China is one big clothes factory that produces a wide variety of clothing items that may interest visitors. Look for shirts, tops, coats, jackets, sweaters, jeans, scarves, neckties, and shoes in Friendship Stores, department stores, and markets. However, you may find the styles, designs, and sizes limited. Several of the street markets in Beijing are especially popular with tourists who visit them to pick up inexpensive designer label clothes that are actually overruns or knock-offs of such famous names as Tommy Hilfiger, Gianni Versace, Polo, Nike, Esprit, Adidas, Levi Strauss, and Calvin Klein.

❑ **Linens and tableware:** Many shops offer a wide selection of linens and tableware that are probably more appealing to Europeans than to North Americans. While the hand work may be good, styles tend to be uninspired.

❑ **Furniture:** If you are looking for inexpensive old furniture or copies of old pieces, China has a great deal to offer in this department. Most of the furniture, however, may not be as old as it appears. Much of it has been either refurbished or newly made to look old. Look for big pieces of furniture, such as cabinets, chests, desks, beds, tables, and chairs.

❑ **Home furnishings and accessories:** Along with furniture, you'll find lots of home furnishings and accessories, including baskets, boxes, small decorative pieces, lacquer and carved screens, and paintings.

❑ **Carpets and rugs:** China is a major producer of silk, wool, and cotton carpets and rugs. You'll probably have a chance to visit at least one carpet factory during your stay in China. You'll see the weaving and cutting processes and then visit the display room where you will see lots of carpets. We've not been that impressed with the quality, designs, and colors, and prices. In fact, given the worldwide glut in carpets from China, India, and the Middle East, you can probably do just as well, if not better, back home purchasing a nice carpet from a department store that runs periodic sales and may have purchased from a dealer with designs made especially for export for Western tastes. Just don't get carried away with the demonstration and feel obligated to purchase. If you do find something you like, the factory or shop should be able to arrange shipping.

❑ **Paintings:** If you like art, you'll find some wonderful paintings in China, from traditional style Chinese and folk art to Western style watercolors, oils, and inks. You'll even find unique lacquer paintings in Chongqing. If you visit the right places, you will have opportunities to meet artists at work (try the art institutes in Chongqing and Shanghai) and buy directly from them. Prices on paintings vary dramatically, from inexpensive watercolors in the US$5-10 range to art priced at US$50,000 or more. Master artists tend to command very high prices. However, this whole shopping area falls into what we call the "slippery shopping culture." Galleries selling art often ask absolutely outrageous prices, claiming their artists are world famous (but we've not heard of them before we entered the gallery). This is an area where you need to bargain very hard, even when dealing directly with the artist. Don't be shy to ask for deep discounts. After all, the value of paintings tends to be determined by whatever you are willing to pay, and that could be very little or a lot. Don't be surprised if you can walk away with a 90 percent discount! One of the best buys in Chinese art are the colorful folk paintings that go for US$20 to US$50 each, although don't be surprised if someone tries to convince you that they really sell for US$200. That's the price you may pay for the same paintings in Hong Kong and Paris!

❑ **Calligraphy:** This is an acquired taste amongst those who can read Chinese or who appreciate this ancient and popular art form. Calligraphy is usually displayed in the same manner as traditional Chinese silk scroll paintings—make interesting wall hangings.

❑ **Art supplies:** Most cities have an art supply street lined with several shops selling a wide range of art supplies, including brushes, ink slabs, paints, papers, and books.

Many of these same shops also sell paintings and calligraphy.

❑ **Embroidery:** Chinese artisans are especially famous for their hand embroidery work in silk and wool. Copying famous scenes as well as portraying people and animals, the fine embroidery work is especially interesting to observe in factories and at demonstrations in department stores and art institutes. On more than one occasion you'll probably have a chance to see artisans at work producing this traditional art form that requires great skills and attention to detail. While interesting to observe and admire, you may find this embroidery work too ethnic in motif to purchase for your own home. Also, look for colorful embroidered collars, panels, shoes, vests, hats, opera costumes, and robes which can make interesting decorative pieces if properly mounted and displayed.

❑ **Chops:** The famous Chinese chops, both antique and new, are widely available in most Friendship Stores, hotel shops, and department stores. In many places you can have your own personalized chop carved with your name in Chinese characters. Made of soapstone, you can choose different sizes and colors. Use your chop to stamp your name in ink or press it in a wax seal. Chops make inexpensive gifts that can be easily carried in your suitcase. If you need to pick up 20 gifts for relatives and friends back home, 20 personalized chops might be the perfect "quick and easy" gift to give.

❑ **Jade and Agate:** You may be overwhelmed by the amount of jade and agate jewelry, carvings, and bowls you'll see throughout China. Jade and agate come in many different colors, shapes, and sizes. If you visit a jade factory or arts and crafts emporium with a demonstration area, you will have a chance to watch artisans at work fabricating and carving the jade. Buying jade, however, can be somewhat bewildering since you see so much of it everywhere you travel. Furthermore, not all jade sold is real jade. Jadeite, nephrite, and soapstone are sometimes substituted for real jade. Be very careful where and what you buy. If you don't know much about jade, especially the value of different qualities and colors, you may be best off buying in a Friendship Store or in a reputable joint venture department store such as Nextage

(Yaohan) Department Store in Shanghai. We especially like the beautiful agate pieces (bowls and carvings) available in China. In fact, we prefer the agate to the jade, and agate is more expensive than inferior jade.

❑ **Jewelry:** You'll find lots of traditional gold and jade jewelry as well as silver Tibetan and tribal jewelry. Also look for pearls in Beijing, especially inexpensive strands of pearls that can be made into jewelry.

❑ **Cloisonne:** This unique craft uses copper wires and an enameling process to produce beautiful vases, pots, beads, bracelets, pill boxes, plates, trays, and animal figures.

❑ **Sandalwood fans:** Look for intricately carved sandalwood hand fans that range in price from very inexpensive (less than US$2.00) to very expensive (more than US$1000). The most expensive ones are basically works of art which include intricate paintings. Most Friendship Stores have a separate section displaying these fans. The inexpensive models may not be made of sandalwood, but of less expensive woods and then sprayed to smell like sandalwood.

❑ **Soapstone carvings:** Soapstone is a relatively inexpensive soft stone that is used to make carvings similar in design to those made from jade and agate. If you are not familiar with the different types of stones used for carving figures and making jewelry, you could confuse soapstone with jade and thus pay ten times more than what you should be paying. After you've seen an example of soapstone in comparison to jade, you'll know the difference. Soapstone carvings can be quite beautiful, but make sure you pay soapstone prices.

❑ **Teapots:** If you are a collector of teapots, you'll be in teapot heaven. Shops everywhere offer all shapes and sizes of teapots for collectors. Most are very small one-cup teapots. Most Friendship Stores have a separate section devoted to this unique art form. Also, look for collectible teapots in various flea markets that offer antiques and curios.

❑ **Porcelain and ceramics:** There's a good reason why much of the world's tableware is called China. The porcelain and ceramic traditions are well and alive in today's China. Plates, cups, pots, bowls, and pillows made of porcelain and ceramics are ubiquitous throughout the country. Look for the distinctive blue and white pottery and white porcelains as well as the beautiful pale blue, gray, or blue-green glazed and crackled Caledon ceramics. Prices can be very high depending on the size and age of various pieces. Collectors of antique ceramics should visit the municipal and provincial antique stores and Friendship Stores where they will find pieces stamped with the official red or brown wax seals for export approval. Most markets offer lots of porcelain and ceramics. However, you really need to know what you're doing in this department because of the numerous fakes on the market. In fact, you may have difficulty finding genuine antique ceramics. The fakes are so good they even fool the experts. China has a long tradition of making fake antique ceramics. Indeed, you may encounter some ceramics that are even presented by shopkeepers as being genuine 200 year old fakes—a cut above the ubiquitous "made yesterday" fakes! This copy tradition has been going on for centuries. And the quality of fakes is very very good. If there is one shopping area where you can easily get scammed, it's ceramics. Watch your wallet and don't trust strangers who tell you stories about the true age of the pieces. And remember, there are genuine antique fakes in China!

❏ **Leather goods:** China produces a tremendous amount of leather goods. Look for jackets, handbags, wallets, luggage, and gloves. The leather is of average to mediocre quality. Prices tend to be inexpensive. If you're looking for cheap leather, China is a good place to buy. If you're looking for good quality leather, except for expensive designer lines, it will be difficult to find.

❏ **Furs:** You'll find inexpensive furs in several shops and markets. However, don't expect stylish tailoring or quality furs. Some of cheapest furs are found in Beijing's Russian Market which is frequented by Russians who buy in large volume for resale back home.

❏ **Toys:** You'll find lots of toys offered by vendors near major sightseeing attractions as well as in department stores and markets. Look for kites, dolls, tops, and stuffed animals.

❏ **Childrens' clothing:** Most department stores have a childrens' section which offers a wide range of clothes, from cute silk pajamas and dresses to knitted sweaters and jackets. Prices tend to be inexpensive compared to what you may pay back home. Many of the clothes, such as the colorful and embroidered silk pajamas, make nice gifts.

❏ **Luggage:** China's many markets offer a wide range of soft-sided and hard-sided luggage at reasonable prices. If you need an extra bag, you should be able to pick up one for one-half to one-third the price you might pay back home. The quality may not be great, but the prices are right, and the bags should get you back home in style.

❏ **Musical instruments:** If you collect musical instruments, China has some unique pieces, especially sting and wind instruments, you'll want to survey. You'll occasionally come across tribal instruments that make wonderful home decorative items.

❏ **Music:** If you're interested in traditional or modern Chinese music, visit a music or bookstore where you will find lots of CDS and tapes. Although ostensibly illegal, some stores still offer inexpensive pirated CDS of Western music.

❏ **Curios:** Too numerous to mention. They are everywhere, from vendor stalls and shops at major sightseeing attractions to flea markets and Friendship Stores.

❏ **Painted snuff bottles and eggs:** This particular art form involves producing traditional miniature paintings on the inside of small glass snuff bottles and on eggs. The attention to detail is incredible.

❏ **Papercuts:** This popular art form involves cutting figures from colored paper with a scissor. An interesting and fascinating art form that is uniquely Chinese. If you have a chance to meet a papercut artist at work, chances are you can directly purchase a personalized papercut.

❏ **Dough modeling:** Another unique Chinese art form involving the use of clay dough to make a variety of miniature figures, from panda bears and children to fruits and vegetables. The dough figurines are usually brightly painted. An intriguing art form that many people love to collect.

❑ **Micro carvings and paintings:** Another unique art form produced on bamboo, ivory, porcelain, rice grains, and other mediums. Usually involves carving or painting Chinese characters in miniature form. The characters are so small that you need to see them with a magnifying glass.

❑ **Traditional medicines:** Many markets, department stores, and street shops offer a wide range of traditional medicines. Most of these places do a good local business. You may want to visit them more for the cultural experience than for shopping. What do you do with a pickled snake?

❑ **Tea:** China is famous for its many variety of teas. Look for packaged teas in Friendship Stores and department stores. These can make nice gifts for your tea drinking friends.

❑ **Wine and liquor:** Each province produces its own unique varieties of wines and liquors. You'll see many of these on display in Friendship Stores and department stores.

The list of products goes on and on as you explore China's many department stores, shopping arcades, shops, and markets. Wherever you go, you're bound to discover something unique and interesting.

WHERE TO SHOP

You may be amazed at all the different shopping venues available to both locals and visitors. Shopping opportunities seem to be everywhere, from hotel lobbies and museums to historical sites and airport shopping arcades. Everywhere you seem to visit, there's shopping for similar types of items.

China's major shopping centers are found in Beijing, Shanghai, and Guangzhou and to a lesser extent in Chongqing which is famous for its many art galleries. The old days, which were not too long ago, when shopping was designated as a tourist activity for generating foreign exchange and thus primarily confined to government-run Friendship Stores and transacted via a separate currency, are gone. The New China is all about making money which translates into lots of venture capitalists, joint ventures, private shopkeepers, street vendors, upstart entrepreneurs, and shopping courtesy of linkages with the wealthy Chinese investment communities in Hong Kong, Taiwan, and Singapore (they love investing in multi-storey department stores). You'll still find the ubiquitous Friendship Stores, but many of them have been transformed into modern department stores which must compete with a profusion of new joint venture department stores and shopping arcades modeled after those found in Hong Kong, Taiwan, Singapore, and Bangkok.

❑ China's major shopping centers are found in Beijing, Shanghai, and Guangzhou.

❑ Friendship Stores must now compete with new joint venture department stores and shopping arcades modeled after those found in Hong Kong, Taiwan, Singapore, and Bangkok.

❑ Look for our "Mao's Malls" in Shanghai, Guangzhou, and Beijing.

❑ Few museums operate their own arts and crafts shops. Watch out for aggressive salespeople who may misrepresent their products.

❑ One of the most delightful shopping experiences involves visiting the arts and crafts institutes in Chongqing and Shanghai.

You'll be faced with numerous shopping choices in the New China, ranging from glitzy hotel shopping arcades, shopping centers, joint venture department stores and shops, museum shops, private street shops, and trade shows to the more traditional Friendship Stores, street vendors, and markets. Wherever you travel in China, chances are you will find many opportunities to shop for arts, crafts, and local products along with imported and locally produced international designer label clothes and accessories. As China's economy continues to expand, so does its shopping choices. The trend is to build more and more hotel shopping arcades and multi-storey shopping centers modeled after those elsewhere in Asia.

Here's what you can expect to find when shopping in China's major cities and tourist destinations:

❑ **Hotel Shopping Arcades:** More and more five-star joint venture hotels are developing upscale shopping arcades that primarily showcase designer label clothes and accessories. While some are manufactured in China under licensing agreements, others are imported from the world's major fashion houses in Italy, France, Germany, and England and especially appeal to Asian visitors, expatriates, and China's newly monied upper class. In Beijing it's the **Palace Hotel Shopping Arcade**; in

Shanghai it's the **Portman Ritz-Carlton** and **Jin Jiang Tower**; and in Guangzhou it's the **Garden Hotel Shopping Arcade**.

❑ **Upscale Shopping Centers:** Few cities other than Shanghai have developed stand-alone upscale shopping centers. In Shanghai it's **Maison Mode** and the **Jin Jiang Dickson Center** as well as the two adjacent underground shopping malls collectively known as the **Magnolia Underground Shopping Center**. But if Shanghai, like Hong Kong, is a pacesetter for things to come, more and more air-conditioned shopping centers should appear in other cities of China, especially Beijing and Guangzhou.

❑ **Friendship Stores:** These are convenient one-stop-shop government department stores and arts and crafts emporiums. Every major city has at least one "real" Friendship Store, and they all look very similar in terms of their product mix and services. While for years (until the early 1980s) literally the "only shop in town" for tourists who arrived by bus loads to do their China shopping in a special tourist currency, today these stores still remind one of the old communist shopping culture reserved for foreigners. These multi-level department stores are jam-packed with clothes, accessories, arts, crafts, antiques, jewelry, furniture, carpets, and foods. Although many are somewhat worn and service is often lethargic, they still remain convenient and reliable for tourists. Prices are fixed and usually reasonable, and they offer money exchange desks, packing and shipping services, and taxi stands. If you want to do comparative shopping, especially to get a good sense of current market prices on various items, there are not better places to start than at the local Friendship Store. Chances are you will also find some good buys in these places. Now facing intense competition from more modern and service oriented joint venture department stores, many of the Friendship Stores look like they have fallen on hard times or they have modernized to remain competitive. A good contrast in found in Beijing between the old Friendship Store on Jianguomenwai Street and the newer one called You Yi (Friendship) Shopping City at the Beijing Lufthansa Center adjacent to the Landmark and Kempinski Hotels. The former represents the old shopping culture while the latter represents China's new shopping culture. Then contrast any Friendship Store throughout China with the huge Nextage (Yaohan) Department Store in Shanghai (Pudong area), which represents a joint venture with Japan. The differences are striking; they do not bode well for the future of government-run Friendship Stores.

❑ **Government Department Stores:** The government still operates many departments stores that primarily appeal to local residents. Most of them are filled with inexpensive clothes and household goods that look dated. Others, especially in Shanghai, were originally established to primarily cater to Overseas Chinese. While you may want to visit some of these places, don't expect to buy much. For most visitors, these are more cultural experiences than places to make purchases. Expect many of these department stores to be very crowded. Local residents are avid department store shoppers.

❑ **Joint Venture Department Stores:** During the past few years several new department stores have been built by joint venture operations in China's major cities. Most are very modern multi-level structures, complete with escalators and elevators, air-conditioned, and offering the latest in fashions, accessories, make-up, jewelry, arts and crafts, music, electronics, and household goods, many of which are produced by joint ventures in China. These department stores especially appeal to China's new class of affluent young people, many of whom are employed with joint ventures where they make relatively good salaries (three to four times that of government employees). These department stores, too, can be cultural experiences—observe what China's new class of young shoppers prefer in this new "communism with a capitalist face" economy. Modeled after similar department stores in Hong Kong, Taiwan, and Singapore, they are relatively upscale compared to the older and more lower middle class government-run department stores. Many of these department stores include grocery stores which you may want to visit to stock up on drinks and snacks. The grandest of these department stores are found in Shanghai (**Nextage**) and Guangzhou (**Guangzhou World Trade Centre Complex**).

❑ **Underground Shopping Malls:** Here's the ultimate capitalist commentary on the Sino-Soviet conflict of the 1960s and 1970s and the ending of the Cold War—

underground bomb shelters converted into shopping malls. We call them "Mao's Malls". Some are flea markets whereas others are upscale joint venture shopping complexes. The most interesting and upscale one is found in Shanghai, an underground labyrinth of more than 200 joint venture shops. Look for less upscale underground shopping complexes in both Beijing and Guangzhou. We'll examine this unique shopping venue in the Chapters on Shanghai, Beijing, and Guangzhou.

❑ **Private Street Shops:** All cities have commercial streets lined with a large variety of private shops offering everything from food and electronic goods to clothes, arts, crafts, and music. While most of these shops cater to the consumer needs of local residents, others may be of interest to tourists. In Beijing the major shopping street is **Wangfujing Street**; in Shanghai the major shopping streets are **Nanjing and Huaihai Roads**; in Guangzhou it's **Beijing and Wende Roads**. Most major cities, such as Beijing, Shanghai, and Xi'an, also have their own cultural streets or sections which are lined with arts, crafts, and antique shops that especially appeal to tourists. In Beijing it's **Liulichang Culture Street**; in Shanghai it's the Old City or **Yu Yuan** (Jade Garden); in Xi'an it's the **Ancient Culture Street**; and in Shenzhen it's the whole **China Folk Culture Village** complex.

❑ **Factories and emporiums:** Invariably you'll end up visiting a silk, carpet, jade, embroidery, or cloisonne factory where you will be taken initially on a tour of the manufacturing section, where you can see artisans at work, and then finish with a stop at the factory shop where you are expected to buy. While interesting to see the artisans at work, prices and selections are not necessarily any better at the factory shop than in Friendship Stores and department stores. Indeed, many of these factories are "tour bus stop shops" that pay tour guides and drivers commissions to bring tourists to their doors. Knowing you'll probably end up in such places, be sure to know your comparative prices before making such purchases. Also, even if prices are displayed on items, don't conclude these are fixed prices. Bargain hard for anything you purchase at one of these factories or emporiums.

❏ **Vendor Stalls and Shops:** Many of China's new entrepreneurs can be found along major streets and at most sightseeing attractions operating small vendor stalls from which they sell a large variety of items, from clothes to curios and toys. Others operate shops that offer a wide range of arts, crafts, and curious. Be sure to bargain in these places. Some may claim "fixed prices," but try bargaining anyway.

❏ **Museum Shops:** Few museums operate their own arts and crafts shops. Since museums have had to become more entrepreneurial in generating additional operating funds, they have "privatized" their commercial operations—the so-called museum shops and galleries. Consequently, don't assume a museum's shops belong to museum or the government and thus should be trusted for quality and value. On the contrary, many museum shops are owned and operated by private concessions. While many of these shops offer excellent quality and value and are very reliable (Beijing and Shanghai), others may be less so (Chongqing). Salespeople at some museum shops and galleries can be very aggressive. Unfortunately, some also tend to take advantage of unsuspecting tourists by quoting outrageous prices on various arts and crafts. It's not unusual to pay 100 to 1000 percent more for similar items you can purchase at the fixed-price Friendship Stores. Our advice: know want you are doing and be wary of merchants, however nice they may appear. And bargain very hard if you suspect the shop is being run by a private concession. Forget the old 40 to 50 percent discount rule. Try 70, 80, or 90 percent. You may just get it!

❏ **Art Institutes:** One of the most delightful shopping experiences in China involves visiting various arts and crafts institutes where you will have a chance to see artists and craftspeople at work and in some cases purchase items directly from them. Two of our favorite such places are the **Painter's Village** in Chongqing and the **Shanghai Arts and Crafts Institute** in Shanghai. In both cases you will get a close-up view from master artists and craftspeople on how various art and craft forms are produced. You'll also have a chance to meet these talented people and learn about their work. Many of the older artists and craftspeople literally survived the Cultural Revolution, giving up their work to labor in fields as farmers for years and then being rehabilitated as master artists and craftspeople. Don't be timid about bargaining in these places, even when you're dealing directly with the artist who may or may not know the real market value to his or her work. Like many privatized museum shops, prices in these places can also be unexpectedly high. It's up to you to bring them in line with reality!

❏ **Private Collectors:** At least in the case of Shanghai, which is famous for being a city of collectors, you can pursue another shopping avenue—private collectors who sell from their homes. If you're interested in collecting stamps, old watches, miniature boats, shells, or match boxes, you may want to seek out these private collectors. We'll survey this shopping option in the chapter on the treasures and pleasures of Shanghai.

❏ **Traditional Markets:** Since supermarkets and grocery stores have yet to make major inroads in China, most local residents visit their local market each day to buy fresh meats and produce (welcome to early morning rush hour traffic!). Each city has several of these traditional markets that service various neighborhoods. In addition to offering lots of interesting food in seemingly unsanitary conditions, these markets also sell a variety of additional items, such as appliances, kitchen items, and even pets. Visiting these markets is more a cultural experience (great photo opportunities) than a venture into quality shopping. At the same time, you will find other types of traditional markets, offering everything from clothes and accessories to furniture, antiques, and collectibles. Some basically function as large flea markets where you can occasionally discover a unique treasure. In Beijing, which is gradually moving its traditional markets into multi-storey buildings, it's **Beijing Curio City, Hong Xiao Market, Liang Ma Antique Market, Chao Wai Market, Xui Shui Market, Russian Market,** and **San Li Tun Market**; in Shanghai it's the **Dong Tai Market** and **Fuyou Flea Market**; in Xi'an it's the **Beiyuanmen Street Antique Bazaar**; and in Guangzhou it's the **Qing Ping and Daihe Road markets**. Markets are meant for bargaining, some more so than others.

❑ **Airport Shopping Arcades:** Most major airports offer a wide range of shopping opportunities. Look for small airport shops offering local food products as well as arts, crafts, jewelry, and books.

Rules For Success

S hopping in China follows its own set of rules and logic that differs from shopping in most other countries. On the one hand, there's lots of shopping available for all kinds of local handcrafted products, which ostensibly makes China a shopper's paradise. On the other hand, procuring these items can at times be difficult because of uncertainty about the pricing and quality of products.

Our task in this chapter is to make some sense out of China's new shopping culture so that you can acquire your treasures with confidence and ease. Properly oriented, you should be better able to effectively navigate your way through China's many department stores, shops, and markets.

TWO PRICING AND PRODUCT CULTURES

The three shopping cultures we identified in Chapter 5 revolve around two pricing and product cultures. Depending on where you shop, expect to encounter two very distinct styles of shopping, each with its own set of rules and related pitfalls. The first one appears more like the one you are probably used to back home—fixed prices where items are displayed with price tags and purchases result in signed receipts. This shopping culture is primarily found in department stores and joint venture shops—especially designer label boutiques. You'll probably feel comfortable shopping in these places because you know exactly what to pay for particular items and you feel confident that the goods presented are genuine. The best examples of such shops are the Friendship Stores and upscale shops attached to four- and five-store hotels. Occasionally you may encounter a special sale in these places or you may be offered a discount, but in general prices are fixed and product integrity is relatively predictable.

The second shopping culture involves price uncertainty and questionable product integrity. Once you shop outside department stores and upscale boutiques, you'll encounter much of this culture. Markets, factories, and private shops, including many concessions at museums and tourist stops, are part of this unpredictable shopping culture. In general, most prices are not displayed or, if they are, they may be meaningless—a form of wishful thinking on the part of merchants. You should never pay the initial asking price in these places. If you do, you will be overpaying what may be an astronomical price. In these places, final pricing is arrived at through the process of bargaining. However, unlike bargaining in many other parts of the world, including Hong Kong, where the rule of thumb is to counter with one-third or one-half of the initial asking price and then settle for a final price somewhere in between, in China the bargaining process can involve a totally absurd range, with discounts sometimes as much as 90 percent of the initial asking price. In addition, the quality and authenticity of products, especially antiques and jewelry, is often misrepresented to unsuspecting tourists. Consequently, you may feel good at purchasing an item at 30 percent of the asking price but then later discover your still paid two or three times the actual value because the quality or authenticity of the item was misrepresented. Nonetheless, shopping in this second culture, especially in traditional street and flea markets, can be a great deal of fun, and you can often get unique items and good buys—if you know your products and you are a savvy bargainer. While most visitors enjoy shopping in these places, few are savvy bargainers;

> ❑ The fixed-price culture primarily operates in department stores and joint venture shops.
>
> ❑ The second shopping culture involves price uncertainty and questionable product integrity and is primarily found in markets, factories, and private shops.
>
> ❑ While most visitors enjoy shopping in the second shopping culture, few are savvy bargainers; many overpay and get cheated.
>
> ❑ Do your initial comparative shopping at Friendship Stores where prices are fixed and product integrity is good.
>
> ❑ Special sales are rare, except in Hong Kong during June and December.

visitors enjoy shopping in these places, few are savvy bargainers; many overpay and get cheated in the process.

Our first shopping rule of thumb is to assume that all prices in shops and markets are subject to bargaining unless you are in an obvious fixed-price department store or joint venture shop; factory shops and handicraft emporiums are not department stores. Our second rule of thumb is that many goods are likely to be misrepresented either out of ignorance (some merchants really don't know about the product but want you to feel confident and thus give inaccurate information) or by deliberately scamming customers (many merchants believe if the tourist is so gullible he thinks he can buy an early dynasty porcelain or quality jade for practically nothing, he deserves what he gets).

PLAN AND COMPARE PRICES

We strongly recommend that you approach China with a well organized shopping plan. Your plan should include a list of items you want to purchase as well as a list of shopping areas and specific shops you wish to visit. Use this book as a starting point for identifying possible products and specific shops. List the items you wish to purchase and the people for whom you are buying as well as the comparison prices you gathered before you left home. This well organized shopping plan will enable you to make the most of your shopping time in China.

However, if you're uncertain about what to buy in China and decide to "wait and see" what's available, you can quickly do your planning and comparative shopping immediately upon arriving in China. We strongly recommend visiting the Friendship Stores in each city prior to venturing into the markets or private shops, factories, and handicraft emporiums. These shops, which resemble department stores and handicraft emporiums, are stocked with a wide range of products at fixed prices. By surveying their offerings and prices, you'll have a solid information base from which to compare prices and products in other shops. In the end, after you've shopped around and discovered the price advantages and convenience of Friendship Stores, you may decide to return to them to do much of your shopping. They also offer the added advantages of exchanging money, packing, and shipping.

PRICE TAGS JUST FOR YOU

Bargaining is a way of life in many places you will visit in China. While most stores display price tags on items, except for the truly "fixed price" department stores and name-brand designer shops, don't take such labeling as a sign of the final price you should pay. Rather, treat stated prices as starting prices from which you begin a bargaining process to determine the final price **you** will pay. In fact, many shops put price tags on items because they know tourists tend to pay what's marked on the tag. Don't let these tags dissuade you from negotiating a price that can be 30, 50, or 70 percent of what is marked on the tag.

DETERMINE FAIR MARKET VALUES

Before you can effectively play the bargaining game, you need to have some idea of the fair local market value for various items. Since Chinese department stores have fixed prices, begin identifying fair market values for comparable items by visiting department stores. Keep in mind that small shops selling the same items should be 10 to 20 percent less than the department stores simply because their overhead is less. Once you have department store pricing information, begin visiting shops on your list. But before making a purchase, try to visit three shops to get comparative prices for the same items. Check these prices with your home and department store pricing information and then begin bargaining in earnest for your best deal. If the price is no different than the department store price, buy it at the department store where you will encounter fewer problems should you need to return the item.

PREPARE FOR PRICE UNCERTAINTY

Most North American and European tourists come from fixed-price cultures where prices are nicely displayed on items. The only price uncertainty may be a sales tax added to the total amount at the cash register. Only on very large-ticket items, such as automobiles, boats, houses, furniture, carpets, and jewelry, can you expect to negotiate the price. If you want to get the best deal, you must do comparative shopping as well as wait for special discounts and sales. Bargain shopping in such a culture centers on comparative pricing of items. Shopping becomes a relatively passive activity involving the examination of printed advertisements in newspapers and catalogs.

Expert shoppers in fixed-price cultures tend to be those skilled in carefully observing and comparing prices in the print advertising media. They clip coupons and know when the best sales are being held for particular items on certain days. They need not be concerned with cultivating personal relationships with merchants or salespeople in order to get good buys.

Like fish out of water, expert shoppers from fixed-price cultures may feel lost when shopping in China. Few of their fixed-price shopping skills are directly transferable to the Chinese shopping environment. Except for department stores, shops seldom advertise in the print media or on TV and radio. Special sales are rare, except in Hong Kong during June and December.

You will find plenty of opportunities to practice your bargaining skills in China, especially in small shops and markets. The general guideline is this: **unless you see a sign stating otherwise, you can expect prices of most goods in small shops to be negotiable**. And even if you see a "fixed price" sign, prices may still be negotiable; you really won't know until you try to bargain. You can safely assume that all stated prices are the starting point from which you should receive anything from a 10-50 percent discount, and perhaps much higher, depending upon your haggling skills, level of commitment to obtain reduced prices, and the merchant's original pricing strategy.

- ❏ Many price tags are meaningless for determining the price you should pay. View them as starting prices from which to start the bargaining process.

- ❏ Most goods in small shops are negotiable.

- ❏ Expect to receive at least 10 to 20 percent discount on most items in stores willing to discount.

- ❏ Tailors normally quote a fixed price subject to little or no negotiation.

- ❏ Bargain on ready-made items you can carry out of the shop.

- ❏ Never accept the first price offered.

- ❏ Be sure to get a receipt as well as observe the packing process.

The structure of prices on certain goods and services varies. The prices on items in department stores are fixed. Taxi prices may be negotiable, but negotiate before you get into the cab. Hotel prices are subject to a variety of discounts for different categories of travelers—VIP, business, government, weekend, and tourist.

When in doubt if a price is fixed, negotiable, or subject to discounts, **always ask for a special discount**. After the salesperson indicates the price, ask one of three questions: *"Is it possible to do any better on this price?"*, *"What kind of discount can* *you give me on this?"* or *"What is your best price?"* If the person offers a discount, you can either accept it or attempt to negotiate the price through a bargaining process.

While skilled shoppers in fixed-price cultures primarily compare prices by reading ads and listening to special announcements, the skilled shopper in bargaining cultures is primarily engaged in face-to-face encounters with sellers. To be successful, the shopper must use various interpersonal skills. Once you know these and practice bargaining, you should become a very effective shopper in China.

ESTABLISH VALUE AND PRICE

Not knowing the price of an item, many shoppers from fixed-price cultures face a problem. What is the actual value of the item? How much should I pay? At what point do I know I'm getting a fair price? These questions can be answered in several ways. First, you should have some idea of the value of the item, because you already did comparative shopping at home by examining catalogs and visiting discount houses, department stores, and specialty shops. If you are interested in a name-brand designer watch, for example, you should know what that same item or comparable watch costs back home.

Second, you have done comparative shopping among the various shops you've encountered in various cities of China in order to **establish a price range** for positioning yourself in the bargaining process. You've visited a department store in Beijing or Shanghai to research how much a similar item is selling for at a fixed price. You've checked with a shop in your hotel and compared prices there. In your hotel you might ask *"How much is this item?"* and then act a little surprised that it appears so expensive. Tell them that you are a hotel guest and thus you want their *"very best price."* At this point the price may decrease by 10 to 20 percent as you are told this is *"our very special price,"* *"our first-customer-of-the-day price,"* or *"our special hotel guest price."*

Once you receive a discounted *"special price"* from your first price inquiry, expect to get another 10 to 20 percent through further negotiation. But unless this is a one of a kind item and you are certain that you want to purchase it, do not negotiate any more at this time. Take the shop's business card and record on the back the item, the original price, and the first discount price; thank the shopkeeper, and tell him or her that you may return. Repeat this same scenario in a few other shops. After doing three or four comparisons, you will establish a price range for particular items. This range will give you a fairly accurate idea of the going discount price. At this point you should be prepared to do some serious haggling, playing one shop off against another.

Effective shoppers in China quickly learn how to comparative shop and negotiate the best deal. In learning to be effective, you don't need to be timid, aggressive, or obnoxious—extreme behaviors frequently exhibited by first-time practitioners of the Asian art of bargaining. Although you may feel bargaining is a defensive measure to avoid being ripped off by unscrupulous merchants, it is an acceptable way of doing business in many Asian cultures. Merchants merely adjust their profit margins to the customer, depending on how they feel about the situation as well as their current cash flow needs. It is up to you to adapt to such a pricing culture.

One problem you may soon discover is that every situation seems to differ somewhat, and differences between items and shops can be significant. For example, you can expect to receive larger discounts on jewelry than on shoes. Discounts on jewelry may be as great as 50 to 60 percent whereas discounts on home furnishings may be only 10 to 20 percent.

The one major exception to bargaining concerns tailors. Tailors normally quote you a fixed price subject to little or no negotiation; you merely trust that you are getting a fair price and, after all, it is not a good idea to make your tailor unhappy by bargaining when he doesn't want to. He may compensate by cheapening the quality of your clothes. Only in tailor shops do we avoid forcing the price issue by bargaining. At best ask *"Is it possible to do any better on the price?"*, use a common friend's name as reference, or ask for an extra shirt—but don't risk being short-changed on quality just to save a few dollars. If you comparative shop among a few tailor shops, you will quickly identify what should be the fair market rate for tailoring services assuming the use of comparable quality materials.

Our general rule on what items to bargain for is this: bargain on ready-made items you can carry out of the shop. If you must have an item custom-made, be very careful how you arrive at the final price. In most cases you should not bargain other than respond to the first price by asking *"Is this your best price?"* Better still, drop a few names, agree on a mutually satisfactory price, and then insist that you want top quality for that price.

Except for custom-made items, department stores, and shops displaying a "fixed price" sign, never accept the first price offered. Rather, spend some time going through our bargaining scenario. Once you have accepted a price and purchased the item, be sure to get a receipt as well as observe the packing process. While few merchants will try to cheat you, some tourists have had unpleasant experiences which could have been avoided by following some simple rules of shopping in unfamiliar places.

GET THE BEST DEAL POSSIBLE

Chances are you will deal with a Chinese merchant who is a relatively seasoned businessperson; he or she is a family entrepreneur who thrives on status and personal relationships. As soon as you walk through the door, most merchants will want to sell you items then and there. Sometimes shop personnel follow you around so closely that you may inadvertently step on them. If you occasionally back up abruptly, you can discourage this closeness and give yourself some personal space. Some shopkeepers will be aggressive and pester you, trying to sell you anything and everything in their store; this may make you feel uncomfortable and you quickly attempt to flee from the shop! Others are very low-keyed, letting visitors wander around on their own and then slowly engage them in conversation. They know that once you leave their shop, you probably will not come back. Before you leave, the merchant must convince you that you are getting the best possible deal and that you should not waste your time talking to others. In many cases you will, in fact, get the best possible deal in such a shop.

The best deal you will get is when you have a personal relationship with the merchant. Contrary to what others may tell you about bargains for tourists, you often can get as good a deal—sometimes even better—than someone from the local community. It is simply a myth that tourists can't do as well on prices as the locals. Indeed, we often do better than the locals because we have done our comparative shopping and we know well the art of bargaining—something locals are often lax in doing. In addition, some merchants may give you a better price than the locals because you are "here today and gone tomorrow"; you won't be around to tell their regular customers about your very special price or expect it again next month.

PRACTICE 12 RULES OF BARGAINING

The art of bargaining in China can take on several different forms. In general, you want to achieve two goals in this haggling process: **establish the value of an item and get the best possible price**. The following bargaining rules generally work well.

1. **Do your research before initiating the process.** Compare prices among various shops, starting with the fixed-price items in department stores. Spot-check price ranges among shops in and around your hotel. Also, refer to your research done with catalogs and discount houses back home to determine if the discount is sufficient to warrant purchasing the item abroad rather than at home.

2. **Determine the exact item you want.** Select the particular item you want and then focus your bargaining around that one item without expressing excessive interest and commitment. Even though you may be excited by the item and want it very badly, once the merchant knows you are committed to buying this one item, you weaken your bargaining position. Express a passing interest; indicate through eye contact with other items in the shop that you are not necessarily committed to the one item. As you ask about the other items, you should get some sense concerning the willingness of the merchant to discount prices.

3. **Set a ceiling price you are willing to pay.** Before engaging in serious negotiations, set in your mind the maximum amount you are willing to pay, which may be 20 percent more than you figured the item should sell for based on your research. However, if you find something you love that is really unique, be prepared to pay whatever you must. In many situations you will find unique items not available anywhere else. Consider buying **now** since the item may be gone when you return. Bargain as hard as you can and then pay what you have to—even though it may seem painful—for the privilege of owning a unique item. Remember, it only hurts once. After you return home you will most likely enjoy your wonderful purchase and forget how painful it seemed at the time to buy it at less than your expected discount. Above all, do not pass up an item you really love just because the bargaining process does not fall in your favor. It is very easy to be *"penny wise but pound foolish"* in China simply because the bargaining process is such an ego-involved activity. You may return home forever regretting that you failed to buy a lovely item just because you refused to "give" on

the last $5 of haggling. In the end, put your ego aside, give in, and buy what you really want. Only you and the merchant will know who really won, and once you return home the $5 will seem to be such an insignificant amount. Chances are you still got a good bargain compared to what you would pay elsewhere if, indeed, you could find a similar item!

4. **Play a role**. Shopping in China involves playing the roles of buyer and seller. Asians tend to be terrific role players, more so than Westerners. In contrast to many western societies, where being a unique individual is emphasized, high value is not placed on individualism in China. Rather, the Chinese learn specific sets of behaviors appropriate for the role of father, son, daughter, husband, wife, blood friend, classmate, superior, subordinate, buyer, seller. They easily shift from one role to another, undergoing major personality and behavioral changes without experiencing mental conflicts. When you encounter a Chinese businessman, you are often meeting a very refined and sophisticated role player. Therefore, it is to your advantage to play complementary roles by carefully structuring your personality and behavior to play the role of buyer. If you approach sellers by just "being yourself"—open, honest, somewhat naive, and with your own unique personality—you may be quickly walked over by a seasoned seller. Once you enter a shop, think of yourself as an actor walking on stage to play the lead role as a shrewd buyer, bargainer, and trader.

5. **Establish good will and a personal relationship.** A shrewd buyer also is charming, polite, personable, and friendly. You should have a sense of humor, smile, and be light-hearted during the bargaining process. But be careful about eye contact which can be threatening to Asians. Keep it to a minimum. Asian sellers prefer to establish a personal relationship so that the bargaining process can take place on a friendly, face-saving basis. In the end, both the buyer and seller should come out as winners. This cannot be done if you approach the buyer in very serious and harsh terms. You should start by exchanging pleasantries concerning the weather, your trip, the city, or the nice items in the shop. After

exchanging professional cards or determining your status, the shopkeeper will know what roles should be played in the coming transaction.

6. **Let the seller make the first offer.** If the merchant starts by asking you *"How much do you want to pay?"*, avoid answering; immediately turn the question around: *"How much are you asking?"* Remember, many merchants try to get you to pay as much as you are willing and able to pay—not what the value of the item is or what he or she is willing to take. You should never reveal your ability or willingness to pay a certain price. Keep the seller guessing, thinking that you may lose interest or not buy the item because it appears too expensive. Always get the merchant to initiate the bargaining process. In so doing, the merchant must take the defensive as you shift to the offensive.

7. **Take your time, being deliberately slow in order to get the merchant to invest his or her time in you.** The more you indicate that you are impatient and in a hurry, the more you are likely to pay. When negotiating a price, **time** is usually in your favor. Many shopkeepers also see time as a positive force in the bargaining process. Some try to keep you in their shop by serving you tea, coffee, soft drinks, or liquor while negotiating the price. Be careful; this nice little ritual may soften you somewhat on the bargaining process as you begin establishing a more personal relationship with the merchant. The longer you stay in control prolonging the negotiation, the better the price should be. Although some merchants may deserve it, **never** insult them. Merchants need to "keep face" as much as you do in the process of giving and getting the very best price.

8. **Use odd numbers in offering the merchant at least 40 percent less than what he or she initially offers.** Avoid stating round numbers, such as 60, 70, or 100. Instead, offer $62.50, $73.85, or $81.13. Such numbers impress upon others that you may be a seasoned haggler who knows value and expects to do well in this negotiation. Your offer will probably be 15 percent less than the value you determined for the item. For example, if the merchant asks $100,

offer $62.50, knowing the final price should probably be $75.00. The merchant will probably counter with only a 10 percent discount—$90. At this point you will need to go back and forth with another two or three offers and counter-offers.

9. **Appear disappointed and take your time again.** Never appear upset or angry with the seller. Keep your cool at all times by slowly sitting down and carefully examining the item. Shake your head a little and say, *"Gee, that's too bad. That's much more than I had planned to spend. I like it, but I really can't go that high."* Appear to be a sympathetic listener as the seller attempts to explain why he or she cannot budge more on the price. Make sure you do not accuse the merchant of being a thief, even though he may be one! Use a little charm, if you can, for the way you conduct the bargaining process will affect the final price. This should be a civil negotiation in which you nicely bring the price down, the seller "saves face," and everyone goes away feeling good about the deal.

10. **Counter with a new offer at a 35 percent discount.** Punch several keys on your calculator, which indicates that you are doing some serious thinking. Then say something like *"This is really the best I can do. It's a lovely item, but $67.25 is really all I can pay."* At this point the merchant will probably counter with a 20 percent discount—$80.

11. **Be patient, persistent, and take your time again by carefully examining the item.** Respond by saying *"That's a little better, but it's still too much. I want to look around a little more."* Then start to get up and look toward the door. At this point the merchant has invested some time in this exchange, and he or she is getting close to a possible sale. The merchant will either let you walk out the door or try to stop you with another counter-offer. If you walk out the door, you can always return to get the $80 price. But most likely the merchant will try to stop you, especially if there is still some bargaining room. The merchant is likely to say: *"You don't want to waste your time looking elsewhere. I'll give you the best price anywhere—just for you. Okay, $75. That's my final price."*

12. **Be creative for the final negotiation.** You could try
    for $70, but chances are $75 will be the final price
    with this merchant. Yet, there may still be some room
    for negotiating **extras**. At this point get up and walk
    around the shop and examine other items; try to
    appear as if you are losing interest in the item you
    were bargaining for. While walking around, identify
    a $5-10 item you like which might make a nice gift
    for a friend or relative, which you could possibly
    include in the final deal. Wander back to the $75
    item and look as if your interest is waning and per-
    haps you need to leave. Then start to probe the
    possibility of including the extras while agreeing on
    the $75: *"Okay, I might go $75, but only if you include
    this with it."* The *this* would be the $5-10 item you
    eyed. You might also negotiate with your credit card.
    Chances are the merchant is expecting cash on the
    $75 discounted price and may add a 2-5 percent *com-
    mission* if you want to use your credit card. In this
    case, you might respond to the $75 by saying, *"Okay,
    I'll go with the $75, but only if I can use my credit card."*
    You may get your way, your bank will float you a loan
    in the interim, and in case you later learn there is a
    problem with your purchase—such as misrepresenta-
    tion—the credit card company may even help you.
    Finally, you may want to negotiate packing and de-
    livery processes. If it is a fragile item, insist that it be
    packed well so you can take it with you on the air-
    plane or have it shipped. If it is a large item, insist
    that the shop deliver it to your hotel or to your
    shipper. If the shop is shipping it by air or sea, try to
    get them to agree to absorb some of the freight and
    insurance costs.

This slow, civil, methodical, and sometimes charming approach to bargaining works well in most of Asia, and with some
modifications, in China and especially Hong Kong. However,
merchants do differ in how they respond to situations. In some
cases, your timing may be right: the merchant is in need of cash
flow that day and thus he or she is willing to give you the price
you want, with little or no bargaining. Others will not give more
than a 10 to 20 percent discount unless you are a friend of a
friend who is then eligible for the special "family discount." And
others are not good businessmen, are unpredictable, lack moti-
vation, or are just moody; they refuse to budge on their prices
even though your offer is fair compared to the going prices in

other shops. In these situations, unless it's a unique item you can find nowhere else, it is best to leave the shop and find one which is more receptive to the traditional haggling process.

Bargaining in traditional markets requires a different approach and may result in larger discounts. In contrast to the numerous polite merchants you encounter in shops, sellers in open-air markets tend to be lower-class, earthy, expressive, pushy, persistent, and often rude as they attempt to sell you many things you cannot use or have no desire to even inspect. They may joke a great deal, shout at you—"*Hey, you mister*"— push and shove, and pester you. These markets are similar to a great big carnival.

In contrast to our previous bargaining rules, successful bargaining in open-air markets should involve **little time** and a great deal of **movement**. If you are interested in an item, ask the price, counter with a price you are willing to pay, and be relatively firm with this price. Since there is a great deal of competition in these markets, it is to your advantage to spend very little time with any one vendor. State your offer and slowly move on to the next vendor. Sellers know they will probably lose you to the competition, so they need to quickly conclude a deal before someone else gets to you; they are motivated to give you large discounts. You also can be a little more aggressive and obnoxious and less charming in these places. If, for example, an item is quoted at $10, offer $4 and move on toward the next vendor. Chances are the seller will immediately drop the price to $7. If you counter with $5 and are moving while stating your offer, the seller will probably agree to your offer. But be sure you want the item. Once your offer is accepted, you are expected to carry through with the purchase. Open-air stalls are great places to accumulate junk while successfully practicing your bargaining skills!

Many of our shopping rules need to be modified in different places you visit in China. In Chapter 7 on Beijing, for example, we outline many additional tips for successful shopping in China, especially Beijing and Chongqing. Be sure to incorporate these with the list in this chapter.

BARGAIN FOR NEEDS, NOT GREED

One word of caution for those who are just starting to learn the fine art of Asian bargaining. **Be sure you really want an item before you initiate the bargaining process**. Many tourists learn to bargain effectively, and then get carried away with their new-found skill. Rather than use this skill to get what they want, they enjoy the process of bargaining so much that they buy many unnecessary items. After all, they got such *"a good deal"* and thus could not resist buying the item. You do not need to fill your suitcases with junk in demonstrating this ego-gratifying skill. If used properly, your new bargaining skills will lead to some excellent buys on items you really need and want.

EXAMINE YOUR GOODS CAREFULLY

Before you commence the bargaining process, carefully examine the item, being sure that you understand the quality of the item for which you are negotiating. Then, after you settle on a final price, make sure you are getting the goods you agreed upon. You should carefully observe the handling of items, including the actual packing process. If at all possible, take the items with you when you leave the shop.

BEWARE OF SCAMS

Although one hopes this will never happen, you may be unfortunate in encountering unscrupulous merchants who take advantage of you. This is more likely to happen at private shops and markets that are set up to cater to the tourist trade. The most frequent scams to watch out for include:

1. **Misrepresenting quality goods.** Be especially cautious in jewelry stores and antique shops. Sometimes so-called expensive antiques are excellent copies and worth no more than US$20. Precious stones, such as rubies, may not be as precious as they appear. Accordingly, you may pay $2,000 for what appears to be a ruby worth $10,000 back home, but in fact you just bought a $25 red spinel. Pearls come in many different qualities, so know your pearls before negotiating a price. Real jade is beautiful, but many buyers unwittingly end up with green plastic, soapstone, or aventurine at jade prices. Some merchants try to sell "new antiques" at "old antique" prices. Many of the fakes are outstanding reproductions, often fooling even the experts. Indeed, the Chinese have been in the reproduction business for over 2,000 years, and they are very good at making new things look old. Since there is a thriving business in copies, you may want to simply shop for reproductions.

2. **Goods not shipped.** The shop may agree to ship your goods home, but once you leave they conveniently forget to do so. You wait and wait, write letters of inquiry, and receive no replies. Unless you insured the item and have all proper receipts, you may never receive the goods you paid for.

Your best line of defense against these and other possible scams is to be very careful wherever you go and whatever you do in relation to handling money. A few precautions should help avoid some of these problems:

1. **Do not trust anyone with your money** unless you have proper assurances they are giving you exactly what you agreed upon.

2. **Do your homework** so you can determine quality and value as well as anticipate certain types of scams.

3. **Examine the goods carefully**, assuming something may be or will go wrong.

4. **Watch very carefully how the merchant handles items** from the moment they leave your hands until they get wrapped and into a bag.

5. **Request receipts** that list specific items and the prices you paid. Although most shops are willing to "give you a receipt" specifying whatever price you want them to write for purposes of deceiving Customs, avoid such pettiness because Customs officials know better, and you may need a receipt with the real price to claim your goods, seek a refund, or put in an insurance claim. Be sure to make your own notation on the back of the receipt indicating the item and its cost in dollars. Many receipts will be written only in Chinese and you may have difficulty a week later determining what receipt was for which item. The approximate dollar value will help you keep track of your spending as you go as well as assist as you fill out your Customs declaration.

If the shop is to ship, be sure you have a shipping receipt which also includes insurance against both loss and damage.

6. **Take pictures of your purchases.** Before anything gets packed, be sure to take a photo of the item with the person who sold it to you. If you later have a problem with your purchase, you'll at least have visual evidence of what you purchased and with whom.

7. **Gain possible protection against scams by using credit cards** for payment, especially for big ticket items which could present problems, even though using them may cost you more. Though credit card companies are not obligated to help you, many will assist if a shop has defrauded you. However, you must be able to substantiate your claim.

If you are victimized, all is not necessarily lost. You should report the problem immediately to the local authorities or your credit card company. While inconvenient and time consuming, nonetheless, these steps should help you get satisfactory results.

PART III

The China Connections

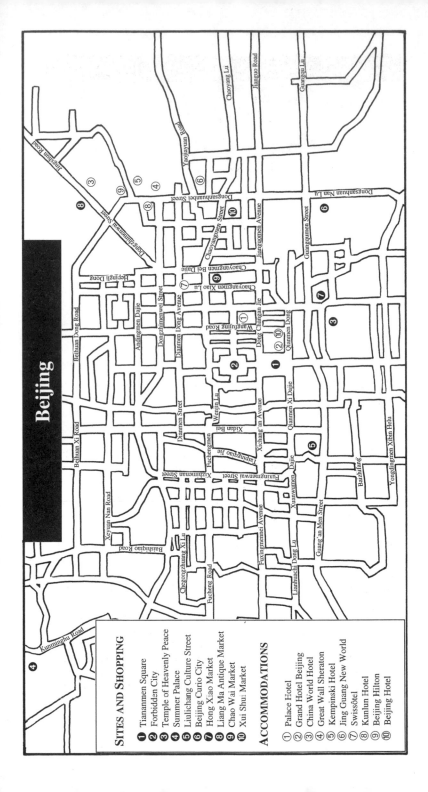

Beijing

Welcome to one of the world's great cities. If you're looking for China's major attractions along with some terrific hotels, restaurants, and shopping, look no further than Beijing. Undergoing rapid transformation, this city is one of those "must visit" destinations in Asia. Indeed, it's difficult to grasp the enormity of China without spending at least a few days experiencing the unique treasures and pleasures of this important city.

GETTING TO KNOW YOU

Beijing is to China what Rome is to Italy, Paris is to France, and London is to England—its historical, cultural, political, and administrative center. To visit China without visiting Beijing is like going to France without at least seeing the treasures and pleasures of Paris.

Within the context of China, Beijing is where the power is, where it gets accumulated and dispensed to other parts of China and the world. It has been the capital of China for the past 500 years. Yes, it was once the city of ruthless emperors and empresses, the scene of the Boxer Rebellion, and a city occupied by foreign troops. Today, it's the city of new emperors and empresses who belong to the political factions that comprise today's powerful ruling Communist Party of China and who are variously allied with new foreign occupants, the joint venture capitalists with their hotels, factories, shopping centers, and high-rise office buildings. Say what you may about the changing politics and economics of China, Mao Zedong still looms large in today's China as his larger than life portrait hanging in Tiananmen Square will quickly remind you.

Beijing is a huge, flat, and sprawling city of 11 million inhabitants who boast an often grand and controversial 3,000+ year history. It's the city that gave rise to many of China's great dynasties and empires that, in turn, shaped much of ancient and contemporary Asian history. For centuries Chinese rulers considered Beijing to be the center of the earth and they accumulated power, built massive armies, and subjugated much of the world according to myopic Chinese geography.

❑ To visit China without seeing Beijing is like going to France without visiting Paris.

❑ Beijing is a city of new-found wealth brought about by recent economic reforms that welcomes joint ventures and encouraged local entrepreneurship.

❑ This is not a beautiful city, although it does have its pockets of beauty, especially the historic Imperial sites.

❑ The longer you stay here, the more it grows on you.

❑ Beijing has a similar location as Madrid, Philadelphia, and Rome.

❑ September and October are probably the best times to visit Beijing because of the pleasant climate.

Today Beijing has all the evidence of a still grand city wielding power over its hinterland as well as playing an increasingly important international role with a booming economy oriented toward greater industrialization, western investment, and exporting "Made in China" goods. This is a city that has preserved some of its glorious and sometimes decadent history as evidenced in the massive Tiananmen Square, the sprawling Forbidden City, and the grand Museum of Chinese History as well as the nearby Ming Tombs, Summer Palace, and Great Wall. It's a gateway city to many of China's most alluring historical treasures. For history buffs, this is heady stuff that makes for great travel adventures. You'll need at least four days here to really see and experience this fascinating city and its outlying areas.

This also is a city of new-found wealth brought about by recent economic reforms that welcomed joint ventures and encouraged local entrepreneurship. The resulting economic boom has meant higher incomes which, in turn, have helped fuel a decidedly consumer economy and a rapidly expanding middle class. The evidence is everywhere, from crowded department stores and fashionable shopping centers to busy restaurants and shops. The popularity of clothing and accessory stores reflects local residents' preference for spending money on the latest in fashion.

BEAUTY IN EYES OF BEHOLDER

By any stretch of Eastern or Western imagination, Beijing is not a beautiful city. It reminds us of Bangkok ten years ago—a rather ugly sprawling urban metropolis of chaotic traffic, concrete buildings, worn two-storey shophouses, crumbling urban infrastructure, and helter-skelter neighborhood settlement patterns. For first-time visitors, this can be a rather disorienting city. The feeling of being lost and the urge to discover greater order in the midst of all the teeming chaos are common amongst visitors. But, then, about the third day the city begins to feel different—you get into the flow of things and begin enjoying what just a few hours earlier was an intimidating environment.

Beijing is a rapidly transforming city where the old is making way for the new. Old worn, crumbling, and makeshift buildings are being torn down in favor of modern concrete and glass construction. Such chaos gives Beijing a unique charm, or perhaps a distinct character, similarly found in many other rapidly developing Asian cities. As the old gives way to the new, construction cranes and new high-rise commercial and residential buildings continue to dramatically alter the city's budding skyline each year.

While Beijing's living chaos gives it a certain Asian charm, its rapid redevelopment is changing the city forever into a modern Western city complete with expressways, ring roads, five-star hotels, department stores, and architecturally adventuresome high-rise commercial buildings. The traditional congested residential communities with their narrow and colorful alleys, the *hutongs*, give way to huge apartment complexes. Within a few years, the old Beijing will most likely disappear under the constant hammering of construction crews intent on transforming this place into a modern 21st century city. All that will be left is to untangle its growing automobile and bus traffic that attempts to transverse a road system designed for an urban era best noted for its bicycle and pedestrian traffic.

If you're looking for beauty in Beijing, you'll have to get off the streets and explore its many historical sites. Worlds apart from the chaos of urban living, beautiful and tranquil monuments of past empires, such as the Forbidden City and the Temple of Heaven, demonstrate the importance of beauty, symmetry, grandness, and power in the life of Beijing and China. Emperors, too, desired to escape the chaos of Beijing's streets! Like Bangkok, Beijing is one of Asia's two truly Asian cities, places where 18th and 19th century colonial powers did not have an opportunity to impose their notions of urban design on such cities. Beijing's exotic charm is found in the chaos of its meandering streets and lanes, in its juxtaposing of the old and new, and in its traditional markets and haggling culture spilling out onto its many streets and lanes. Beijing has its pockets of beauty, but they tend to be in the eye of the beholder. To us, Beijing's beauty lies in its vibrant street life where the old and new constantly come into contact. The longer you stay here, the more it grows on you, and perhaps the more beautiful Beijing becomes in the eyes of the beholder.

THE BASICS

LOCATION

Beijing is located in the southern part of the North China Plain at latitude 39°56'N and longitude 116°20'E or about the same as Madrid, Philadelphia, and Rome—but without the Mediterrean climate and with more wind and dust than elsewhere. The Shanxi and Inner Mongolian plateaus lie to the west and northwest of the city and the Bohai Sea is to the east. The city covers an area of 16,807 square kilometers of which 750 square kilometers is classified as "urban." Five rivers run through the city and empty into the Bohai Sea to the east. The city is 43.71 meters about sea level with hills and mountains found in the northwestern part of the city.

 ## CLIMATE AND WHEN TO GO

Beijing's climate is similar to that of Philadelphia but with more extremes and irritants. It has decidedly hot summers and cold winters. The best times to visit are late spring and early summer, between May and mid-June, and in fall, between late August and early November. Autumn is really the ideal time, especially mid to late October. Spring tends to be short and dry with dusty winds blowing from the Gobi desert. Winter tends to be dry, cold, and windy, and it occasionally snows—not a good time for most visitors. Winter temperatures average -5°C and sometimes fall to -20°C. Spring can be windy with frequent dust storms descending on the city from Central Asia. June and July can be rainy. And July and August is often oppressively hot and humid with temperatures reaching 100°F or higher; average summer temperatures are in the range of 26-30°C. September and October are probably the perfect times to visit Beijing.

POPULATION

Beijing is China's second largest city with a population of approximately 11 million. Because city boundaries encompass rural areas, the population is classified as being 7.1 million urban and 3.9 million rural. Approximately 3 million residents are considered transient laborers, many of whom work in the many construction sites that continue to transform this city's skyline and streets. The Han are the dominant ethnic group comprising over 96 percent of the population. China's 55 other ethnic minorities number over 300,000 and the Huis, Manchus, and Mongolians are the largest minorities. Many of the ethnic groups live in special neighborhoods with their own distinct cultural and linguistic characteristics.

GETTING THERE

Beijing is one of Asia's major transportation hubs. It's serviced by 84 international, 13 regional, and 630 domestic air routes which connect it with 54 cities in 39 countries. More than 40 international airlines maintain booking offices in Beijing. Several major international airlines fly direct from many cities in Asia and Europe. Many travelers from the U.S. arrive after stopovers in Tokyo, Seoul, Hong Kong, or Taipei. However, flying via these major gateway cities can be a long and tiring flight involving a stopover between continuing on to Beijing— 17 to 24 hours from New York City or Washington, DC. Here's one of the best tips for getting to Beijing: take Northwest Airline's direct flight from Detroit to Beijing—13 hours and 15 minutes non-stop. It's the best flight available from the U.S., especially if you are flying from the East Coast, Midwest, or Southeast. We've flown to Asia numerous times, but this is the first flight we've ever taken that has gotten us to Asia so quickly and relatively refreshed. We saved nearly nine hours flying Northwest! Our usual 24-hour travel time to Asia (with layovers on the West Coast or/and Japan's Narita) was cut to just 15 hours 35 minutes. A one hour 20 minute light from Washington Dulles International to Detroit, about an hour on the ground in Detroit and a 13 hour 15 minute flight non-stop and we were in Beijing.

China's regional airlines can carry you to Beijing from other cities within China.

Be sure to confirm your onward or return flights as soon as you arrive in Beijing. Otherwise, your airline reservation could be canceled for failure to reconfirm. Ask you hotel concierge, travel desk, or front desk to do this for you. This is a service you should expect from your hotel.

You also can reach Beijing by rail. Beijing also is connected by train to most major cities within the country. The train trip from Hong Kong to Beijing takes two days (nearly 36 hours) and requires sleeping accommodations. The city has five railway stations with lines connecting to most provincial capitals. The new West Railway Station opened in February 1996 and is Asia's largest rail terminal. You can purchase 1st, 2nd, and 3rd class tickets. Contact your hotel travel desk for information on rail schedules as well as for purchasing tickets. While the hotel desk charges a small commission for this service, it's well worth paying it just to avoid the confusing and time-consuming process of purchasing your own tickets at the railway station.

Hong Kong also is connected to Guangzhou by boat, hovercraft, and bus. If Guangzhou is your first or last connection with Beijing, you may want to take one of these transportation options with Hong Kong. You can get a train or flight between Guangzhou and Beijing.

ARRIVAL

Most visitors to China arrive at the Beijing International Airport, also known as Capital International Airport, which is located 17 miles (27 kilometers) northeast of the city center. Depending on traffic, it usually takes about 30 to 60 minutes to go from the airport to the major hotels. An older and somewhat worn airport designed to accommodate smaller planes, arrival on a 747 can overtax its aging facilities. Immigration and Customs procedures are relatively efficient, as good as any we've experienced in Hong Kong or even super-efficient Singapore. Baggage retrieval, however, leaves much to be desired given the antiquated equipment best designed for handling luggage from small planes. Indeed, it takes three people to operate the system, which must be continually stopped and started in order to make it function properly for large groups arriving on 747s. Expect to spend some time between Immigration and Customs trying to get your baggage from this aging baggage retrieval system.

Just before passing through Immigration, look for the hotel reservation desk next to baggage retrieval and just before Customs. This desk can assist you with reservations should you arrive unprepared. After leaving Customs, you will exit into the rather crowded arrival hall. If you've made arrangements to meet someone here, look for your name on a hand-held sign. Your party should meet you in this area. If not, proceed to the hotel transportation desk in the arrival hall where you can make your transportation arrangements. You'll also find a taxi queue just outside the door to the left of the transportation desk where you can get a metered taxi. A typical trip from the airport to the downtown area takes 30 to 60 minutes and costs about 200 yuan. Depending on which hotel you booked and whether you made prior arrangements, you may find a hotel courtesy van representative in the arrival hall. Look for your hotel sign or go to the hotel counter desk for information on where you can connect with the courtesy van. Forget about renting a car unless you have a valid Chinese driver's license.

If you plan to arrive in Beijing on a domestic flight, make sure you book your flights well in advance. Many flights are fully booked. The overtaxed domestic airport can be extremely crowded.

GETTING AROUND

Beijing is and isn't easy to get around in. It's a very large and sprawling city where distances between the major hotels and sites can be great and involve heavy traffic. If, for example, you stay in the northeast section of the city (Sheraton Great Wall, Landmark Towers, Kempinski, Kunlun, Hilton hotels), you'll be at least a half-hour from such major attractions as the Forbidden City and Tiananman Square and the major shopping streets of Wangfujing Avenue and Liulichang. During rush hour traffic, which seems to go on for several hours during the day, you may spend nearly an hour going between your hotel and these areas. Consequently, you may want to select a hotel closer to these prime areas, especially near Wangfujing Avenue (try the Palace, Grand, Beijing, Holiday Inn Crown Plaza, Overseas Chinese Prime, Peace, Novotel). From there you are within a 15-20 minute walk to the Forbidden City, Tiananmen Square, and major shops. Within this area, plan to do lots of walking.

The quickest and most convenient way to get around Beijing is to hire a guide and driver which can be arranged through your hotel for 200 to 700 yuan per day. Taxis are readily available. If you know where you're going and can understand signs, you might want to use the less expensive buses and metro to get around, although they are often crowded. However, unless you speak Chinese, always take a hotel card with you that has its name and address in Chinese along with a map of the city. If you get lost, you can always show your hotel card to a taxi driver or head for the nearest hotel where someone will speak English and give you directions.

TRANSPORTATION

Since few people outside the major hotels and shops speak English, you're on your own with the local transportation system. It will most likely be an adventure if you decide to flag down taxis and minivans or use buses and the subway to get around the city. But if you have limited time and you're not in the mood for an adventure with the local transportation system and learning the local language, it's best to hire a car and driver. It may cost a lot more, but you'll be glad you made this choice.

While you can easily arrange a car and driver through your hotel, it may be less expensive to call **Capital Taxi Company** directly (Tel. 6461-6688) to arrange for a car and driver. They charge 300 yuan a day, but you're also expected to feed the d river which is another 40-50 yuan for the day.

Taxis are metered and charge according to their size and distance traveled. Luxury sedan taxis cost 12 yuan for the first four kilometers and 2 yuan for each additional kilometer. Small sedan taxis cost 10.4 yuan for the first four kilometers and an additional 1.6 to 2.5 yuan per kilometer thereafter. **Minivans or yellow taxis** (*miandi*)—rather small and uncomfortable—charge 10 yuan for the first 10 kilometers and 1-1.5 yuan per kilometer thereafter. With over 60,000 of these vehicles cruising the streets of Beijing, you can easily flag them down along streets or at street corners. Taxis have a surcharge for waiting or low-speed driving during traffic jams; after 11pm they charge 20 percent more.

Buses (*gonggong qiche*) and **electric buses** (*dianche*) are cheap (5 or 8 mao) but they also tend to be very crowded, especially during rush hours (6:30-8:00am and 5:00-6:30pm). Buses numbered between 1 and 100 only run within the city. Most tourists use bus numbers 1, 4, 37, 52, and 57 which pass near the major hotels and sites. Electric buses numbered in the 100s

❑ Beijing is a large and sprawling city where distances between major hotels and sites can be great and involve heavy traffic.

❑ The easiest way to get around is by hiring a car and driver.

❑ Taxis are metered and charge according to their size and distance traveled.

❑ Most major hotels maintain tour desks that offer standard tours of Beijing and the outlying areas.

❑ Tip when you feel it's appropriate to do so. Doing so will help improve the service ethic in China's budding hospitality industry.

run within the city. Bus No. 103 is popular with tourists because it passes by some of the city's major landmarks, such as the Wangfujing commercial district, Wenjinjie (former Capital Library), the Forbidden City, and the White Pagoda of the Beihai Park. Most tourist maps include the bus lines.

Double decker buses and **mini buses** also provide transportation alternatives. Double decker buses cover five different routes which are popular with tourists. Twelve-passenger mini buses (*xiao gonggong*) are relatively inexpensive (1 to 6 yuan) and essentially cover the same routes as the large public buses.

Beijing's **subway** is very fast and convenient, except during rush hour. Operating from 5:30am to 11:00pm, its two lines circle the city (1) and extend to the far western suburbs (2). The city line stops at several tourist sites: Beijing Railway Station, (Qianmen) Tiananmen Square, Xizhimen (Beijing Zoo), Yonghegong (Lama Temple), Dongsi Shitiao (Workers' Stadium), Xidan (shopping center), and Jianguomen (Ancient Observatory and Friendship Store). One-way fares are 2 yuan.

If you want to join the masses and get around faster than many taxis and buses, you may want to rent a **bicycle**. They can be rented at large bicycle repair shops or from most hotels. Rentals run from three yuan per hour for the best bicycle to 40 yuan for 24 hours for an ordinary bicycle; you'll also be expected to leave a 200-300 yuan deposit. An ordinary one-speed bicycle is more than adequate for navigating the streets of Beijing since the city is very flat. Master Wang at the front of CVIK Plaza is one of the largest bicycle rental places in the city. Since the majority of Beijing residents get around by bicycle, the streets are well organized with bicycle lanes and bicycle parking spaces. However, be very careful in navigating the streets and we cautious about bicycle thieves. Bicycle lanes tend to be very congested and accidents are frequent between bicycles and with pedestrians, cars, and buses.

TOURS

Most major hotels maintain tour desks that offer standard tours of Beijing and the outlying areas as well as can arrange a car and driver. Most have a book which includes descriptive materials on the various tours. You also can contact the China International Travel Service (CITS) office for information on their tours: Travel Arrangement Counter, Lobby Floor of Beijing Tourism Tower, 28 Jianguomenwai Street, Chaoyang District, Beijing 100022, Tel. 6515-8565 or 6515-8844. They also have tour desks at the Lido, Great Wall, Beijing-Toronto, Jianguo, Beijing, and Tianlun hotels.

WATER AND DRINKS

The water in Beijing is not potable except at a few top hotels. Drink it and you will most certainly end up ill. Most hotels provide either bottled water or have an in-house purification system with separate faucets for safe drinking water. When in doubt, ask the front desk about their water system. You may want to carry bottled water with you. You'll find plenty of small shops and grocery stores stocking a wide range of canned soft drinks, beers, fruit juices, and mineral water. We usually make the grocery store one of our first stops to stock up on our favorite drinks. By putting a few of our own in the mini-bar refrigerator, we can avoid the high charges by the hotel for such items.

TIPPING

Tipping is not officially encouraged which may be one reason service has been so bad for so long in China! But this does not mean you should not tip in Beijing. While it is true that tipping is not a widespread practice and people do not expect to receive tips, it's also true that tips are widely and gratefully accepted—especially at the four- and five-star hotels patronized by Western visitors who tend to tip where tips are now often expected. Contrary to what others may tell you or what you have read elsewhere, do tip when you feel it is appropriate. However, you should not corrupt the local economy by engaging in excessive tipping—standard 10 to 15 percent tipping would be excessive outside the major hotels. Cut your normal tipping behavior in half—leave extra change at a restaurant or 5 percent of the total bill or tip 25¢ per bag rather than 50¢ or a $1.00 per bag. Especially in China, good service should be recognized and rewarded, but not excessively. As local personnel in the newly emerging hospitality industry more and more become drawn into a tipping culture tied to service performance, they should improve their service accordingly. Keep in mind that many hotel personnel only make US$100 to US$150 per month, so don't tip the equivalent of a day's or week's wages which is excessive and potentially corrupting. As in most other countries, money talks and walks in China.

RESOURCES AND VIRTUAL BEIJING

Once you arrive in Beijing, check with your hotel concierge for literature on the city. Depending on the hotel, they may have

English copies of *Beijing This Month, Business Beijing, Welcome to China: Beijing, Beijing: The Official Guide*, and a map of the city. The English-language newspapers *China Daily* and *Beijing Weekend* (published on Friday only) also are available at major hotels. Bookstores should have copies of a few popular English-language publications, such as *Beijing Review, China Pictorial, China Today*, and *Women in China*.

If you are Internet savvy and enjoy preparing for your trip by gathering online information before you depart, you might use one of the major search engines to identify sites relevant to "Beijing." Our favorite, Altavista *(http://www.altavista.digital.com)* generates more than 120,000 sites relevant to Beijing! We always have good luck with one of the most popular travel sites on the Internet that has links to major cities around the world: *http://www.city.net*. Go directly to Beijing by entering the following URL: *http://www.city.net/countries/china/beijing*. Also look at: *http://chinatour.com* and *http://chinatoday.com*. If you're interested in surveying major Beijing hotels that also have CNN service, go to this URL: *cnnhotels.com/hotels/asia/china/beijin01.htm*. This site will give you photos of the hotels along with telephone and fax numbers and rates. If you're interested in the Grand Hotel Beijing, go to their site: *www.chinatour.com/ghb/a.htm*. You can gather a great deal of information on Beijing via the Internet by visiting these and many other sites.

THE STREETS OF BEIJING

The first thing that strikes visitors to Beijing is the people and the traffic—lots of both! Beijing is a busy and congested city with people everywhere. The streets seem crowded throughout the day as pedestrians, bicycles, taxis, cars, trucks, and an occasional horse-drawn cart vie for ever decreasing road space.

The good news is that the streets of Beijing are largely devoid of noisy and polluting motorbikes and motorcycles (they are restricted by law), and you'll see no mangy dogs or other animals roaming the streets. Despite the heavy presence of police ostensibly directing traffic in robot-like style, the streets still remain chaotic—too few expressways, flyovers, and one-way streets and too many liberal turn areas, a great deal of jaywalking, too many bicycles amongst the many cars and buses, and just bad "king of the road" driving habits. The traffic cops simply can't cope with the volume of chaotic traffic attempting to negotiate intersections in ten different directions. At times it's bewildering as you feel the traffic is coming at you from every possible direction! Thank god for drivers who can dodge the thousands of bicycles that weave in and out of the traffic in what is an intriguing and elegant form of urban street dance.

Beijing also has a dramatically changing skyline due to the rapid construction of high-rise hotels and commercial buildings responding to a booming economy. Old worn and dilapidating two and three-storey shophouses are being torn down to make way for the new symbols of modernity—the tall Western commercial building of glass and elevators. Every year seems to result in a transformation of the city's skyline with bold architectural designs that attempt to blend traditional Chinese and contemporary Western architectural styles. The result is a unique blend of styles. It also means that Beijing is constantly under construction which generates a great deal of dust, dirt, and noise. It also generates greater traffic congestion as thousands of workers head for construction sites each day and as the city attempts to expand its water and sewerage services by tearing up streets.

Despite a well developed public transportation system consisting of a subway, buses, and taxis, getting around the streets of Beijing remains difficult. Too many cars and buses compete with too many bicycles on streets designed for lighter traffic and with rules that seem nonexistent. Streets that should be one-way and intersections that should have turn restrictions are markedly absent for a city of 11 million. As a result, short trips between the center city and the northeast that should only take 10 minutes instead take 25-40 minutes through a maze annoying stop-and-go traffic. And a 59 kilometer trip from the city to the Great Wall that should only take 45 minutes often becomes a tedious 2-hour journey. The city is in great need of new traffic designs and rules rather than more robotic corner cops attempting to give the impression of taking control of the hopeless traffic.

Whenever you decide to take to the streets of Beijing, be sure to factor in the congested traffic. In many places you may be better off walking rather than taking a car. Better still, use the underground Metro to quickly get you from one destination to another. But it, too, tends to be congested.

When you navigate the streets of Beijing, be sure to do so with a good map. Most hotels have maps for their guests. Ask at the concierge desk. Since many streets are not well marked in English, it's best to pay particular attention to various landmarks appearing on the map, from hotels to major sights. Also, take a hotel card with you in case you need to take a taxi back to your hotel or ask directions from shopkeepers or others. Some hotels provide a handy card which is actually a checklist of all the major sites and shopping areas. With this card you will be better able to communicate with taxi drivers and others for getting around the city and then returning to your hotel. While many shopkeepers and personnel in the heavy touristed areas speak English, most people do not. A map and hotel card with Chinese characters should prove helpful should you get lost walking the streets of Beijing. You'll rarely get lost for more than ten minutes.

SHOPPING TREASURES

Shopping has become of age in Beijing within the past few years as the city has made major strides in becoming an international city attracting thousands of business people and tourists each year. With the construction of new four and five-star hotels has come classy shopping malls, hotel shopping arcades, and upscale shops. In Beijing you can now visit the boutiques of famous name brand European designers.

Like so many other things in China during the past ten years, the transformation of shopping in Beijing has been dramatic. Only ten years ago shopping here was rather drab and unexciting—confined to the official Friendship Store and a few department stores and shops offering inexpensive local goods of little interest to international visitors other than many Overseas Chinese.

Today's shopping arcades, department stores, Friendship stores, and markets brim with both locally produced and imported goods. You'll find everything from inexpensive clothes, souvenirs, and crafts to high quality arts, antiques, jewelry, and fashion clothes and accessories. While Beijing is by no means a shopper's paradise, it has enough interesting treasures to offer dedicated shoppers, keeping them occupied for at least three days of shopping and sightseeing.

SIXTEEN TIPS FOR SAVVY TREASURE HUNTING

Shopping in Beijing is by no means an easy task. If ever the saying "buyer beware" were true, it certainly is in the case of Beijing. You really need to know what you're doing when shopping in Beijing. Otherwise, you can easily get ripped off in this ostensibly socialist paradise where the worst evils of eighteenth and nineteenth century capitalism have supposedly been eradicated. They haven't.

In addition to the general shopping rules we identified in

Chapter 6, we recommend following a few rules that should make your shopping adventure go relatively well. These tips should come in handy as you make your sojourns into the streets and shopping centers of Beijing:

1. **Wear a good pair of walking shoes.** The streets and sidewalks of Beijing can be tough on regular shoes. Since you will probably be doing a great deal of walking, make sure you treat your feet right with comfortable walking shoes.

2. **Take a calculator to communicate with merchants.** Keep in mind that you may have difficulty communicating with merchants, shopkeepers, and market vendors in English. A calculator can become your main means of communication. Not only does it help you figure prices and make offers, it also com-municates that you are probably a savvy shopper.

3. **Watch your money.** While crime against tourists is not widespread in Beijing, pickpockets do have a life in any city, especially in market areas. Take sensible precautions in carrying money—securely and out of sight. Also, avoid displaying U.S. dollars. In many places, once people know you have U.S. dollars, they may pester you to death trying to get you to exchange your dollars on the black market.

4. **If approached by strangers who want to exchange money or sell you something, it's best to simply ignore them.** You may be approached by some very persistent individuals who want to exchange your dollars on the black market, sell you postcards, or offer you counterfeit CDs. These people can be relentless. When approached by such individuals, it's best to ignore them; if you engage them in a conversation, you'll have difficulty shaking them. Once you start talking with the individual, they seem to own you. If you do start a conversation and the person will not let up, stop and very dramatically emphasize *"No," "I don't want any," "Go away,"* or *"I want you to disappear, now. Go quickly!"* You may need to get loud, rude, and emotional—draw a crowd if necessary—to make the pest go away. Remember, these are not nice people you need to be culturally sensitive with. They are the bottom-feeders of the shopping world who deserve all

the contempt you can heap on them to make them disappear.

5. **Use U.S. dollars sparingly and discretely.** This is the corollary to Rule #3. While you should avoid flashing U.S. dollars, many shopkeepers are eager to accept them in lieu of local currency and credit cards. After all, they can get a better exchange rate on the black market. Do such purchasing discretely since you don't want to attract others who will want your U.S. dollars.

6. **Always start bargaining in the local currency (RMB or Yuan) rather than in U.S. dollars.** While some merchants want to initially quote prices in U.S. dollars, you will be at a psychological advantage if you keep your transactions in the local currency. Avoid the temptation to start bargaining in U.S. dollars. Once you've reached what appears to be your final offer in yuan, use your calculator to convert into U.S. dollars. Make your final offer in U.S. dollars if you wish. If, for example, the merchant's final price is ¥4,300, use your calculator to convert this amount to U.S. dollars, which in 1998 would be $519.95. Now switch the bargaining process to U.S. dollars by offering $500. This gives you a new psychological advantage in the bargaining process. Merchants will often agree to your final offer when you make it in U.S. dollars. They also prefer receiving U.S. dollars which will command more on the black market than the official rate of exchange.

7. **Use credit cards whenever possible.** While major shopkeepers readily accept Visa, MasterCard, and American Express, they may also add 5 percent to your bill for the privilege of using this plastic money. You may be tempted to pay cash in order to avoid paying their credit card commission. However, think twice before doing so. If you do encounter a problem with a shop, your credit card company may be able to assist you with your purchase, which may end up being a cheap form of "buyer's insurance." Better still, bargain for a cash price, then ask how much the credit card price will be, and then as part of your final deal insist that you be given the cash price for using your credit card. Many shopkeepers will finally agree to give you the same price.

8. **Don't trust anyone with your money.** Many shop-keepers are very good at establishing friendly and ostensibly trusting relationships with relatively naive foreign visitors. Despite many years under Communist rule, many Chinese merchants are still very expert at making "a deal" that is very much in their favor and that is deceitful and dishonest. Indeed, they seem expert at making the buyer "feel good" about the developing personal relationship and what is supposed to be a real bargain price. For example, you may be told a US$1,000 item is very old and of excellent quality and that the shopkeeper can discount it to US$700—but absolutely not more because they are hardly making any profit. In reality, the item is proba-bly a reproduction worth no more than US$30. You'll be treated to an interesting show of deception, even when you catch the shopkeeper in the act of lying. They always have another equally convincing story. Many of these people are nothing more than expert con men (but mainly women) who will tell you any-thing to get you to buy. The problem is especially widespread when it comes to buying antiques. Shop-keepers are notorious for lying about the age of items, knowingly offer fakes as originals, and play bait and switch games. Indeed, during our first day in Beijing we managed to nearly get cheated three times in a single day at three different shops. Fortunately, we were able to immediately recover from some poten-tially big mistakes because we had either used our credit cards or insisted that certain language appear on receipts for Customs purposes. In each case we had clear evidence of being created and these were some of the sweetest people we encountered. Also, use your intuition. If you feel uncomfortable about making a purchase because of potential misrepresentation, chan-ces are your intuition is right: don't buy.

9. **Shop in government shops whenever possible.** When in doubt, buy from government shops which can be trusted for quality and reliability. The govern-ment shops, especially Friendship Stores, have rela-tively good selections and quality. Better still, they can be trusted. The problem is knowing what is truly a government store. Merchants have figured out that Westerners tend to trust the Friendship Stores. These were the only stores for foreigners before privatization

began about 15 years ago, and most visitors have encountered them on previous visits, heard or read about them. In today's China it is hard to find a shop around heavily touristed areas that doesn't have "Friendship Store" somewhere in its name. Most of these shops as well as those whose personnel claim they area a government store have no government connection other than that the government issues them a permit to operate—something like a business license, but in no way provides assurance that the shop doesn't misrepresent its merchandise.

Unfortunately, Beijing growing private sector of merchants and shopkeepers often tend to fit into the stereotypical "buyer beware" syndrome associated with misrepresentation, exploitation, and con artists. Two decades ago when all the shops were truly government shops, one could be fairly assured that goods were what they were purported to be. What incentive was there for the shopkeeper to misrepresent goods when he was paid a salary for hours worked—no sales commissions, and the profits went not into his pocket, but to the government. Since privatization, we have learned to be cautious. Our advice: when making a purchase outside a government shop, make sure all your red flags go up before handing over your money. And if they say they are a government store, they may not be. The only ostensible government shops we trust are Friendship Stores.

10. **Bargain everywhere except in government shops and designer boutiques.** Despite the presence of price tags on most items, bargaining is a way of shopping life in Beijing. Prices are fixed at government shops, department stores, and designer boutiques, although the vendors leading into these shops will bargain. When in doubt as to which shops are government or not, look for a uniform and name tag which signifies a government shop employee or try to bargain. Always consider a price tag to be the starting point from which it is your duty to reduce the final paid price from 20 to 50 percent, or even more. In markets offer at least one-half the stated price but settle for 60-70 percent of the initial asking price. In other places, expect to receive a 10-30 percent discount, with 20 percent being a standard discount. When making a large purchase, it may even be possi-

ble to get a discount in a department store. Indeed, we observed a department store give a 10 percent discount on a thousand dollar amber bowl because the customer asked and business was slow. Though unusual, it is possible. However, these are not hard and fast rules. In some places, you should ask for an 80% discount. The problem is that prices tend to be all over the place, with many sellers asking outrageous initial prices. Hopefully, you'll get a sense of fair value by visiting the fixed price government operated Friendship Stores. If not, go for the 80 percent and see what happens.

11. **Be very skeptical of claims about authenticity or age of so-called antiques.** The antique business is filled with misrepresentation and reproductions. Indeed, the fakes are so good that they even fool the experts. If you insist on buying antiques, make sure you know what you're doing and buy at reputable places. The best places will be government shops, government-approved shops, and shops at the major hotels which have government-certified seals for export approval. Shops engaged in misrepresentation and outright cheating will tell you all kinds of stories about why their particular 300 to 800 year old piece does not need the government's red seal of approval. Or they will ostensibly get the seal for you and you can pick up the piece in an hour. You probably don't know exactly what the government seal looks like and can't read Chinese characters, so any "chop" mark might be put on a wax seal just for you. Don't believe them however convincing their story may be. You'll potentially be taken advantage of as they sell you a fake at an astronomical antique price. Be extremely skeptical when buying antiques at the many shops that line both the east and west sections of Beijing's major antique street, Liulichang Cultural Street. This area is best shopped for its art and art supplies rather than for its "antiques." If an item is truly made prior to 1795, it cannot legally be taken out of the country anyway.

12. **The best quality products are most likely found in the shops of the top hotels.** Most hotels police their shops for quality and reliability. After all, hotels can't afford to have unhappy guests shopping at shops under their leases. If you have a problem with such a

shop, the hotel will usually assist you in resolving the problem.

13. **Be aware of and prepare your packing and shipping options.** Packing and shipping is something that needs to be arranged rather than avoided. Indeed, many travelers avoid buying large items because they are afraid of shipping. This should not happen to you in Beijing or other places in China. Most shops can arrange packing and shipping by using the post office, Federal Express, or a professional shipper who can consolidate large shipments for sea transport. You'll find a few reliable and inexpensive such shippers in Beijing. Always speak with your hotel concierge about reliable packing and shipping services; they usually can provide you with good advice in these departments.

14. **Ask for a credible receipt and document your purchase on the back of the receipt.** Many shops are reluctant to give receipts. Indeed, some shops may try to charge you for a receipt! Insist that you receive a proper receipt which should include the shop's name, address, the item purchased, and the price. The receipt also should be stamped "Paid" in red Chinese characters. However, getting all this information on a receipt can be difficult. Many small shops only offer a generic receipt form, which does not include their name and address. In this case, ask them to write their name and address on the receipt. You, in turn, should write in English, on the back of the receipt, the item you bought, when, where, and for how much. You may need this receipt when you leave China. In addition, it gives a record of what you purchased when you pass through Customs in your own country. The reluctance of merchants outside government shops to issue receipts is probably due to tax issues.

15. **Use your hotel concierge for assistance.** Concierges tend to be very knowledgeable about the city and offer some additional services unique to China. For example, most should be able to help you with shipping— putting you in contact with reliable shippers—and recommending specific shops. They also can assist with getting antiques approved for export (you may have to leave these items with them to be approved, packed and shipped after you leave Beijing). Also,

given the rapid transformation of the city and its shopping venues, many of our recommendations may become quickly dated as shops move, markets close, and new shops and shopping centers and plazas open. Be sure to tip the concierge accordingly for such special services.

16. **Get a car and driver to take you shopping**. Trying to shop on your own without the assistance of a car and driver can be frustrating. Some of the markets and shopping centers are difficult to find even with a good map. Unless you speak fluent Mandarin and know where everything is located in Beijing, you are well advised to hire a car and driver to take you to the various shopping locations. It's easiest to arrange for a car and driver through your hotel; their drivers are familiar with many of the shopping areas and are used to working with guests that have special shopping needs. Contact the hotel concierge for assistance in arranging this service. Also, ask the concierge to mark the major shopping locations on your map so the driver will know where to go. Many drivers are not familiar with our shopping areas and thus may need to ask for directions along the way. If you have the areas marked on your map (in English and Chinese), your shopping adventure should go relatively smoothly.

 SHIPPING WITH EASE

Shipping from Beijing is relatively easy. If you find something that is too large to take with you, consider having it shipped rather than passing it up as something too difficult to get back home. Many shops will arrange shipping for you. Alternatively, you can contact a shipper and have them consolidate your purchases into one combined shipment. You also can ask your hotel concierge for assistance.

If you decide to arrange your own shipping, consider whether you want to ship your goods by air or sea. Air shipments are normally figured on the basis of weight, although volume may be included in the rates. Sea freight shipments are figured by volume or cubic meters. Expect one cubic meter from Beijing to New York to cost about US$250 plus documentation and handling fees. If you plan to buy furniture, shipping by sea freight will be relatively inexpensive. Such shipments normally take from five to eight weeks to receive. Two very reliable shippers in Beijing include:

Beijing Friendship: Tel. 6532-4827. Ask for Ms. Lui Hui Min.

TCI Trans China International: Tel. 6513-3047 or Fax 6513-3054. Ask for Mr. Ian Chin.

If you want to ship by air, contact the local office of Federal Express or DHL. Both of these companies provide efficient shipping services. In the case of Federal Express, ask about their 7-10 day Economy Service.

WHAT TO BUY

ANTIQUES

Beijing abounds in antiques, or least what are supposed to be antiques. In actual fact, there are few genuine antiques for sale in the shops of Beijing. Shopkeepers make all kinds of claims about the age of ceramics, paintings, carvings, and sculptures as well as the procedures for exporting antiques (few stories are true). More often than not they misrepresent the pieces and attempt to sell copies at antique prices. The copies are so good that they can even fool the experts, especially in the case of ceramic plates and bowls. Our advice: know what you're doing or assume what you're buying is probably a reproduction and therefore bargain for fake prices. If you want a real baptism on the fake business, head for the many shops that line both the east and west sides of **Liulichang Road**, Beijing's so-called "culture" or "antique" street. Except for a small shop that appears very reputable, Shop #103 East Liulichang, and the fun flea market atmosphere of the **Rongxing Antique Market** (across from the Art Book Store, #34), we have nothing to recommend here. You can probably find some genuine antiques here, but you really need to be an expert's expert to determine authenticity, quality, and value. It's "buyer beware" when shopping for antiques in Beijing, or for that matter, anywhere in China.

If you're in the market for antiques and related home decorative items, be sure to visit Beijing's four markets that offer a large variety of so-called antiques: Beijing Curio City, Hong Xiao Market, Liang Ma Antique Market, and Chao Wai Furniture Market. **Beijing Curio City** is the largest antique market with over 250 shops. We especially like the antique shops on the third floor of the **Hong Xiao Market**. The **Liang**

Ma Antique Market offers some interesting antiques and curios; but go there only after visiting Beijing Curio City and Hong Xiao Market. The **Chao Wai Furniture Market** primarily deals in large pieces of furniture—chests, tables, and cabinets; it may soon be razed and relocated to another location.

PAINTINGS AND CALLIGRAPHY SUPPLIES

Beijing abounds with paintings and calligraphy supplies, from fine brushes and ink slabs to inks and papers. Galleries have proliferated throughout the city. In addition, art exhibits and auctions are periodically held in some of Beijing's major hotels, such as the Grand and Kunlun. Several shops that line **East Liulichang Street**, such as the China Book Store, are especially well noted for such items (just don't buy their antiques). The **Friendship Stores** have reasonably priced paintings and calligraphy supplies. Some of the best art galleries in the city are found at the **National Art Gallery** (shop on the left side of the third floor), **Wan Fung Art Gallery** (136 Nan Chi Zi Dajie, east of the Forbidden City), **Art Palace Shop** (Holiday Inn Crowne Plaza), **CFLAC Cultural Gallery** (third floor of the China World Hotel Shopping Arcade), **Songphoenix Gallery** (Beijing Hotel), and the **Beijing Art Gallery** (289 Wangfujing Street, 2nd floor). Many of the shops mentioned in the section on antiques also offer paintings and calligraphy supplies.

ARTS AND CRAFTS

This shopping category covers numerous types of products found in Beijing's many markets, shops, and department stores, from wood and jade carvings to kites and embroidery. You'll find an overabundance of arts and crafts throughout Beijing. For a quick overview of the types of arts and crafts available, be sure to visit the **Friendship Store** on Jianguomennei Avenue and the Friendship Store at You Yi Shopping City (Beijing Lufthansa Center) adjacent to the Kempinski Hotel. The **Beijing Curio Market** and the **Hong Xiao Market** also have interesting selections of arts and crafts. Some of the best quality arts and crafts will be found in hotel shops.

FURNITURE

If you are in the market for Chinese furniture, Beijing has a lot to offer. While much of the furniture is ostensibly antique, most of it is not as old as it is supposed to be. Many pieces are reconditioned with perhaps as much as 80 percent being new wood. Nonetheless, much of this furniture is very attractive and the prices are good, even after adding shipping. The most popular place for furniture is the **Chaw Nai Market** which consists of one large warehouse on Ritan Lu, one block north of Ritan Park which is near Jianguomenwai. One of the best places for good quality antique and reproduction furniture is the **Hua Yi Chinese Antique Furniture Company** (contact office located across from the Kempinski Hotel and United Airlines office at the rear of the Liang Ma Antique Market, Tel. 6460-8461 or Fax 6576-0126). Also look for furniture on the fourth floor of the **Beijing Curio Market** which is primarily devoted to large pieces of furniture. Overseas shipping can be easily arranged at both the Chaw Nai Market and the Hua Yi Chinese Antique Furniture Company.

FOODS AND DRINKS

If you're interested in purchasing local or imported foods and drinks, you're best off visiting the supermarket sections of department and Friendship stores. One of the best supermarkets is located at the lower level of the **You Yi Shopping City** (Beijing Lufthansa Center) which is attached to the Kempinski Hotel. The Wellcome supermarket chain in Hong Kong operates supermarkets in the Holiday Inn Lido and in the shopping arcade of the China World Trade Centre (China World Hotel).

CLOTHES AND ACCESSORIES

Shops, departments stores, and markets in Beijing offer a wide range of clothes and accessories, from inexpensive locally produced clothes to very expensive imported designer clothes and accessories. Most visitors to Beijing love to shop the street markets, such as the **Xiu Shi Market** (Silk Market) near the embassies (runs south from Xiu Shui Street to Jianguomenwai Street) and the smaller **San Li Tun Market**, for inexpensive shirts, coats, jackets, shorts, sweaters, gloves, and shoes. These crowded markets are jam-packed with factory overruns and knock-offs of name brand clothes and accessories such as Levi Strauss, Tommy Hilfiger, Timberland, Polo, Converse, Nike, Esprit, Adidas, Calvin Klein, and Gianni Versace which you may or may not find stylish and compatible with your color tastes. At the other end of this clothing spectrum are the many boutiques offering genuine imported designer clothes and accessories. The largest concentration of such shops are found in the upscale shopping arcade of the **Palace Hotel** (8 Goldfish Lane, Wangfujing). Here you'll find Italian, French, and German designer shops such as Hugo Boss, Versace, Givenchy, Gucci, Ferragamo, Prada, Louis Vuitton, Celine, and Bally. The shopping arcade attached to the **China World Hotel** (next to exhibition center) includes such designer shops as Ermencgildo Zegna, Cerruti 1881, and Trussadi. In between these two are the many clothing offerings available at Beijing's numerous department stores. You'll usually find a good selection of locally produced clothes, especially cashmere sweaters, coats, shirts, and dresses, at the Friendship Stores where prices are relatively reasonable and where you also can get tailoring done. The best such store for clothes is the Friendship store which is called **You Yi Shopping City** (Beijing Lufthansa Center) adjacent to the Kempinski Hotel at 52 Liangmaqiao Road (Tel. 6465-1851). The **Parkson Department Store** carries many popular labels such as Benetton, Esprit, Elle, and Bonia. CVIK Plaza offers such brand names as Nautica, Pierre Cardin, Valentino, Stachi, Playboy, Crocodile, Charles Jourdan, Esprit, Dunhill, and Guy Laroche. If you're interested in silk clothes for both adults and children, silk yardage (US$9 a yard!), cashmere sweaters, jackets, and tailoring services, as well as carpets and porcelains, you should visit the popular **Yuan Long Embroidery and Silk Company** (55 Tiantan Lu or Temple of Heaven Road, Chongwen District, Tel. 6702-0682, but check current address at your hotel since this shop is in the process of being relocated to a new building). This store offers good selections at relatively reasonable prices. You also may want to explore the many shops found in the major hotels, especially the shopping complexes that link the old **Beijing Hotel** with the new **Beijing Grand Hotel** and the shops in the new **Sun Dong An Plaza** on Wangfujing Avenue. For a unique shopping experience for what may be best termed novelty clothes, try the Red Army's clothing store: **Army Store 3501** (Hujialou 3501), just down the street from the Jing Guang Center which houses the Jing Guang New World Hotel. While the clothes here are not particularly fashionable, they are cheap and utilitarian. Indeed, you can buy big green army coats for US$21.00! You'll also find a wide range of typical Army surplus goods here: shoes, boots, camouflage T-shirts, caps, backpacks, canteens, and lights. The inexpensive (47 yuan) T-shirts are especially popular. This store has a particularly good selection of binoculars and telescopes—just in case you're in the market for these products.

SOUVENIRS AND GIFTS

Beijing, and most places in China, abound with souvenir and gift items ranging from paper cuts, dolls, and chops to jade carvings, lacquer boxes, and sandlewood fans. Since few genuine antiques can be found in or exported from China, handicrafts now reign supreme in Beijing's many shops. You can't miss these ubiquitous items which are especially found in and around the major tourist sites. The Forbidden City and Great Wall, for example, have hundreds of shops and vendor stalls offering a wide range of souvenir and gift items. While many hotel shops will offer such items, the best selections and prices often will be found at the Friendship and department stores. For the best one-stop-shopping for souvenirs and gift items, visit the **Friendship Store** at 17 Jianguamenwai Dajie (Tel. 6500-3311) and **You Yi Shopping City** (Beijing Lufthansa Center) adjacent to the Kempinski Hotel at 52 Liangmaqiao Road (Tel. 6465-1851). Also, be sure to explore the handicraft stalls on the third floor of the **Hong Xiao Market**. If you're looking for something unique, visit the **Shard Box Store** at 1 Ritan Bei Road, Chaoyang District (Tel. 6500-3712). Popular with expatriates, this shop offers a wide selection of jewelry and decorative boxes made from old porcelain shards. They also sell Tibetan style jewelry, snuff bottles, loose gemstones, and other antiques.

WHERE TO SHOP

You'll find lots of places to shop throughout Beijing. While only a few years ago most shopping was confined to the ubiquitous Friendship stores, today shopping has proliferated to include many other places. However, most shopping of interest to international visitors will be found in shops and department stores located along a few major streets, hotel shopping arcades of four and five star hotels, a few street and shopping complex markets, and shops and vendor stalls found at major sightseeing attractions.

MAJOR SHOPPING STREETS

❏ **Wangfujing Avenue:** Beginning at the Beijing Hotel and running north, this has been long considered Beijing's main shopping street. Also the location for the country's busiest McDonald's restaurant (near the corner with the Beijing Hotel), today this street is lined with more than 130 shops offering a wide variety of goods, from clothes to food products. Here you'll find lots of restaurants, leather coat kiosks, optical shops, arts and crafts shops, and department stores. You also may encounter a few persistent beggars along this street. Somewhat old, worn, and dated, the shops here remind one of Beijing of more than a decade ago. The landmark **Beijing Department Store**, for years the city's main shopping center, lacks the upscale look and products of Beijing's newer department stores. Frequented primarily by local residents (all signs are in Chinese), it appears to be a tired relic of a bygone era (doesn't even have an elevator or escalator to navigate its levels). Nonetheless, the new **Sun Dong An Plaza** complex, should help transform shopping along this street. Indeed, the whole street is undergoing a major renovation that should breathe new life into the whole area, from the Beijing Hotel to Goldfish Lane. We found few shops here worth spending more than a few minutes visiting. The only one of any note is the **Beijing Art Gallery** (289 Wang Fu Jing Street) for jewelry, jade carvings, paintings, art supplies, and eyeglasses.

❏ **Liulichang Culture Street**: Rebuilt in the early 1980s in traditional Chinese architectural style reminiscent of Old Beijing, the buildings lining the two sections (east and west) of this pedestrian street are packed with "old" and "new" antiques, from ceramics and jade carvings to bronzes. Once the center for scholars and art connoisseurs during the Qing Dynasty, this street is best noted as a center for art and art supplies—traditional Chinese scroll paintings, calligraphy, rubbings, writing brushes, ink sticks and inkstones, and handmade paper. While long noted as a major center for good quality antiques (and for some strange reason still recommended in several guide books as such) most of the ostensible antiques in this area should not be trusted. It's best to assume everything is a reproduction here unless you can be thoroughly convinced otherwise (you're well advised to trust no one, however sweet and trusting their personality). Indeed, this is the one place in China where you can really get "burned" buying antiques. Since many are fakes, you really need to know what you are doing before making a substantial purchase. Most shops claiming to be selling antiques simply lie, but their reproductions are quite good (try Zheng Pin Zhai, B36 West Liulichang, and Ji Gu Ge Antique Shop, 136 East Liulichang, for good examples of reproductions—both nearly ripped us off with "new antiques" to the tune of US$2500!). For some real fun shopping in an enclosed market-stall atmosphere, be sure to stop at the **Rongxing Antique Market** (across from the Art Book Store, #34) which has a big colorful gate at its entrance. This expansive building is crammed with vendor stalls selling art, antiques, and collectibles. Many visitors find this market to be the highlight of their visit to Liulichang. The whole area is best trusted for its art and art supplies (reproduction paintings, calligraphy, books, paint brushes, and ink pads) than for its antiques. To that end, try **Rongbaozhai** on West Liulichang for art supplies, woodblock prints, and copies of noted calligraphy and paintings. Also **Jiguge** at 136 East Liulichang has an good supply of stone rubbings, jade carvings, production paintings, and reproduction clay tomb figures.

SHOPPING CENTERS AND DEPARTMENT STORES

❏ **CVIK Plaza:** Located near the American Embassy and the Xui Shui Market, this is a rather upscale shopping center offering name brand clothes under labels such as Nautica, Pierre Cardin, Valentino, Satchi, Playboy, Crocodile, Charles Jourdan, Esprit, Dunhill, and Guy Laroche. You may be most interested in what's available on the fifth floor. Here you will find a good selection of quality handicrafts, arts, rugs, silk fabric, chops, and cashmere products. You'll also find some very fashionable leather and fur coats.

❏ **Sun Dong An Plaza:** This newest addition to upscale shopping in Beijing is located directly across the street from the old Beijing Department Street on Wangfujing Street. Slated to open in 1998, it is supposed to house more and more name brand shops of the quality found at the Palace Hotel shopping arcade.

❏ **Friendship Stores:** Beijing has several Friendship Stores which are basically expensive department stores. Once open only to tourists and diplomatic personnel, they are now open to local residents who frequently shop in these stores because of their reputed quality and pricing. The oldest is located on Jianguomenwai Street just adjacent to Baskin-Robbins and Pizza Hut. An old and somewhat worn building, it offers four-floors of products of interest to visitors, from fabrics to antiques. We recommend starting at the top floor, which primary includes clothes, and work your way down to the attractive third and second floors. The third floor houses an excellent selection of arts and crafts. The newest and largest branch of the Friendship Store is the Beijing Lufthansa Center which is also known as the You Yi (Friendship) Shopping City. Located adjacent to the Landmark and Kempinski Hotels, the store is jam-packed with upscale products of interest to both visitors and local residents who frequent it in large numbers. This is reputed to be Beijing's best department store.

❑ **Parkson Department Store:** Located at the corner of Fuxingmennei Avenue and Fuchengmenman Street (several blocks west of The Forbidden City) this Malaysian owned six-storey shopping complex is filled with good quality clothes and household products. You'll find lots of name brand clothes on the first floor such as Benetton, Esprit, Elle, and Bonia. The sixth floor is of special interest to visitors with its food court and nice quality, selections, and displays of folk art, ceramics, carvings, art, tea pots, and calligraphy. This floor also houses the China National Arts and Crafts Museum (admission fee).

❑ **Beijing Department Store:** Located in the heart of the shopping district along Wangfujing Street. Open from 8:30am until 8:30pm. This used to be Beijing's major department store. It has seen better days, or perhaps the days before were never as good as today! It's worn. While it's still popular with many locals, we have nothing to recommend about this place other than it's at best a cultural experience. All signs are in Chinese and there are no elevators or escalators. You won't spend time here.

HOTEL SHOPPING ARCADES

You'll find several shopping arcades attached to some of the major hotels in Beijing. Each has its own distinctive character. Other hotels have one or two shops that may be of interest to visitors. Most, however, primarily service the immediate shopping needs of their own guests who may not have time to shop for clothes, arts, crafts, or jewelry elsewhere in the city. Some of the major hotel shopping arcades worth visiting include:

❑ **The Palace Hotel:** *8 Goldfish Lane.* Looking for the latest in European fashion and accessories, or do you want a glimpse of the future for shopping in Beijing? Look no further than this plush three-storey marbled shopping arcade housed in one of Beijing's finest hotels. Elegant and fashionable, the shops here don't seem to belong in Beijing. Opened seven years ago but only recently reoriented to luxury fashion and accessories, this arcade is what Hong Kong is all about and it reminds one of the management control of this hotel — the Peninsula Group from Hong Kong. Here you'll find the big names in the fashion worlds of Italy, France, and Germany, just like you'll find at the Peninsula Hotel in Hong Kong: **Gianni Versace, Gucci, Prada, MCM, Gentlemen Givenchy, Yves Saint Laurent, Bruno Magli, Escada, Mondi, Gieves & Hawkes, Canali, Christian Dior Clarins, Sofia, Etienne Aigner, Escada, Dormeuil, Versace Classic V2, Louis Vuitton, Hermès, Celine, Ferragamo, Bally, Celine, Givenchy,** and **Hugo Boss.** For excellent crystal and glassware, try **Baccarat.** The arcade also has two adjacent antique shops left over from the previous mix of arcade shops—**Ju Ya Zhai** and **Ze Ya Tang.** Located at the very end of the bottom floor, they offer some interesting selections, although you will be better off shopping for similar antiques along Liulichang street, and in Beijing Curio City and the Hong Xiao Antique Market where the selections and prices are much better. Upstairs, just off the lobby near the concierge desk, are **Ermenegildo Zegna** for men's fashion, **Davidoff** for tobacco products, and the **Palace Boutique** for books, magazines, bottled water, and odds and ends.

❑ **China World Hotel Arcade:** *Jian Guo Men Wai Avenue. Open daily from 9am to 9pm.* Located adjacent to the Exhibition Hall of the China World Trade Center, this three-storey marble shopping arcade connected by escalators offers several shops of interest to international visitors. Unlike the exclusive shops found in the shopping arcade of the Palace Hotel, this one is a mixture of upscale fashion and accessory, clothing, and arts and crafts shops along with airline offices, banks, restaurants, and service centers. In the fashion department, look for the classy shops of **Ermenegildo Zegna, Cerruti 1881,** and **Trussadi** on second floor. The most interesting shops are found on the third floor (second level). We especially like the arts, crafts, jewelry, and carpet selections at the large **Arts and Crafts Shop** (L201A) located just inside the front entrance to the arcade; look for a small kiosk in front of this shop operated by an artist producing interesting detailed paintings on goose eggs. The **CFLAC Cultural Gallery** (L219) offers excellent quality paintings, including the fine but very expensive watercolors of Huo Genzhong. The nearby **Marco Polo Carpet Shop** offers a large selection of Chinese carpets. **Europe** is a small but good quality shop offering leather and fur coats primarily for women, although it does have a few leather jackets for men.

❑ **Beijing Hotel/Beijing Grand Hotel:** This can be one of the most confusing hotel shopping arcades in Beijing. Two hotels, the older four-star Beijing Hotel and the newer five-star deluxe Beijing Grand Hotel are linked by a long and at times circuitous corridor that also changes levels and is lined with clothing, arts and crafts, food, jewelry, and antique shops and kiosks. The best way to shop this area is to begin at the Beijing Hotel lobby and turn left into the corridor and begin exploring the many shops that line this eclectic area. At times you may think you've entered a souk or bazaar! The shops nearest the Beijing Hotel also include some interesting antique and art shops tucked away along side corridors. Indeed, two art shops offering numerous quality paintings (Song-phoenix Gallery) are found in this section along with a small antique stall (Liyuan Antique Shop) offering ceramics, chops, jewelry, tea pots, paintings, and Tibetan pipes. Be sure to bargain hard in these places. As you approach the section that leads into the lower level of the Beijing Grand Hotel, you'll find additional clothing, antique, and arts and crafts shops. Take the escalator up one flight to the atrium section of the Grand Hotel. At the top of the escalator, just behind you, is a small upscale hotel shopping arcade that is difficult to find unless you're looking for it. Here you will find a few small clothing boutiques (Woolsey, Hi-Five, Calypso) and a jewelry shop. If you are in the lobby of the hotel, look for signs mentioning any special art exhibits. These are often held on the second or third floors of the hotel.

❑ **Other hotel shopping arcades:** Many other major hotels (four and five star) have small shopping arcades with shops primarily offering clothes, accessories, jewelry, and arts and crafts. The **Holiday Inn Crowne Plaza** is especially noted for its monthly art exhibits in the first floor art gallery and the Art Palace Shop on second floor. The **Overseas Chinese Prime Hotel** (previously known as the Guangdong Regency Hotel) has a small shopping arcade which offers a good selection of clothes, arts and crafts, jewelry, and silk yardage. The huge **Sheraton Great Wall Hotel** has one large but well appointed shop offering excellent quality clothes, jewelry, arts, crafts, and carpets. The nearby **Kunlun Hotel** has a few art and craft shops on first and second floor and it occasionally hosts major art exhibits. Next to the hotel in a separate building is the Kunlun Shopping Centre which is actually a small department store offering a wide range of clothing, accessories, leather goods, jewelry, jade, and luggage.

MARKETS

Beijing has numerous markets. Many are of little interest, or are prohibited, to visitors, such as the ad hoc, chaotic, and seemingly unsanitary morning fresh fruit, vegetable, and meat markets that are held daily in the *hutong* or cheap clothing and accessory markets primarily appealing to locals. Several other markets are of great interest to international visitors. In fact, market shopping in these places is often the highlight of many visitors' stay in Beijing. These places can be fun to shop in and often yield good bargains, if you know how to bargain properly. Make sure you bargain hard in these markets. The rule of thumb should be to offer 50 percent of the asking price and then be willing to settle for 30 or 40 percent, although 50 percent may be just right. Many of them specialize in particular goods, such as antiques, furniture, curios, or clothes. Unfortunately, many of the markets are disappearing as they are uprooted by new commercial buildings and apartment complexes; a few are being relocated. The trend is to consolidate the street markets and vendor stalls under a single roof in a modern air-conditioned multi-level commercial building, such as the Beijing Curio City which now has over 250 antique dealers operating from small shops. While the traditional worn and chaotic market loses its colorful character in such well organized settings, nonetheless, the market and its products manage to survive. They also are more convenient to find and shop.

Some of Beijing's most interesting markets for visitors include the following. Hopefully, all of these markets will survive during the next five years. However, we will not be surprised to learn that a few, such as the Chao Wai Market, may soon close and relocate in multi-level commercial buildings or disappear altogether. Before venturing into any of these markets, be sure to check with your hotel concierge to make sure the market is still operating and verify its current location and hours of operation.

❑ **Beijing Curio City:** *Located west of the Huawei Bridge, Dongsanhuan Nanlu, Chaoyanag District. Open daily from 9:30am to 6:30pm. Tel. 6773-6098.* If you're in the market for antiques, collectibles, rugs, art, or home decorative items, put this market at the top of your shopping list. It doesn't get much better for variety and selections. This is one of China's largest and best antique markets. It's jam-packed with over 250 antique dealers operating from a labyrinth of small shops found on four floors of this multi-level shopping complex accented with a central atrium for special exhibits. You enter the building by first passing through a large duty-free store, the **Beijing Downtown Duty Free Shop**. This upscale shop is filled with attractive imported watches, hand-bags, shoes, perfumes, cosmetics, jewelry, clothes, and candy. It includes such designer labels as Gucci, Ferragamo, Burberrys, Paloma Picasso, Christian Dior, Nina Ricci, and Bally. As you pass through the frosted sliding glass doors at the rear of this shop, you enter into the large atrium of the four-story antique and curio complex. This whole area is simply overwhelming. The 250+ antique and curio shops are filled with all types of antique market items. The quality tends to be more upscale than in other antique markets. At the same time, there's a high level of redundancy in products offered. Indeed, most shops seem to offer the same range of products. If you don't mind the mind-numbing redundancy, you can easily spend a few hours here poking through the many dusty and cluttered shops. On the first floor you'll find small shops offering jade carvings, pearls, baskets, traditional Chinese paintings, tea pots, blue and white porcelain, Tibetan art, and lots of small collectibles and objets d'art. The second and third floors have more of the same, although you'll find more Tibetan rug and art shops on these floors. The fourth floor is primarily devoted to furniture. You'll find desks, beds, cabinets, chests, tables, chairs, and screens packed on three sides of this floor, from simple to extremely ornate designs. The friendly merchants all seem to greet you in either Chinese (*ni hao* for *"hello"*) or in English (*"Hello, come in please"*). Whether or not you will find real antiques here is another question. Remember at least three of our shopping rules for Beijing: there are few legitimate antiques in Beijing; merchants have a propensity to misrepresent their products to buyers; and it's always "buyer beware" whenever shopping for anything proported to be more than 50 years old! While the product selections at Beijing Curio City are good, we cannot vouch for the honesty nor reliability of merchants. We always assume the worst in such places—they are likely to misrepresent their wares.

❏ **Hong Xiao Market:** *Located near the North Gate of the Temple of Heaven. Open 8:30am to 7pm.* This is one of our favorite markets and it may well become your favorite because of its wide selection of inexpensive products and its friendly and festive atmosphere. Hong Xiao offers a lot more than just antiques and curios. Like Beijing Curio City, it's housed in a multi-level (three-storey) building. But unlike other markets, this one has a real mix of products, from clothes, jewelry, and leather goods to luggage, pearls, and antiques. Don't be turned off by what you encounter on the first floor—lots of cheap curios, from watches to tea and neckties, offered in an extremely crowded and congested area. Head for the escalator! The good stuff is found on the second and third floors. Take the escalator to the second floor where you will find a large selection of inexpensive shoes, handbags, briefcases, belts, and luggage. You'll find one large enclosed wholesale shop on this floor offering a good selection of luggage and handbags. Indeed, one of the best deals on luggage in Beijing is found in this shop (¥150 for a large hard-sided piece with wheels and handle—the identical piece was selling for ¥240 in the Xui Shui Market). But the third floor is our favorite place to shop. Here you'll find numerous vendors selling pearls spread out on tables in the middle section of this floor, adjacent to the escalators. In fact, this is one of Beijing's best pearl markets for both selection and price. The one end of the floor is devoted to small antique shops that offer some good selections of porcelain, boxes, carvings, old clothes, embroidered neck pieces, and small colorful shoes. The merchants here appear more honest, although again it's "buyer beware." We managed to find the same porcelain pillow here for US$60 that had been offered to us the previous day at a large shop in Liulichang Culture Street for US$390. The other end of this floor is devoted to handicraft shops offering a wide selection of items, from sandlewood fans to lacquer screens.

❑ **Liang Ma Antique Market:** *Liangmaquiao Road, Chaoyang District, small entrance directly across the street from the Kempinski Hotel and United Airlines office. Open 9am to 10pm.* Somewhat difficult to find (entrance directly across the street from the United Airlines sign), this rather worn antique and curio market is divided into two sections—an outdoor covered shop area and a main enclosed building. Similar to the shops found in Beijing Curio City, the shops here offer a wide variety of blue and white porcelain, paintings, clocks, rugs, and curios. At the rear of this market is the **Hua Yi Furniture Company**, one of the largest furniture dealers in China. They have a large showroom and warehouse elsewhere in Beijing. The **Liang Ma Collectors Market**, the separate building on the left, has several shops under one roof offering more of the same—rugs, porcelain, paintings, furniture, and collectibles. Many of the shopkeepers seem preoccupied with gambling in the hallways! Overall, this is an interesting market on a much smaller scale than Beijing Curio City. It does have more of the traditional market atmosphere than the newer antique market locations.

❑ **Chao Wai Market:** Located in one long narrow warehouse on Ritan Road (just one block north of Ritan Park, near Jianguomenwai Street) this is one of Beijing's most popular markets for good quality antique and reproduction furniture. Numerous vendors offer a wide selection of large furniture pieces (chests, cabinets, tables, chairs) as well as lacquer boxes, bird cages, ceramics, and carpets. This old market may soon close since it is surrounded by new residential (apartment) construction which may eventually claim this property. In fact, some vendors have already moved to the fourth floor of the Beijing Curio Market since one of the two buildings that used to constitute the Chao Wai Market was closed two years ago. Don't worry about shipping your purchases abroad. It's easy to arrange since the Beijing Marine Shipping Company is conveniently located at the very end of this building.

❑ **Xui Shui Market:** Located along Jianguomenwai Dajie, just adjacent and behind the U.S. Embassy. Open 9am to sunset (6-7pm). Clothes, clothes, and more clothes everywhere. This is real market shopping that makes for happy shoppers looking for the latest bargains in name-brand clothes. In fact, this is the favorite clothing market for many visitors to Beijing. It's large, it's crowded, and it's jam-packed with goodies that appeal to foreign visitors. Located adjacent to the U.S. Embassy, the official name for this market is Xiu Shui Market. However, it also is known under three other names—the Silk Market, the Xiushui Silk Alley, and the Yong An Li Market. It's called the Silk Market by English speakers because it's easier to say than Xui Shui or Yong An Li, and the market has a disproportionate number of silk products, from shirts to scarves. This can be both a fun and bewildering market. It seems to go on and on, with the level of product redundancy being extremely high. The market consists of two sections, one with stalls lining one side of two streets and the other lining both sides of a long and narrow alley, including side lanes. Here you will find lots of clothes, especially shirts, slacks, jackets, sweaters, and vests under such labels as Tommy Hilfiger, Guess, Hugo Boss, J. Crew, NAF NAF, Converse, and Polo. The product mix also includes shawls, gloves, silk pajamas, blouses, carpets, furs, quilts, shoes, and luggage. You can easily spend a couple of hours pushing and shoving your way through the crowded stalls. You'll see many visitors pushing their way through the alley laden with plastic bags fattened with bargain purchases. Watch your wallet here just in case you encounter a pickpocket. Also, avoid those who approach you with the lines *"Change dollar?"* and *"Want CD?"* They are the local pests.

❑ **Russian Market:** *Located near Xui Shui Market and Ritan Park, just 200 yards from Chao Wai Market.* It's called the "Russian Market" because Russians come here to buy very cheap goods for resale in Russia. You'll see Russians laden down with huge bags stuffed with furs and pelts. This is largely a dying market since fewer and fewer Russians now come to Beijing. An interesting cultural experience but you probably won't find much here that you will purchase for yourself. The quality here is at best mediocre.

❑ **San Li Tun Market:** *Locate 10 minutes north of the Xui Shui Market.* Similar to the Xui Shui Market but much smaller in scale and much easier to navigate. Includes several stalls lining one side of the street. Popular with foreign visitors, the stalls offer a wide selection of shirts, jeans, quilts, jackets, sweaters, and shoes. The clothes include such popular labels as Levi-Strauss, Tommy Hilfiger, Timberland, Polo, Calvin Klein, Gianni Versace, Converse, Nike, Esprit, and Adidas. Some claim these are the real thing rather than knock-offs. However, we've yet to be impressed by the styling and colors of such name-brand products.

❑ **Other Markets:** Beijing also has a few other markets, such as the Bird or Guanyuan Market (northwest part of city opposite Guanyuan Park), night markets, and Sunday markets. Check with your hotel for the times and locations of these markets.

STREET STALLS AND VENDORS

Streets stalls and vendors proliferate throughout the city. You'll find numerous stalls lining major streets. Popular with local shoppers, most of these stalls offer inexpensive clothing and footwear which are of little interest to foreign visitors. These places are more of a cultural experience than destinations for serious shoppers.

MUSEUMS, GALLERIES, SITES

More and more of Beijing's major tourist attractions have become shopping centers. Some places are crowded with street vendors, hawkers, and stalls offering the same types of souvenirs. Others include quality arts, crafts, and antique shops. Whatever you do, don't dismiss shopping in these areas. You may find a "diamond in the rough!" Of the major sites with good shopping opportunities include:

❑ **The Forbidden City:** You can actually do some good shopping here, especially in the main arts and crafts shops. As you walk through the main gate, you'll pass by numerous vendor stalls and shops that line both sides of the walkway. They offer clothes (from T-shirts to leather coats), books, food, and typical tourist trinkets. You'll also be approached by several postcard vendors attempting to sell you books of postcards. Offer them 50% of their first asking price. Once inside the Imperial Palace grounds, look for an arts and crafts shop opposite the clock building. This shop has a nice collection of paintings (represent 40 artists) along with numerous arts and crafts. Just inside the north gate is a row of shops offering a good selection of arts, crafts, paintings, carpets, and books.

❑ **Temple of Heavenly Peace:** East Gate. You'll find lots of vendor stalls inside the East Gate. The best place to shop here is the **Qing Shan Ju Antique Shop** which is located at the very end of the vendor stalls and to the left. It's housed in a very old and historically important building. The shop offers nice reproductions (though they may tell you they are old) of terracotta figures, porcelain, bronze, old wood baskets and boxes, and a few small furniture pieces. Also look for cloisonne, jade, coins, and paintings. Expect 20-30 percent discounts if you bargain.

❑ **National Art Gallery:** Located at 1 Wu Si Street, Dong Cheng District. The only permanent exhibits here are found in the shops on the third floor. Take the elevator to the third floor which is devoted to arts, crafts, clothes, and food. Collectively known as the **Art Exhibition Shopping Centre of the Chinese Art Gallery** (Tel. 6403-4950), the shop on the left has one of Beijing's largest collections of traditional and modern Chinese paintings and calligraphy along with prices starting at ¥400. The shop on the right has a good selection of jewelry, cloisonne, carvings (stone, wood, ivory, bone), jade, pearls, jewelry, lacquerware, enamel works, fur tapestries, embroidery, silk, carpets, screens, fans, kites, and food.

❑ **The Great Wall:** The main entrance to the Great Wall at Badaling is crowded with shops offering a wide range of tourist trinkets along with some good quality arts and crafts. Here you can buy the ubiquitous "I climbed the Great Wall" sweat and T-shirts along with fur hats, umbrellas, quilts, stuffed panda bears, paintings, film, and soft drinks. One of the oldest shops here, the **Long Qing Antique Store**, offers a good selection of ceramics.

❑ **The Ming Tombs:** Not much here worth recommending for shopping. Look for several vendor shops lining the walkway to the tombs that offer typical tourist products such as hats, puppets, food, and drinks.

SPECIAL EXHIBITIONS AND AUCTIONS

Several of the major hotels have special exhibitions and public auctions where you can usually purchase art and jewelry. The Kunlun Hotel tends to sponsor several such exhibitions and auctions, although other hotels also sponsor such events. To learn about current or upcoming exhibitions and auctions, it's best to check with your hotel concierge and review tourist literature on what's going on in Beijing.

SPECIAL INTEREST SHOPS

A few shops warrant special attention because of the quality or uniqueness of their products. We especially recommend the following shops which are found outside the major shopping areas mentioned above:

❑ **Yuan Long Silk:** *55 Tian Tan Lu, Chongwen District, Tel. 6702-0682* (near Temple of Heaven). Since this shop has been in the process of relocating because of renovation work of their building, please check with your hotel for their current location (they should now be back at their original location). This is one of Beijing's oldest and most famous silk shops. Open from 9am to 6:30 pm, it offers a wide range of fabric, clothes, and handicrafts. It offers very good buys on silk yardage (around US$10 a meter) and children's clothes, especially colorful silk pajamas at prices better than in the government's Friendship Stores. Also look for pillow covers, table cloths, tapestries, shawls, paintings, jade carvings, lacquer screens, carpets, dolls, fans, pens, cloisonne, furs, jackets, and cashmere sweaters. The shop also does tailoring, although don't commission anything unless you have at least a week in Beijing.

❑ **The Army Store:** *3501 Hujialou (across the street and down a few shops from the Jing Guang Center).* This is not your normal shopping place for quality goods. More like an Army surplus store, products offered here have become fashionable for some visitors. Yes, it's the Red Army's supply store. It's jam-packed with boots, shoes, shirts, T-shirts, caps, backpacks, jackets, and coats. The large long green Army coat with fur collars go for an incredible 170 yuan or US$21.00. Camouflage shirts and T-shirts go for as little as 60 yuan. The store stocks a good selection of quality binoculars, just in case you left yours at home.

❏ **Hua Yi Antique Chinese Furniture Company:** *Office at the rear of the Liangma Antique Market (across from Kempinski Hotel).* Also has a showroom and warehouse 20 minutes away. This is one of Beijing's largest dealers in antique furniture.

ACCOMMODATIONS

Beijing offers a wide range of accommodations for international travelers. During the past seven years, several five-star hotels—stars are awarded by the National Tourist Administration—have come on line to service the needs of the growing number of business people and tourists visiting Beijing. Most of these properties include a full range of dining, conference, fitness, and entertainment facilities. Their concierge services tend to be first-rate, helpful for visitors in search of Beijing's many treasures and pleasures, including assistance with shipping questions and services. Some of these hotels sponsor special events for their guests. Prices at these hotels range from US$150 a night (double) to over US$300 a night. Watch for special Winter or weekend packages. Beijing's best five-star hotels include:

❏ **Palace:** *8 Goldfish Lane, Wangfujing, Beijing 100006, Tel. (86-10) 6512-8899 or Fax (86-10) 6512-9050.* Managed by the Peninsula Group and member of both The Leading Hotels of the World and Preferred Hotels and Resorts Worldwide, and rated the best hotel in Beijing by the readers of *Business Traveller Magazine,* The Palace Hotel gets our vote as "best of the best" in Beijing. Located a short walk from the shops of Wangfujing Street and The Forbidden City, the hotel offers every amenity for the business traveler or tourist to Beijing. Offers 530 guest rooms, including 52 suites which feature marble bathrooms and a dispenser for chilled drinking water. Ten food and beverage outlets offer a wide range of cuisines. The Roma Ristorante Italiano features superb Italian specialities, Bavaria Bierstube serves German favorites, The Palace Restaurant highlights spicy Sichuan cuisine while the Future Garden serves the delicate flavors of Cantonese cuisine. The Palm Court Coffee House serves international dishes with a changing buffet selection.

On the three Executive Floors guests enjoy private check-in and check-out, complimentary clothes pressing, use of the satellite business center, breakfast in the Club Lounge, plus complimentary afternoon tea and cocktails and canapes in the evening. A welcome fruit basket and personalized stationery offer a personal touch.

A 24-hour Business Center and a full fitness center are available to guests. Airport transfers can be provided via two Rolls Royces or 12 Mercedes Benz 280s.

The shopping outlets available at the Palace Hotel Arcade offer the best selection of upscale shops, together under one roof, in the city (see Hotel Shopping Arcades section).

❑ **Grand Hotel Beijing**: *35 East Chang An Avenue (Dong Chang'anjie), Beijing 100006, Tel. (86-10) 6513-7788 or Fax (86-10) 6512-0049.* Terrific location within the grounds of the former Imperial City, within a short walk of Tiananman Square and the Great Hall of the People, and near Beijing's famous shopping street, Wangfujing. Attached to the western end of the grand dame Beijing Hotel, this is one of Beijing's two top luxury hotels (5-star). It's also a member of The Leading Hotels of the World. Completed in 1992 and operated by the government, this elegantly furnished 10-storey, 218 room hotel (includes 57 suites), the hotel boasts several good Chinese restaurants (Ming Yuan, Old Pekin, Rong Yuan), fully-equipped health facilities, and is attached to a shopping arcade and long corridor that links it to the Beijing Hotel. Often sponsors special art exhibitions. Offers an unobstructed view of the Forbidden City from the roof terrace.

❑ **China World Hotel**: *No. 1, Jian Guo Men Wai Avenue, Da Bei Yao, Beijing 100004, Tel. (86-10) 6505-2266 or Fax (86-10) 6505-0828. Toll-free U.S. reservation system: Tel. 1-800-942-5050.* Managed by Shangri-La Hotels and Resorts, China World Hotel exudes a distinct oriental flair. The main lobby is flanked on either end by two huge floor to ceiling oriental screens in restful hues of green and blue on gold leaf. The hotel offers 739 guest rooms of which 56 are suites. Specialty rooms include 88 with unique Chinese interior design, two for handicapped guests, and four Horizon Club executive floors featuring larger rooms, butler service, special amenities, and two private lounges. Full range of guest services as well as 24-hour Business Center. 11 food and beverage outlets, discotheque, 12 lane bowling alley, Fitness Center and Tennis and Golf Center. China World Hotel's meeting facilities are augmented by the China World Trade Center's adjoining 10,000 square meter Exhibition Hall—the largest in China. For the avid shopper, the hotel is joined on the other side by a three-level shopping arcade which includes a mix of some designer shops, a small art gallery, and an arts and crafts emporium. The hotel also sponsors a variety of sumptuous entertainment events, including "The Emperor's Banquet" and "The Beijing Food Street Party" which offer musical and dance performances centered around an evening of dining.

❑ **Great Wall Sheraton:** *10 North Dong San Huan Road, Beijing 100026, Tel. (86-19) 6500-5566 or Fax (86-10) 6500-1938. Toll-free U.S. reservation system: Tel. 1-800-325-3535.* The first of the five-star hotels in Beijing to open under Western management (1983), the Great Wall Sheraton has just undergone extensive renovation. It's a huge and imposing windowed complex. The hotel has 1007 rooms and suites which include the ITT Sheraton Club International Floor and a Japanese floor. With five restaurants, a 24-hour coffee shop, and sun deck snack bar, atrium dining, and a barbecue area, one is unlikely to go hungry here. The hotel is nicely located for business people and shoppers: adjacent to the business and diplomatic communities; across the street from the Landmark Towers and the huge You Yi Shopping City (Beijing Lufthansa Center); five minutes from the Agricultural Exhibition Centre and the China International Exhibition Centre; and within 25 minutes of the Forbidden City, Tiananmen Square, and Beijing Airport. The hotel includes a very nice moderate-sized shopping emporium offering excellent quality clothes, jewelry, arts, crafts, and carpets. The hotel provides many special opportunities for entertainment both in the hotel and at nearby tourist venues.

❑ **Kempinski Hotel Beijing:** *50 Liangmaqiao Road, Chao-yang District, Beijing 100016, Tel. (86-10) 6465-3388 or Fax (86-10) 6465-3366. Toll-free U.S. reservation system: Tel. 1-800-426-3135.* Located in the Diplomatic Quarter, ten minutes from the airport and city center. With 530 rooms and suites, the Kempinski adds its Paulaner Boutique Brewery to its many western and Chinese food Outlets. The Brewery offers home brewed beer and Bavarian specialties. For Chinese cuisine, try the Imperial Garden and Dragon restaurants. One of Beijing's finest and most popular western restaurants, Symphony, is found here. Select accommodations on an Executive Floor and receive priority check-in and a private lounge for complimentary breakfast and cocktails. A business center, conference and meeting facilities, fitness center, and its own attached Shopping City (Beijing Lufthansa Center Complex) round out the many offerings of this well located hotel.

❑ **Jing Guang New World Hotel:** *Hu Jia Lou Yang Qu, Beijing 100020, Tel. (86-10) 6501-8888 or Fax (86-10) 6501-3333. Toll-free U.S. reservation system: Tel. 1-800-468-3571.* With 52 floors, this hotel is part of the tallest building in Beijing. Located in the diplomatic and commercial center of Beijing, the New World Hotel has 446 rooms and suites as well as 246 apartments. The Executive Floors offer a hotel within the hotel with separate check-in and express check-out facilities and exclusive use of a boardroom. The Executive Lounge offers complimentary drinks and continental breakfast, plus tea and coffee all day. Its seven restaurants offer a range of cuisines. It has a 24-hour business center and a full range of fitness facilities. Its Arts and Crafts Shopping Arcade on the second floor is one expansive shop selling a wide range of clothing, handicrafts, carved stone pieces, jewelry, and paintings. One of the better hotel shops which also has aggressive sales personnel.

❑ **Swissôtel:** *Dong Si Shi Tiao Li Jiao Qiao, P.O. Box 9153, Beijing 100027, Tel. (86-10) 6501-2288 or Fax (86-10) 6501-2501.* Conveniently located at the Hong Kong Macau Center in the heart of the diplomatic and business district, the Swissôtel offers 500 guest rooms including specially designed facilities for limited-mobility guests. The Swiss Executive Floor provides upscale rooms, complimentary breakfast and cocktails in a private lounge as well as a host of special business services. Culinary selections include Continental and Asian fare of Café Suisse, an Italian buffet in the Veranda, Cantonese and Shanghainese specialities in Happy Valley, and Portuguese and Macanese cuisine in the Macau Grill. A Business Center and Health Club with qualified trainers are available. A second floor shop offers a wide selection of Benetton clothes and Swatch watches. A first-floor handicraft shop, located behind the lobby bar, offers paintings, clothes, silk, jewelry, cloisonne, and rugs.

❑ **Kunlun:** *2 Xin Yuan Nan Lu, Chao Yang District, Beijing, Tel. (86-10) 6500-3388 or Fax (886-10) 6500-3228.* The Kunlun Hotel is located along the Liang Ma River, 30 minutes from the airport and 25 minutes from downtown. The hotel has more than 900 guest rooms and suites with 11 restaurants offering a wide variety of Western, Chinese, Japanese, and Korean cuisines—even a revolving restaurant at the top. It also includes a Business Center, Fitness Center with tennis court, and a large shopping center next door to the hotel. Look for special exhibitions (art) and auctions (art and jewelry).

❑ **Holiday Inn Crowne Plaza:** *48 Wangfujing Avenue, Deng Shi Xi Kau, Beijing 100006, Tel. (86-10) 6513-3388, Fax (86-10) 6513-2513. Toll-free U.S. reservation system: Tel. 1-800-426-4329.* Located within 10-minute walking distance of the Forbidden City and in the heart of Wangfujing Street's shopping, the Holiday Inn Crowne Plaza has a bright, cheerful atrium lobby with many rooms opening onto the delightful and often chamber music-filled atrium. The Crowne Plaza offers 385 rooms and suites including the Crowne Plaza Club executive floors with two lounges. Other facilities include a fitness center and a 24-hour business center. Its three restaurants serve a variety of both western (Plaza Grill) and Chinese cuisine (Pearl Garden). A unique venue is an Art Gallery that features changing exhibitions of both traditional and contemporary Chinese art. Indeed, art and music are constant themes in this unique hotel which is often filled with paintings, sculptures, and chamber music. The atrium lounge is a pleasant place to enjoy noon time or late afternoon piano and harp musical performances.

❑ **Overseas Chinese Prime:** *Huaqiaodasha 2 Wangfujing Avenue, Beijing 100006, Tel. (86-10) 6513-6666 or Fax (86-10) 6513-4248.* Formally known as the Quangdong Regency Hotel until its ownership and name changed in October 1996. Located in the city center with 400 guest rooms and suites. The Executive Floor offers separate check-in, a continental breakfast, and happy hour in a separate lounge. The property includes a Business Center and Health Club with gymnasium, saunas and swimming pool. Its four restaurants offer a range of Western and Chinese food.

Beijing also has several four-star hotels worth considering. Most lack the full range of amenities found at the five-star properties but they are more than adequate to meet the needs of most travelers:

❑ **Beijing Hilton International:** *1 Dong Fang Road, North Dong San Huan Road, Chaoyang District, Beijing 100027, Tel. (86-10) 6466-2288 or Fax (86-10) 6465-3052. Toll-free U.S. reservation system: Tel. 1-800-468-3571.* Set in the commercial district and within easy access by car to Tiananmen Square. The lobby has a warm but spacious feel provided by an open atrium. 365 guest rooms and suites offer a sumptuous traditional Chinese setting. Executive Floors offer a private retreat in the Clubroom, complimentary continental breakfast, afternoon tea selection and cocktails, as well as separate check-in/ check-out services. Six food and beverage outlets include Louisiana Western Restaurant for American favorites, Sui Yuan for Chinese food and Genji Japanese Restaurant. A Business Center is available and the Fitness Center offers an outdoor tennis court and two squash courts. An A. Testoni shop and a newsstand are found in a small shopping area. While officially classified as a four-star hotel, its services and amenities appear to be up to five-star caliber.

❑ **Landmark Tower:** *8 North Dongsanhuan Road, Chaoyang District, Beijing 100004, Tel. (86-10) 6501-6688 or Fax (86-10) 6501-3513.* Part of an office, apartment, and hotel complex, the Landmark Hotel is located in the commercial district just across the street from the Sheraton Great Wall Hotel. It includes 488 guest rooms and a shopping arcade with 20 retail shops. Its many restaurants include Beijing's first Hard Rock Cafe,

Hunan Garden, Jade Garden, Pub, and food court. Additional features include a Business Center and a Fitness Center.

❑ **Traders Hotel:** *1 Jian Guo Men Wai Avenue, Beijing 100004, Tel. (86-10) 6505-2277 or Fax (86-10) 6505-0818.* Adjacent to and affiliated with the well located China World Hotel and the China World Trade Centre, this four-star Shangri-La property includes 298 guest rooms and suites. Guests have access to the facilities available at the China World Hotel (see above), including the Fitness Centre, tennis courts, swimming pool, and bowling alley. The three-storey hotel shopping arcade along with the nearby You Yi Shopping City (Beijing Lufthansa Center) make this an excellent choice for shoppers.

❑ **Jianguo:** *Jianguomenwai Dajie, Beijing 100020, Tel. (86-10) 6500-2233 or Fax (86-10) 6500-2871.* A Swiss-Belhotel International located adjacent to the Jianguo-menwai diplomatic quarter, in the heart of the city's business and administrative center, is only 20 minutes from Beijing Capital Airport and 10 minutes from Tiananmen Square. The Jianguo Hotel was the first joint venture hotel in China. Built in 1982, it was completely renovated in 1996, and is comprised of 67 suites, 66 executive rooms with king or queen sized beds, and 266 superior rooms. The Jianguo Club Floor offers separate check-in, breakfast in the executive lounge, and other attractive features. The hotel also includes seven food outlets including a counter service gourmet take-away for quick treats or lunch on the run; and a 24-hour business center and fitness center. Its major restaurants include Justine's Restaurant for fine French and European cuisine and the Four Seasons Restaurant for Cantonese cuisine and daily dim sum. It also includes the popular outdoor Jianguo Beer Garden and Charlie's Bar with its daily international (British, Indian, Arabian, Mexican, Italian) dining themes. The hotel shop is larger than it initially appears. It has a mini-arts and crafts section that sells the usual along with some nice neck pieces of carved semi-precious stones and beads.

❑ **Beijing Hotel:** *33 East Chang An Avenue (Dong Chang'-anjie), Beijing 100004, Tel. (86-10) 6513-7766 or Fax (86-10) 6513-7703.* Built in 1900 and centrally located within walking distance of the Forbidden City, this is one of Beijing's grand old hotels. While somewhat worn in comparison to the newer and more modern properties, it still has old world charm. It has seen a lot of history pass through its doors. Includes 900 rooms as well as meeting facilities, restaurants, and a large shopping arcade offering everything from arts, crafts, and antiques to clothing, accessories, and cosmetics. Includes a post office and a Bank of China branch. A long corridor that functions as a shopping arcade attaches the Beijing Hotel to the five-star Grand Hotel Beijing.

❑ **Holiday Inn Lido:** *(Lido Fandian) Jichang Road, Jiang Tai Road, Beijing 100004. Tel. (86-10) 6437-6688 or Fax 6437-6237. Toll-free U.S. reservation system: Tel. 1-800-HOLIDAY.* Located a few kilometers northwest of the Great Wall Sheraton, Landmark, Kempinski, China, and Kunlun hotel center and approximately 35 minutes from the city center, this is Holiday Inn's largest property worldwide. A 5-storey, 1000-room hotel located across from Lido Park. Includes several restaurants, entertainment facilities, complete business services, and a supermarket.

Beijing also has several additional four-star hotels as well as numerous three- and two-star hotels. If you arrive in Beijing without a hotel reservation, check with the hotel reservation desk which is conveniently located adjacent to the baggage retrieval area. This desk includes a full range of hotels, from five-star to budget accommodations. However, don't expect much in the budget category. Most hotels in Beijing tend to be three-, four-, or five-star properties which go for US$120 to US$300 a night.

RESTAURANTS

Beijing has a wide range of eating establishments, from local street shops and Western fast food restaurants (McDonald's Pizza Hut, and KFC) to fine Chinese and Western restaurants. More and more excellent quality restaurants are opening to cater to the growing international traffic of business people and tourists. The best restaurants, which also are the most hygienic, are found in the top hotels. While you can find some excellent local restaurants, please be forewarned that they may not meet your exacting health standards. You may want to pay more and concentrate your dining in the major hotel restaurants which also tend to have the best chefs and range of selections. Some of the best restaurants, including Chinese, will be operated by international chefs from Europe, North America, and other parts of Asia, including Hong Kong, Taiwan, Singapore, and Bangkok. For a quick overview of Beijing's best restaurants, pick up a copy of the latest issue of the monthly English and Chinese language *Gourmet World* that features numerous restaurants of interest to foreign visitors as well as the current issue of *Welcome to China: Beijing* for its restaurant listings.

CHINESE

❑ **Palace Restaurant:** *The Palace Hotel, Wangfujing, Tel. 6512-8899, ext. 7900. Open daily, 11:30am-2:30pm and 6-11pm. Reservations essential.* One of China's best Sichuan restaurants for both food and service.

❑ **Ming Yuan:** *Grand Hotel Beijing, 35 East Chang An Avenue, Tel. 6513-7788.* Dine in Ming-style in this sumptuous Chinese restaurant offering authentic cuisine from various regions in China.

❑ **Fang Shan:** *Beihai Park (on Qiong Hua Island), Tel. 6401-1879. Open daily, 11am-1:30pm and 5-7pm.* Open since 1925, this popular restaurant specializes in the Imperial cuisine of the Qing Court. Popular for banquets. Great setting in a restored courtyard on the lake.

❑ **Quanjude Hepingmen Roast Duck:** *Intersection of Hepingmen Lu and Quianmen Xidajie (Chonwen District), Tel. 6301-8833. Open daily, 10:30am-2:30pm and 4:30-9pm.* Also referred to as "Big Duck." This world famous Beijing duck restaurant is huge. Nothing fancy. An unforgettable dining experience.

❑ **Rong Yuan:** *Grand Hotel Beijing, 35 East Chang An Avenue, Tel. 6513-7788.* One of Beijing's finest Chinese restaurants specializing in traditional imperial Sichuan cuisine.

❑ **Beijing Palace:** *130 Chaonie Dajie, Tel. 6524-4202. Open daily, 11:30am-2:30pm and 5:30pm-9:30pm.* Beijing cuisine. Noted for its stew rib with bean paste and seafood dishes.

❑ **China Garden:** *Holiday Inn Lido Hotel, Jichang Road, Jiang Tai Road, Tel. 6437-6688, ext. 2700. Open daily, 11:30am-2:30pm.* Cantonese cuisine. Known for its seafood dishes and dim sum.

❑ **Sui Yuan Restaurant:** *Beijing Hilton Hotel, 4 Dong Sanhuan Bei Road, 1 Dongfang Road, Tel. 6466-2288, ext. 7416. Open daily, 11:30am-2pm and 5:30-10pm.* Cantonese cuisine. Dum sum at lunch time.

❑ **Happy Valley:** *Swissôtel, Dong Si Shi Tiao Li Jiao Qiao, Tel. 6501-2288, ext. 2146. Open daily, 11:30am-2pm.* Cantonese cuisine. Popular for dim sum and seafood.

❑ **Shanghai Flavour Restaurant:** *Kunlun Hotel, 2 Xin Yuan Nan Road, Tel. 6500-3388, ext. 5394. Open daily, 11:30am-2pm and 5:30-9:30pm.* Shanghai cuisine prepared by Shanghai chefs.

❑ **Quanjude Kaoya Dian Restaurant:** *Wangfujing Branch, 13 Shuaifuyuan, Tel. 6525-3310. Open daily, 10:30am-1:30pm and 5-8:30pm.* Serves some of the best Peking Duck in Beijing.

❑ **Sichuan Fandian:** *51 Xirongxian Hutong. Tel. 6603-3291. Open daily, 11am-2pm and 5-8pm.* Famous for its Sichuan cuisine. Served in elegant courtyard rooms of a former emperor's residence (General Yuan Shikai). Popular for banquets.

❑ **Yuen Tai Restaurant:** *Great Wall Sheraton Hotel, Donghuan Bei Road, Tel. 6500-5566, ext. 2162. Open daily, 11:30am-2pm and 6-10pm.* Authentic Sichuan cuisine with a good view of the city.

ITALIAN

❑ **Roma Ristorante Italiano:** *The Palace Hotel, Wangfujing, Tel. 6512-8899, ext. 7492. Open daily, 11:30am-2:30pm and 6:30-11:00pm. Reservations essential.* If you're looking for great Italian cuisine produced by Italian chefs and a restaurant managed by Italian expertise and usually crowded, Roma Ristorante Italiano doesn't get any better for Beijing. Served in a luxurious, elegant, romantic, and intimate setting, you'll forget you are actually dining in

Beijing. Everything is top quality, from pasta to veal and seafood dishes. Be sure to try the delectable desserts, especially the terimasu and chocolate brulee. The creamy house-made ice creams, especially chocolate, are outstanding. Helpful maitre de who knows his kitchen well.

❑ **Toula:** *Beijing International Hotel, Jianguomenwai Dajie, Tel. 6512-6688, ext. 1569. Open daily, 6-10pm.* Elegant restaurant serving traditional Northern Italian cuisine.

❑ **Peppinos Restaurant:** *Shangri-La Hotel, 29 Zizhuyan Road, Tel. 6841-2211, ext. 2727. Open daily, 11:30am-2:30pm and 6-10:30pm.* Good selection of pasta dishes.

FRENCH

❑ **Symphony:** *Hotel Kempinski, Lobby Level, 50 Liangmaqiao Lu, Chayang District, Tel. 6465-3388, ext. 4155. Open daily, 12:00-2:00pm and 6:00pm to 10pm. Reservations required.* Beijing's top French restaurant. Very popular.

❑ **Justine's:** *Jianguo Hotel, 5 Jianguomenwai Dajie, Tel. 6500-2233, ext. 8039. Open daily, 12noon-2:30pm and 6:00-10:30pm.* Fine French dining in classic ambiance.

❑ **La Fleur:** *China World Hotel, 1 Jianguomenwai Daiji, Da Bei Yao, Tel. 6505-2266, ext. 38. Open daily, 10:30am-2:30pm and 6-10pm.* Deluxe French cuisine.

AMERICAN STYLE

❑ **Hard Rock Cafe:** *Landmark Tower Hotel, 8 Dong San Huan, Tel. 6501-6688, ext. 2571. Open daily, 11:30am - 10:30pm.* Trendy American restaurant with loud music and bar atmosphere.

❑ **Louisiana Restaurant:** *Beijing Hilton Hotel, 4 Dong San-huan Bei Road, 1 Dongfang Road, Tel. 6466-2288, ext. 7420. Open daily, 10am-2pm and 6-10pm.* Attractive setting for this refined American cuisine restaurant. Yes, it serves Cajun food.

❑ **The Texan Bar & Grill:** *Holiday Inn Lido, Jichang Road and Jiang Tai Road, Tel. 6437-6688, ext. 1849. Open daily, 11:30am-2pm and 5:30-10:30pm.* If you're hankering for authentic Tex-Mex food, this is the place to go.

❑ **T.G.I. Friday's:** *Huapeng Dasha, 19 Dongsanhuan Beilu, Tel. 6595-1380. Open daily, 11am-12pm.* American chain restaurant and bar serving a wide selection of popular dishes.

JAPANESE

❑ **Genji:** *Beijing Hilton Hotel, 4 Dong Sanhuan Bei Road, 1 Dongfang Road, Tel. 6466-2288, ext. 7402. Open daily, 11:30am-2pm and 6-10pm.* Top Japanese cooking.

❑ **Miyako:***Beijing Grace Hotel, Jiang Tai Xi Road, Tel. 6436-2288, ext. 2650. Open daily, 11:30am-2:30pm and 5:30-9:30pm.* Authentic Japanese cuisine prepared by a Japanese master chef.

MAJOR ATTRACTIONS

Beijing boasts numerous sightseeing attractions within the city as well as outside the city. Those outside the city are usually within a one to two hour drive. For first-time visitors to Beijing, the Great Wall tends to be the highlight of their visit. They find many other sites are interesting, but these often tend to be overstated and hyped as extraordinary, fantastic, or the biggest. You may or may not get as excited about them as the travel literature and guides make them out to be. Like so many other things in China, you may need to use your imagination to picture the glory of these sites, many of which were previously destroyed but never rebuilt in their original splendor. The problem with many of these major sites is that they are often crowded, major sections are often closed to visitors or viewing areas are limited, their history and significance has little meaning to many visitors, especially westerners, and many sites are overrun by hawkers, vendors, and shopkeepers offering a great deal of tourist kitsch. If you're not an avid sightseer, many of Beijing's sites may quickly bore you. Having forewarned you about why you may not get as excited as you might otherwise think you should, here's the best of the best for sightseeing in and around Beijing. Most sites require an admission fee which ranges from US$.30 to US$.60 for locals and from US$3.50 to US$8.00 for foreigners:

❑ **Tiananmen Square:** Located at the center of the city, this is China's grand pedestrian square which is increasing traversed by cars, buses, and bicycles. Used primarily for ceremonies, the square also has a few major attractions, such as **Chairman Mao Memorial Hall** (Mao's mausoleum with Mao lying in a crystal sarcophagus and a museum), **Gate of Heavenly Peace** (long red structure with Mao's portrait hanging about the entrance gate to the Forbidden City), and the **Great Hall of the People** (houses the People's Congress). Many visitors make this their first stop in Beijing from where they can enter the Forbidden city. The entrance is just below the huge portrait of Chairman Mao.

❑ **The Forbidden City (Gu Gong):** *Open daily, 8:30am to 3:30pm with extended hours in the summer, from 6am to 6pm.* Also known as the Imperial Palace, the Forbidden City is located on the north side of Tiananmen Square. This is where the Ming emperors established their palaces and ruled China until the Qing dynasty displaced them and continued ruling China until their fall in 1911. Considered the largest architectural complex in the world, this city within a city includes over 9,000 rooms and halls. However, only a few of the buildings are open to the public and much of this area is closed to visitors. Somewhat over-hyped, there's really not much to see here except for a few buildings constructed in Ming and Qing style and well preserved for visitors. The area also includes an interesting collection of bronzes, porcelain, jade, and paintings. While this definitely is a "must see" site in Beijing, unless you are a real history or architectural buff, you can easily do the Forbidden City in an hour or two. You will find a few good shopping opportunities within the grounds for arts and crafts, but you'll also find lots of tourist kitsch and pesky hawkers trying to sell you over-priced postcards.

❑ **Temple of Heaven (Tiantan):** *Open daily from 6am to 8:30pm in the summer and from 8:30am to 6pm in the winter.* One of Beijing's most enduring symbols, this expansive walled complex consists of a series of attractive round Ming-style temples with square bases and three levels of blue tiled roofs surrounded by pavilions. Probably the most famous temples in all of China. Originally built in the 15th century, they have been repeatedly restored to their original grandeur. The area near the East Gate includes several small arts and crafts shops. However, the best shop is located in an old building to the right of the East Gate entrance—**Qing Shan Ju Antique Shop**.

❑ **Summer Palace (Yi He Yuan):** *Open daily, 7:30am to 6:30pm.* Located 12 kilometers from the city center, this is one of Beijing's most visited sites. Its spectacular gardens, bridges, pavilions, halls, and towers, all arrayed in a pleasant lake-side setting, emphasizes the once opulent and excessive lifestyle of the Qing dynasty rulers. What you will be seeing is a reconstruction of the original Summer Palace which was burned down by foreign troops in 1860 and rebuilt from funds diverted from the Chinese navy. Also, look for the famous lake-side marble boat, the boat that goes nowhere!

❑ **The Great Wall (Chang Cheng):** *Open daily, 8:30am to 11pm.* If there is only one historical monument a Westerner identifies with China, it's the Great Wall. Reputed to be the only man-made structure visible from space, the Great Wall is over 2000 years old and runs nearly 6,400 kilometers. Located within an hour from Beijing by car or train, most people visit one of two locations:

  ▪ **Badaling:** Located 80 kilometers north of Beijing. This is the most popular as well as most developed section of the Great Wall. This area also is relatively close to the Ming Tombs. Lots of shops and stalls selling everything from old and new "antiques" to fur hats and pelts. You can climb to the wall via congested staircases or take a cable car to the top of the wall.

  ▪ **Mutianyu:** Located nearly 100 kilometers northeast of Beijing. This newer section is preferred by many visitors who wish to avoid the crowds of Badaling. This section is near the Miyun reservoir and includes a cable car. Sections of the wall here also are steeper than at Badaling.

There's not much to do at the Great Wall other than walk along its stone walkways and take photos. Make sure to take good sturdy pair of walking shoes and don't be surprised to discover how exhausting the walk can be because of the steep and slippery inclines. Depending on when you visit, the crowds can be oppressive.

❑ **Ming Tombs:** *Open daily, 8:30am-5pm.* Located 50 kilometers northwest of Beijing, these are the burial sites for 13 of 15 Ming Emperors. Only one of the tombs at Ding Ling (Emperor Wanli, AD 1573-1620) has been excavated, renovated, and opened to the public. The nearby museum displays many artifacts found in the tomb. An interesting area to visit. But be sure to visit the nearby Avenue of Animals ("Sacred Way") which in many respects is more interesting than the tombs with its Longfeng Gate, Dagong Gate, and Stele Pavilion. Here you'll see massive stone-carved animals, such as camels, elephants, horses, and mythical beasts, as well as figures of mandarins, lining both sides of the walkway. A very impressive and tranquil site.

❑ **Fragrant Hills (Xiang Shan):** Located 28 kilometers northwest of Beijing, this used to be a favorite summer retreat of emperors. Its now a very pleasant park for visitors. Take the chair lift to its tallest peak for a panoramic view of Beijing.

❑ **Visit to the Hutong:** The *hutongs* are the traditional densely populated residential areas laced with narrow streets that are found in several parts of Beijing. For a cultural experience, take a morning (departs at 8:50am) or afternoon (departs at 1:50pm) tour by trishaw to visit these interesting areas. For reservations, call 6525-4262 or 6524-8482 or contact your hotel tour desk.

❑ **Princely Palaces:** Beijing at one time had over 40 princely palaces functioning during the Qing Dynasty. While many of them have disappeared, others have been converted into schools, hospitals, factories, and storage buildings. In recent years the remaining palace buildings have been put under government protection as part of China's cultural heritage. The Beijing Tourism Administration provides a map of these properties in their handy little tour guide, *The Beijing Official Guide*. You may want to get a copy of this guidebook which may be available at some hotels and airline ticket offices. If not, contact the Beijing Foreign Cultural Exchanges Service Center (2/F Yin Chun Hall, CVIK Hotel, 22 Jianguanmenwai Dajie, Tel. 6512-3388, ext. 2338 or Fax 6512-3415).

The list of additional sightseeing attractions goes on and on and includes numerous historical sites, landmarks, monuments, museums, art galleries, parks, gardens, and zoos. You'll quickly discover Beijing has plenty of things to see and do. Just make sure you set priorities so you don't find yourself with insufficient time to do what you really came here to do.

Historical Sites and Monuments

- Beijing Ancient Observatory
- Big Bell Temple
- The Drum Tower
- Lama Temple (Yonghegong Lamasery)
- Temple of the Azure Clouds
- Temple of the Reclining Buddha
- White Cloud Temple

Museums

- Beijing Museum of Natural History
- Capital Museum
- China Arts and Crafts Gallery
- China Art Gallery
- Contemporary Art Gallery
- Museum of Chinese History
- Museum of the Chinese Revolution
- Sackler Archaeological Museum at Beijing University

Parks, Gardens, and Zoos

- Beihai Park
- Beijing Zoo
- Prospect Hill (Coal Hill)

ENTERTAINMENT

As the cultural center of China, Beijing has a lot to offer in the traditional and modern arts, from opera and ballet to concerts and exhibitions. As a major business and tourist center, it also offers some western nightlife.

If you're interested in the traditional and modern Chinese arts, plan to attend some of these performances:

❑ **Beijing Opera:** Performed every evening at 7:30 in the Liyuan Theater (Qianmen Hotel, 175 Yungan Road (Tel. 6301-6688). Also performed in several other theaters in the city.

❑ **Puppet Show:** China Puppet Theater, A1 Anhauxili, Tel. 6425-4846; or Hotel Beijing-Toronto every Saturday evening at 8pm (Tel. 6500-2266).

❑ **Acrobatics:** Chaoyang Theater, 36 Dongsanhuan Bei Lu, Tel. 6507-2421.

❑ **Symphony:** Beijing Concert Hall, 1 Bei Xinghuajie, Tel. 6605-7006.

Check with your hotel concierge or the entertainment section of the English-language newspaper *China Daily* for exact times and locations.

Beijing is not known for its hot Western nightlife, but this scene has been changing dramatically within the past few years. Nonetheless, you'll find enough of bars, pubs, and discos to fill your evening. Most are part of the major four- and five-star joint venture hotels. Karaoke fans will feel at home in Beijing. Some of the most popular places include:

Pubs/Bars

- **Alfred's:** Overseas Chinese Prime Hotel, Tel. 6513-6666
- **Beijing Pig & Whistle:** Holiday Inn Lido, Tel. 6437-6688
- **Charlie's:** Jianguo Hotel, Tel. 6500-2233
- **Frank's Place:** Gongrentiyuguan East Road, Tel. 6507-2617
- **Hard Rock Cafe:** Landmark Tower, Tel. 6501-6688
- **Paulaner Brauhaus:** Kempinski Hotel, Tel. 6465-3388
- **Pimm's:** Beijing Hilton, Tel. 6466-2288
- **Spruce Goose:** Mövenpick Hotel, Tel. 6456-5588

Discos/Bars With Karaoke Venue

- **Caesar Palace:** Rainbow Plaza, Tel. 6595-2288
- **Cyclone:** Holiday Inn Lido, Tel. 6437-6688
- **Derby Bar:** Swissôtel, Tel. 6501-2288
- **JJ Disco & Rainbow Karaoke:** 74-75 Xinjiekou, Tel. 6607-9691
- **Jungle Disco:** Tianlun Dynasty, Tel. 6513-8888
- **Moonlight Karaoke:** Jing Guang New World, Tel. 6501-8888
- **Paradise Club Karaoke:** Holiday Inn Crowne Plaza, Tel. 6513-3388
- **Peace Karaoke:** Peace Hotel, Tel. 6512-8833

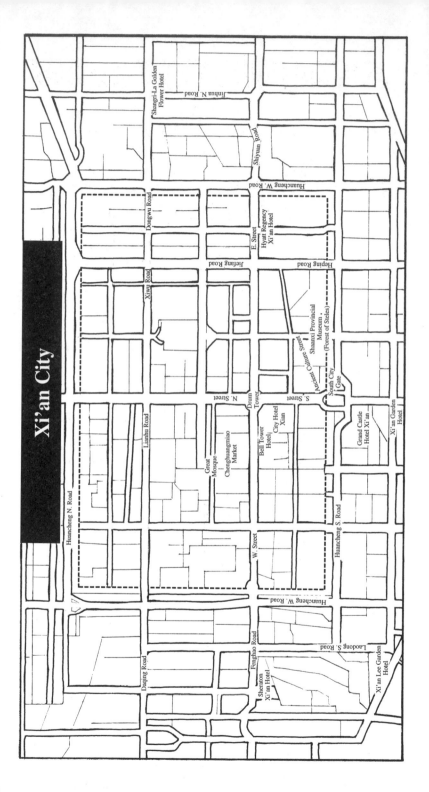

Xi'an City

8

Xi'an

The largest city in northwest China with an urban population of nearly 2.5 million, Xi'an is an exotic and legendary city—an in-your-face city of grand history and culture. Dry, dusty, and often short of water, it's a city from which great dynasties once ruled China; the city where the Silk Road began; a city of great universities; and a city undergoing rapid industrialization. Teeming with people, bicycles, and cars, this city exudes a distinct character with its grand walls, impressive city landmarks, delightful museums, and colorful shops.

One of China's most popular tourist destinations, Xi'an attracts 3.5 million foreign and domestic tourists each year. Most come here for one purpose—view the incredible collection of terracotta warriors unearthed at the village of Lintong, 37 kilometers northeast of Xi'an city. Usually a short two- to three-day visit, Xi'an is often the highlight of any visit to China. Xi'an is different, and it leaves visitors with a true sense of a grand and powerful ancient Chinese history.

SURPRISING XI'AN

Located in northwest China 1,034 kilometers southwest of Beijing, Xi'an is a very special destination for travelers in search of China's unique treasures and pleasures. It's a very old city, tracing its roots for nearly 5,000 years. In many respects, it is the cradle of ancient Chinese civilization, having played a central role in the great panorama of Chinese history. After Beijing, Xi'an is the most interesting and frequented place for exploring ancient Chinese history, archaeology, and culture. If you are a history buff, you'll love Xi'an. And if you're really not into ancient history and archaeology, you'll probably still enjoy the exotic character of this rapidly developing city with its massive walls, hoards of bicycles and cars, and bustling markets and street shops. Its 60,000 Moslems (primarily Hui minority), many of whom trace their ancestors to the Tang-era Silk Road merchants, and their Great Mosque give the city an additional exotic element not found in many other Chinese cities.

While the travel image of Xi'an is closely tied to the famous archeological sites of unearthed terracotta soldiers, Xi'an also is well known as one of China's seven ancient national capitals and a great center for Buddhist scholars, monks, and artists. Previously known as Chang'an, it was once the great political center of China. Its 11 dynasties ruled China for nearly 1100 years, from the Qin Dynasty in 230BC to the Tang Dynasty in the 9th century AD. Now the capital of Shaanxi Province, Xi'an was once the center of the thriving Silk Road trade which began nearly 2,000 years ago. It served as the eastern terminus for the many caravans that transported luxurious Chinese products to the Middle East and Europe. Indeed, by the eighth and ninth centuries (AD), Xi'an had reached its zenith with fabulous palaces, temples, mosques, bazaars, and even universities. Today its massive walls and such historical monuments as the Huaqing Palace, the Big and Small Wild Goose Pagodas, and the Great Mosque testify to Xi'an's once strategic importance in east-west communication and trade. Its many impressive burial grounds and museums along with dazzling Tang cultural performances emphasize the fact that this once was a grand city of great wealth, power, achievement, and importance throughout China.

During the past 900 years Xi'an receded into the background as a provincial city which occasionally asserted an important political role. It was not until the 1970s that Xi'an began regaining its reputation as one of China's most important historical cities. An accidental discovery put Xi'an on the tourist map in a very big way. In 1974 a group of farmers uncovered the first of nearly 6,000 life-size terracotta soldiers and horses while sinking a new well in their field. Within five years of this serendipitous discovery a huge hangar-like building was constructed over what become known as Pit #1. As the outside world learned more and more about this wondrous archeological discovery, more and more archeologists, historians, government leaders, and tourists ventured to Xi'an to observe this unfolding "eighth wonder of the world," a 2,200 year old army of soldiers with weapons in exact formation. The incredible detail and distinct facial expressions of each figure in this silent army of warriors have left lasting impressions on millions of visitors who have ventured to this site during the past two decades. As archeologists continued to dig, they established two adjacent pits which are now enclosed as part of an impressive museum of granite and cement. It is this discovery and ongoing archeological digs that continue to attract nearly 3 million visitors to Xi'an each year. They arrive by train or plane, proceed 37 kilometers northeast of the city, and observe the stunning and still unfolding underground drama of terracotta soldiers and their horses. One leaves this site duly impressed at having viewed one of China's most impressive sites and convinced the long trip to Xi'an was well worth it.

But Xi'an is much more than just a city adjacent to a massive burial ground containing an army of terracotta soldiers and horses. Encircled by 14 kilometers of the best preserved walls in all of China, Xi'an is a bustling old and dusty city of nearly 2.5 million people (6 million if you count a large rural population residing within the extended city); an important manufacturing city with nearly 2,200 joint venture companies producing everything from textiles, autos (Suzuki), and airplanes to electronics and pharmaceuticals; an important center for higher education with nearly 40 universities, colleges, and research institutes; and a city that may soon have its own modern subway system (if the mayor gets his way) to help alleviate its bicycle and auto clogged streets. Plans are underway to turn Xi'an into a high-tech center, drawing on its extensive educational complex and attractive joint venture climate.

- ❏ Xi'an is one of China's most popular tourist destinations which attracts 3.5 million visitors each year.

- ❏ This is one of the world's oldest cities with a history of nearly 5,000 years.

- ❏ Xi'an was once the center for the thriving Silk Road trade that began 2,000 years ago.

- ❏ The discovery of the 2,200 year old army of 6,000 terracotta soldiers and horses in the 1970s put Xi'an on the tourist map.

- ❏ A two- to three-day visit to Xi'an should be sufficient.

Like so many other big cities in China, Xi'an is undergoing a significant transformation from an old city to a modern one with the construction of more and more buildings and major improvements in the city's infrastructure, from streets to power lines and sewers. The city's distinctive walls and bustling streets remain, housing what is one of China's most dynamic cities.

After making the obligatory visit to the museum and

archeological site of terracotta soldiers, you'll find a few things to see and do in the city, from visiting museums and walking the city's massive walls to shopping and taking in a colorful Tang cultural show. Depending on how interested you are in sightseeing, most of the highlights of the city, including shopping, can be covered within a day. All totaled, a two- to three-day visit to Xi'an may be sufficient, especially if you are on a tight schedule visiting other places in China. More than three days in Xi'an may leave you with few stimulating things to see and do.

THE BASICS

CLIMATE AND WHEN TO GO

Xi'an's climate is relatively dry and cool compared to many other parts of China; it's less extreme than in Beijing. Compared to the United States, it's most comparable to that of Kansas, Iowa, or Wyoming. Its distinct seasons result in cold winters (below freezing but not extreme) and hot summers (hits 100°F in July). The best times to visit are Spring and Fall—March, April, September, or October.

GETTING THERE

Xi'an has excellent transportation facilities. Most visitors to Xi'an arrive by plane or train. The city is well serviced by regularly scheduled flights from other major cities within China, especially Beijing, Shanghai, and Hong Kong. The flight from Beijing takes about one hour and 45 minutes. International flights now connect directly to Xi'an from Macau, Osaka, Hiroshima, Nagoya, Singapore, and Bangkok.

Xi'an's relatively new (1991) Xianyang International Airport is located approximately 50 kilometers from the city center. Buses and taxis conveniently connect the airport with the city. The CAAC shuttle bus only goes so far as it city ticket office from which you'll need to take another bus or taxi to your hotel. It's more convenient to just take a taxi from the airport to the city for around Y180. The drive from the airport to the city reveals a very dry, dusty, and eroded landscape punctuated with numerous imperial burial grounds and rural houses with ears of corn strung along their roofs. It's a very different landscape from other parts of China.

TRAIN

Nearly 70 trains run to and from Xi'an. Direct trains connect Xi'an to Beijing, Chengdu, Guangzhou, Quindai, Shanghai, Taiyuan, Urumqui, and Wuhan. If you are coming from Chongqing or Kunming, you must change trains at Chengdu. The train trip from Beijing to Xi'an takes approximately 14 hours; from Chengdu to Xi'an is about 19 hours; and from Guangzhou to Xi'an takes about 22 hours.

GETTING AROUND

The city is well serviced by taxis, buses, trolley buses, mini-buses, and pedicabs. In addition, you can always join the masses by renting a bicycle. It's most convenient to take taxis which are abundant and relatively inexpensive. And bicycles are everywhere, and dangerous for many pedestrians. You can easily arrange taxis and bicycles at your hotel. Since you will most likely be visiting the terracotta archeological site, you can join a tour, take a taxi, or rent a car. Check with your hotel about making these transportation arrangements.

GETTING TO KNOW YOU

Surrounded by mountains and located in the flat Weihe River basin, Xi'an is a relatively cosmopolitan city located at the center of the historic Silk Road. Rich in history, Xi'an first impresses you from a distance as you approach the city—it's encircled with massive walls and gates. Reminiscent of a grand movie set, Xi'an is literally an enclosed fortress city surrounded by a moat. Built in the 14th century, its 14 kilometers of walls form a rectangle encompassing the city. The best preserved walls in all of China, they are truly massive: 12 meters high and 12-14 meters wide. They include 164 watchtowers and four huge gates.

The city itself is laid out in a grid pattern with extremely crowded streets and sidewalks and worn buildings. Like so many other cities in China, this one is not particularly attractive although it does have its moments of architectural beauty. Because of all the new construction and infrastructure projects, many of the streets are often torn up and blocked to traffic. Consequently, you may find yourself going in circles trying to get from one section of the city to another. The city displays a colorful street life in the evening as vendors crowd the sidewalks with small stalls and pushcarts from which they sell everything from food, especially Xi'an's famous dumplings, prepared over charcoal stoves, to clothes and household goods. This is a city of great street theater in the late afternoons and evenings.

One of the best places to orient yourself to the city as well as concentrate your activities is the **South Gate**. Climb the stone stairs to the top of the gate and walk along the wall. You may even want to do some shopping at the nice arts and crafts shop that's conveniently located at the top of stairs. If you look directly to the north along the main street, you'll see the city's major landmark, the distinctive 600-year old **Bell Tower**. The main shopping area tends to be concentrated to the east of this tower. Just to the northwest of the Bell Tower lies the **Drum Tower** and **Great Mosque**. Between these two landmarks is **Beiyuanmen Street** with its popular antique stalls. If you look immediately to the east, just a few minutes walk from the South Gate (watch the traffic as you cross the street!) you'll see the entrance to the one of Xi'an's most important shopping areas, the **Ancient Culture Street**, which also leads to one of Xi'an's major museums, The Forest of Steles or **Shaanxi Provincial Museum**, with its famous Tang Dynasty stone tablets. This recently built street, with its Tang Dynasty style architecture, is lined with arts and crafts shops reminiscent of Liulichang Culture Street in Beijing.

SHOPPING TREASURES

BUYER BEWARE

Xi'an is by no means a shopper's paradise. Nonetheless, it does have a lot to offer to those interested in local arts and crafts, especially the distinctive and colorful folk art of Shaanxi Province. But you must be careful here. Just because you are traveling in one of China's less expensive cities doesn't mean you should conclude everything will be cheaper in Xi'an. You may discover the opposite is true. Like so many other shopping experiences in China, the laws of supply and demand do not necessarily operate in Xi'an. Shops offering tourist items tend to be well organized to handle tourists, and their money. Indeed, we encountered several ubiquitous "bus-stop-shops"— mainly large arts and crafts emporiums—that have reputations for high prices and for giving commissions to tour guides. Most of these shops offer the same types of products, mainly arts and crafts, that you can find much cheaper in Beijing and Shanghai. Many shops have "Friendship Store" in their name. These are not to be confused with the government sanctioned Friendship

Stores. If you are taken to a handicraft emporium or jade factory by a tour guide or driver, chances are they will be getting a commission on what you buy. Our advice: be very cautious in making purchases, and bargain very hard if you find something you really love. Expect to pay more in Xi'an for comparable arts and crafts found in other major cities of China.

WHAT TO BUY

The shops of Xi'an offer a wide variety of unique arts and crafts. Forget about buying any "antique" terracotta figures; all are replicas that more or less look like the real thing. Besides, the real thing would be a bit large for most homes. Xi'an is especially famous for its folk arts and crafts. Colorful folk paintings from the famous town of Huxian in Shaanxi Province (about 50 kilometers from Xi'an) are especially attractive buys and favorites of savvy art collectors who are familiar with this unique and relatively inexpensive art form. The folk paintings in Xi'an cost around US$30 but sell for nearly US$200 in Hong Kong and even more in the United States and Europe. Also look for replicas of tri-colored glazed pottery, stone (steles) rubbings, shadow puppets, ancient Yanzhou porcelain, cloisonne figures, pottery, Qin embroidery, papercuts, colored clay sculptures, jewelry, carpets, jade carvings, calligraphy, and art supplies. Vendors in and around the major tourist sites offer a wide selection of colorful (bright red) children's patchwork waistcoats and shoulder bags as well as embroidered children's shoes, hats, shadow puppets, and painted clay ornaments.

❑ Beware of the ubiquitous "bus-stop-shops" that offer overpriced arts and crafts.

❑ Many shops have "Friendship Store" in their name but they are not really Friendship Stores.

❑ Expect to pay more in Xi'an for comparable arts and crafts found in other major cities.

❑ Forget about buying any "antique" terracotta figures; they're all replicas.

❑ Xi'an is especially famous for its folk arts and crafts. Look for colorful and inexpensive folk paintings from the nearby town of Huxian.

WHERE TO SHOP

Shopping will quickly find you when you visit the major historical sites. Vendors line the walkways offering a wide variety of curios and folk crafts. One of the largest concentration of vendors is found at the **Museum of Emperor Qin's Terracotta Army** which is the site for the army of 6,000 terracotta soldiers and horses. Here, the vendors are organized into an arts and crafts market to the right of the major walkway the leads to the museum. Numerous vendors offer a wide selection a similar brightly colored children's patchwork waistcoats and shoulder bags, embroidered hats, furs, and models of the terracotta figures. Being restricted to this area by the authorities, the vendors do not come out to pester tourists—only shout from the sidelines! Be sure to bargain hard for everything. Since most vendors offer the same products, competition here should result in some fun bargaining and good prices. You'll also find a small antique shop to the left of Pit #1 appropriately called "Antique For Export Shop." The shop offers officially approved antiques, complete with the ubiquitous red seal, that can be exported from China. Most antiques in this shop are old porcelains.

Within the city of Xi'an, the main shopping street is Dong Daji which runs directly east of the Bell Tower. Look for the following shopping areas and shops:

- ❑ **Ancient Culture Street:** Located within a five minute walk northeast of the South Gate, this relatively new and attractive street has been constructed in the style of the Tang Dynasty. The street is lined with shops and street vendors selling art supplies, calligraphy, ink slabs, tea pots, jewelry, chops, paintings, jade carvings, bronzes, and porcelain. As you continue along this street, you eventually come to Shaanxi Museum, or the Forest of Steles, with its famous stone tablets.

- ❑ **Shaan Xi Antique and Curio Store:** Located in the parking lot area of the Shaanxi Provincial Museum, this shop has a nice selection of paintings, porcelain, ceramic figures, jewelry, teapots, wood carvings, and antique reproductions. You'll find some very good quality pieces here.

- ❑ **Beilin Friendship Store:** This huge shop has just about everything you ever wanted in arts and crafts, and then some. Look for nice selections of paintings, scarves, costumes, jewelry, ink slabs, writing brush sets, jade carvings, silk fabric, carvings, books, stamps, chops, silk clothes, ceramics, antiques, and folk art.

- ❑ **Xi'an Cloisonne and Jade Factory:** *No. 9 Yan Ta Road, Tel. 552-2619.* This shop also goes under the name of Cloisonne and Dynasty Jade Carving Factory of Xian China. This is a combination factory and showroom. The downstairs area includes a jade carving workshop and showroom. Here you'll be able to see different qualities and colors of jade as well as jadeite. The floor also includes a large showroom of jade carvings, paintings, antique porcelain, and silk rugs. The upstairs area includes a cloisonne workshop and showroom as well as includes jade carvings, paintings, chops, furniture, and screens. You'll be assigned an English speaking guide to tour this floor. If you decide to buy, be sure to bargain hard here.

❑ **Xi'an Studio Shop of Chinese Cultural Treasures:** *No. 5 Middle Yanta Road, Tel. 553-2380.* Located two doors from the Xi'an Cloisonne and Jade Factory, this is one of the largest arts and crafts shops in Xi'an. The first floor includes paintings, clothes, ceramics, antiques, and jewelry. The second floor offers carpets, lacquer screens and furniture, jade carvings, lacquer boxes, and jade jewelry. The top floor is devoted to reproductions of terracotta warriors, paintings, folk paintings, cloisonne, and workshops producing jade and small terracotta warriors.

❑ **Beiyuanmen Street Antique Bazaar:** Located in the Moslem District, between the Drum Tower and Great Mosque, this is a fun place to visit for "antiques" and collectibles. A typical street market lined with vendors. Bargain hard.

Other shops to look for include the **Xi'an Friendship Store** and **Xi'an Arts and Crafts Store** on Nanxin Street (near Dong Da Jie); **Phoenix Embroidery Factory** (33 Dong Road); **Xi'an Jade Carving Workshop** (173 Xi-1 Road); **Xi'an Luxury Friendship Store** (5 Nan Street); **Shaanxi Cultural Relics Store** (Shaanxi Provincial Museum); and the **Xi'an Cultural Relics Shop** (375 Dong Da Jie). And don't forget the international airport which has lots of shopping opportunities for arts, crafts, food, and clothing available on second floor (after you check in) and in the departure lounge.

ACCOMMODATIONS

You'll have no problem finding decent accommodations in Xi'an. With the growth of both joint ventures and tourism, several new hotels have been built in recent years. Altogether the city has over 40 hotels which accommodate over a million visitors annually. Hotels are both inside and outside the city walls. If you stay inside the city, you'll be conveniently located in relation to the city's major shops and restaurants. However, the downside of staying here is the traffic congestion, noise, and pollution. Hotels outside the city walls may be less conveniently located but you'll avoid many of the negatives associated with being centrally located,

Xi'an's best hotels include the following four and five-star properties:

❑ **Shangri-La Golden Flower Hotel:** *8 Chang Le Xi Road, 710032, Tel. (86-29) 323-29812 or Fax (86-29) 323-5477. In the U.S., Tel. 1-800-942-5050.* Located close to the city center and a 30-minute drive from the Terracotta Warriors Museum, this was Xi'an's first joint venture hotel and still considered by many to be the city's finest. 435 guestrooms and suites offer amenities expected in a deluxe hotel. Upgrade to Shangri-La's Horizon Club floor for additional comforts including Club Lounge check-in and check-out, a deluxe guestroom, complimentary breakfast each morning, and beverages throughout the day. Includes a Chinese restaurant and a coffee shop that serves both Asian and Western cuisine. Complete with a business center, recreation facilities and meeting and banquet facilities. Look for the night market outside the hotel.

❑ **Hyatt Regency Xi'an:** *158 Dong Da Jie, 71000. Tel. (86-29) 723-1234 or Fax (86-29) 721-6799. In the U.S., Tel. 1-800-233-1234.* Located in the center of the city. The lobby atrium is modeled after Xi'an's landmark, the Bell Tower. 404 guestrooms and suites nicely furnished and with expected amenities. Upgrade to Regency Club floors for additional comforts and services. The Chinese restaurant features Sichuanese and Cantonese dishes. The cafe restaurant serves Western food. Includes a business center, fitness center, and conference facilities east of the city walls.

❑ **Sheraton Xi'an:** *12 Feng Hao Road, 710077. Tel. (86-29) 426-1888 or Fax (86-29) 426-2188. In U.S., Tel. 1-800-325-3535.* Located outside the city's walls. 480 rooms and suites and 16 apartments with kitchenettes. Empress Court serves Chinese cuisine. Includes a Western restaurant. Silk Road Cafe serves a variety of foods. Food Street offers fast food options. Full gym and fitness facilities, business center, and secretarial service. Mini supermarket and shops.

❑ **Grand Castle Hotel Xi'an:** *12 Xi Duan Huan Cheng Nan Lu, 710068. Tel. (86-29) 723-1800 or Fax (86-29) 723-1500.* Located just outside the city walls and opposite the South Gate, the Grand Castle is striking because of its classical Chinese roof. The lobby has a large atrium. 359 guestrooms offer expected amenities. Restaurants serve Japanese, Cantonese, and Western foods. Includes a business center and fitness facilities.

❑ **Xi'an Garden:** *4 Dong Yan Yin Road, Da Yan Ta, 710061. Tel. (86-29) 526-1111 or Fax (86-29) 526-1998. In the US, Tel. 1-800-223-6800.* Set in gardens on the southern edge of the city next to the Big Wild Goose Pagoda, the Xi'an Garden Hotel is a member of The Leading Hotels of the World. Each guestroom has a balcony. 301 guestrooms and suites form a pavilion style hotel set in the midst of gardens and ponds. Decorated in Tang Dynasty style. Offers a Tang Dynasty Art Museum and a Tang Theater Restaurant. Restaurants serve Chinese, Japanese, and Western cuisines.

Other places to consider include:

❑ **Grand New World:** *48 Lian Hu Road, 710002. Tel. (86-29) 721-6868 or Fax (86-29) 721-9754.* Located near the West Gate and park.

❑ **Xi'an Lee Gardens:** *8 Laodong Nan Road, 710068. Tel. (86-29) 426-3388 or Fax (86-29) 426-3288.* Located southwest of the city near the Northwest Technical University.

❑ **Bell Tower Hotel:** *Southwest corner of the Bell Tower, 710001, Tel. (86-29) 727-9200 or Fax (86-29) 727-1217. In the US, Tel. 1-800-HOLIDAY.* A three-star hotel. Conveniently located within walking distance of the Drum Tower, Grand Mosque, South Gate, and major shopping streets. Managed by the Holiday Inn.

❑ **City Hotel Xi'an:** *5 Nan Da Street, 710002, Tel. (86-29) 721-9988 or Fax (86-29) 721-6688.* A three-star budget hotel. Conveniently located within walking distance of the Drum Tower, Grand Mosque, South Gate, and major shopping streets.

RESTAURANTS

There's nothing exceptional about the food in Xi'an. It's similar to what you find in many other cities—filling but somewhat uninspired; restaurant sanitation varies and may or may not meet your standards. Xi'an is justly famous for its many varieties of dumplings and crisp fried chicken and duck, and many Overseas Chinese come here to try the noted dumplings.

As in many other cities in China, we play it safe and stay close to our four- and five-star hotel restaurants. This is not to say that Xi'an does not have excellent restaurants. We just haven't had enough good luck to give any definitive recommendations. Our advice: check with your hotel concierge or front desk for current recommendations. Chances are their recommendations will primarily include the best of the hotel restaurants.

MAJOR ATTRACTIONS

Xi'an has several monuments and museums to keep you busy for at least a couple of days of sightseeing. Most of these sites are historical in nature, reflecting Xi'an's long and important dynastic history. The major sites include:

❏ **Museum of Emperor Qin's Terracotta Army**: No visit to Xi'an, or even China, is complete without venturing to the village of Lintong. Located 37 kilometers northeast of the city, this is the primary destination of most tourists. To most visitors, Xi'an is synonymous with the army of terracotta soldiers discovered in the 1970s and subsequently uncovered in three major adjacent excavation areas, known as pits or vaults, enclosed by steel and concrete structures. Sometimes referred to as the "eighth wonder of the world," this somber yet determined looking terracotta army is one of China's most alluring historical sites, second perhaps only to the Great Wall. Pit #1, 62 x 230 meters and 5 meters deep, is enclosed by a massive steal roof structure similar to an aircraft hanger; this pit has the largest collection (numbering over

2,000) of standing soldiers and horses. Many are in remarkably good condition. Originally opened in 1979, Pit #2 is enclosed in a cement and granite building that closely approximates a museum structure. Dimly lighted, this huge pit encompasses nearly 1,400 cavalrymen, archers, infantrymen, and charioteers. It also includes displays of various figures and their weapons. Pit #3 is the smallest excavated area, representing 68 officers; this area was probably laid out as the command headquarters for the army. Opened in 1989, this building also includes a shop where you can purchase arts and crafts as well as a 3-hour CD-ROM of the terracotta army complete with sound and interactive elements. Don't forget to visit the small museum that is housed in a separate building; it includes model terracotta figures with a horse-drawn chariot. You can easily spend two to three hours visiting this archeological and museum site.

❑ **The City Walls:** These massive, both in height and width, walls run for 14 kilometers around the city. Originally built between 1374 and 1378 by the Mings, the walls remain in excellent condition and most sections are accessible to pedestrians. Climb the stairs at the South Gate for a good overview of the city and Bell Tower. Great place to stroll and exercise.

❑ **Dayan Pagoda:** Also known as the Big Wild Goose Pagoda, this 7-storey structure was constructed in 652AD and offers good views of the walled city.

❑ **Little Wild Goose Pagoda:** This 45-meter, 13-storey tall brick pagoda was built in 684 AD. It was an important temple (Da Jianfu Temple) during the Tang Dynasty.

❑ **Bell Tower:** Built in the 14th century, this impressive 36-meter tall Bell Tower stands at the center of the walled city, linking the streets that run directly to the East, West, North, and South Gates. Moved here from another location nearly 200 years ago, the Bell Tower is the city's major architectural landmark. Built by the Mings, the interior ceilings and furniture are distinctly Qing.

❏ **Drum Tower:** Within walking distance of the Bell Tower (go northwest), this tower was built in 1384. Similar in construction to the Bell Tower. Includes an antique shop.

❏ **Great Mosque:** Located just north of the Drum Tower, the origins of this mosque date from the 8th century and symbolize the nearly 60,000 members Muslim community in Xi'an. This is the largest and most famous mosque amongst 14 others in Xi'an.

❏ **Shaanxi Provincial Museum:** Located east of the South Gate and also referred to as the Forest of Steles, this impressive museum includes the largest collection of steles (stone tablets with inscriptions) in China. It's actually housed in an old Confucian temple complex. For calligraphers, this is a fabulous museum. Only a few of the museums more than 2,000 tablets are on display. Be sure to enter all of the various rooms and buildings in this complex. Each yields a different collection of stone carvings. The second room, for example, has an impressive collection of Tang Dynasty stone tablets on the backs of stone carved turtles. The souvenir shop, which is located in the fourth building, is well worth visiting as artisans make black ink rubbings of the steles while you wait. The shop does a brisk business in stone rubbings and the check-out counter will gladly take Visa and MasterCard for payment.

❏ **Shaanxi Historical Museum:** *91 Yanta Zhong Road.* Located south of the walled city, this is one of China's best museums which displays the rich collections of artifacts found in the many archeological sites and tombs that dot the landscape of Shaanxi Province. Some people claim this is China's best museum. You be the judge, especially after seeing the fabulous new Shanghai Museum. Especially strong emphasis on Chinese prehistory and the early dynastic periods. Covers prehistory to the end of the Qing Dynasty. Includes Neolithic pottery, ancient jade carvings, models of granaries and village wells from the Han period, porcelains and figurines from the Sui and Tang dynasty, bronzes from the Warring States period, and numerous stone carvings and terracotta figures. Can easily spend half a day here. Signs in English.

❑ **Banpo Neolithic Museum:** Located to the east of the city walls, this popular museum is located on the site of a neolithic village. Some 6,000 years old, major sections of the village have been excavated to display living quarters, pottery, tools, weapons, graveyards, and even musical instruments. Rich with artifacts.

ENTERTAINMENT

Some of Xi'an's best entertainment is free—just stroll the streets at night and observe all the street vendor activity. This is a lively and colorful city in the evening as local residents busy themselves with eating and shopping. If you stay at a hotel within the city walls, walking the streets at night will be most convenient. Even if you stay outside the city walls at a hotel such as the Shangri-La Golden Flower Hotel on Changle Road, you'll find a huge and crowded wholesale market (Industrial Products Wholesale Market) just around the corner from the hotel.

Most major hotels offer some form of entertainment in the evening, from piano bars, discos, and karaoke to cultural performances (check with the Garden, Royal Xi'an, and Grand New Hotels for scheduled performance dates). But the real entertainment highlight for most visitors is the fabulous **Tang Dynasty Cultural Evening** performance at the dinner theater adjacent to the Xi'an Garden Hotel (39 Changan Road, Tel. 711-633). Dinner starts at 6:30pm and the show begins around 8pm. You can purchase tickets for both the dinner and show or for the show alone. This is a real first-class show well worth the visit. It includes beautiful staging and costumes, with dancers and musicians performing authentic Tang dances accompanied by ancient Tang Dynasty musical instruments. If you can stay awake after a busy day of sightseeing and shopping, this will be one of the most memorable cultural performances you'll attend in China.

BEYOND XI'AN

If you have time and a continuing interest in ancient Chinese history, you'll find several additional archeological sites to visit such as the **Tomb of Emperor Zinshihuang** (on the way to the Museum of Emperor Qin's Terracotta Army), **Maoling** and the **Tomb of Yang Guifei** (40 kilometers northwest of Xi'an), and **Zhaoling** (70 kilometers northwest of Xi'an). If you enjoy temples, you'll find several within an hour's drive of Xi'an:

Caotang Temple (25 kilometers), **Xingjiao Temple** (25 kilometers east), **Quinglong Temple** (southern suburb of Tian Lumiao), and the **Louguan Taoist Temple** (70 kilometers east of Xi'an). If you get bored with archeological sites and temples, you may want to visit the **Xi'an Film Studio** near the Garden Hotel.

If you're interested in the local folk paintings and would like to meet the village artists, then head for Huxian County Town to the southeast of Xi'an. Nearly 2,000 artists in this county produce the distinctive paintings found in the shops of Xi'an and other major cities of China as well as abroad. Be sure to visit the **Huxian Peasant Painting Exhibition Hall** where you will also have an opportunity to visit with the artists.

9

Chongqing and the Yangtze River

What's the seventh largest city in China? You probably would never guess it's the mountainous and riverine metropolis of Chongqing, an old city of very significant historical, cultural, economic, and political importance for China.

Not many visitors to China have heard of Chongqing. However, many students of Chinese history and World War II buffs know it well as "Chungking," the capital of China's Kuomintang government during World War II, the headquarters for General Stillwell, and where Chang Kai Shek and Chou En-lai reached their famous agreement to jointly fight the Japanese rather than each other during World War II. Nearly completely destroyed by Japanese bombing, the city still has an image of literally being in the backwaters of southwest China, an upcountry city now serving as a major departure point for the popular Yangtze River Cruises to the Three Gorges and beyond. Nothing could be further from the truth.

SURPRISING NEW CHONGQING

This is a new city, or at least a 3,000+ year old city in the process of dramatically transforming itself into one of China's great economic powerhouses. It's a city of great contrasts, con-

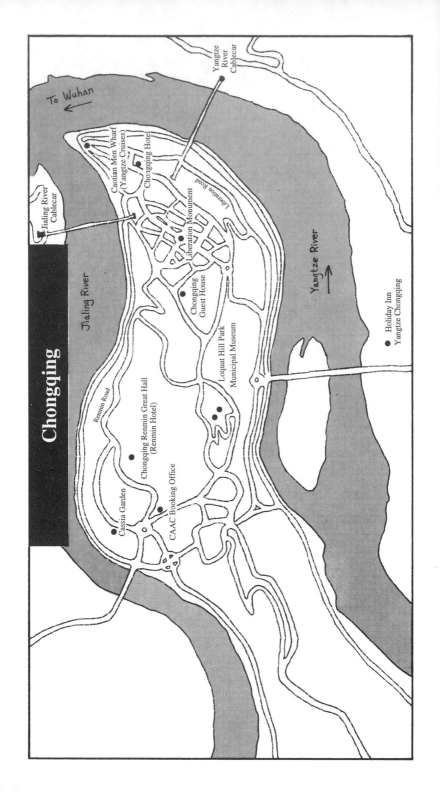

stantly juxtaposing the old and new. Old dilapidating buildings with garbage strewn out their windows cling to sides of steep hills while next door a similar building is demolished to make way for a new modern high-rise building. They coexist for only a year or two. Indeed, the fate of others in the neighborhood is sealed—they are next on the urban renewal chopping block. Shops, restaurants, and residences carved out of caves dot the urban landscape. Peasants in tattered clothes and shoes offer their labor services, from painting and construction to hauling produce, in the midst of a bustling downtown area filled with fashionable shops and department stores frequented by Chongqing's newly emerging, and shopping savvy, middle class. It's old, it's new, and it's definitely a city that is quickly discarding the old for the new. Like so many other large cities in China, there appears to be lots of money moving through the local economy. It's a beehive of activity, from shopping to dining.

Chongqing may be in the backwaters of the Yangtze River, but it's anything but backward. This is a surprisingly modern and vibrant city that is undergoing a rapid transformation as it tears down its old dilapidating residential and commercial buildings and replaces them with new high-rise buildings that are forever altering the city's skyline. Many of the changes have taken place only within the past two years. It many respects, this city looks like Hong Kong on the Yangtze. It's a hard working, driven city of bustling streets, crowded department stores and shops, and colorful markets and

❑ Chongqing is a surprisingly modern and vibrant city undergoing a rapid transformation.

❑ You won't see many bicycles here. This is primarily a city of cars, buses, motorcycles, and pedestrians that crowd its steep and narrow streets.

❑ Chongqing is Southwest China's largest inland port and the major departure point for the popular Yangtze River cruises.

❑ A major industrial center, Chongqing produces nearly 1 million cars and trucks and 2 million motocycles each year.

❑ Avoid Chongqing is the summer—this is one of China's "Three Furnaces" with temperature exceeding 100°F.

❑ Expect numerous traffic jams in downtown Chongqing.

street life. While you may occasionally see a bicycle slowly navigating the steep streets of Chongqing, this is primarily a city of cars, buses, motorcycles, and pedestrians, and now a partially completed subway, who crowd the city's narrow streets. Peasants and laborers carrying bamboo poles with ropes dangling at the end hire themselves by the job (weight and distance) to haul heavy loads up and down the challenging streets of Chongqing. They unload delivery trucks, move products from one part of the city to another, and assist women with their market shopping. They are the local courier service, delivery men, and porters all wrapped up into one. Others lash ropes around their bodies and join one or two other men in pulling heavy-laden two-wheel carts up difficult inclines. No other city in China has such a colorful, practical "human bondage" service.

GETTING TO KNOW YOU

Located in southeastern Sichuan Province at the confluence of the Yangtze and Jialing Rivers, Chongqing is one of China's largest and most important industrial cities. Long known as the "Mountain City" and "River City" and famous as the World War II capital of China, today Chongqing boasts a population of over 3 million, making it China's seventh largest city. It serves as Southwest China's largest inland port and the departure point for the popular Yangtze River cruises that traverse the Three Gorges from Chongqing to Wuhan and back. Most tourists come here because of the popular cruises that begin or end at Chongqing. Without these cruises, Chongqing would remain a popular destination primarily for businessmen involved in the numerous joint ventures that fuel Chongqing's strong manufacturing economy.

CLIMATE AND WHEN TO VISIT

Spread over a mountainous area and on both sides of the Yangtze River, this is a city of many hills and a pleasant climate during winter and spring. Its long hot summer, stretching from May to October, is notorious for its oppressive heat, rain, and humidity. Indeed, Chongqing is known as one of China's "Three Furnaces" with temperatures in excess of 100°F (40°C) in summer; it rarely snows here, and if it does, it's a major phenomenon for local residents who only know snow from pictures. Whatever your plans, try to avoid Chongqing during the heat of the summer; spring is the best time to visit, especially the months of March and April. October to February also is a pleasant time to visit, although the city experiences a great deal of fog and mist during this time. On some days the fog is so thick that it's virtually impossible to see the hills and river, and cruising the Yangtze River during such fogged-in periods can be disappointing.

The most pleasant time of year to visit Chongqing as well as take a Yangtze Cruise, is during the peak tourist seasons of October-November and March-April when daily temperatures range in the 60's to 80's.

TYPOGRAPHY AND ECONOMY

The first thing that strikes visitors as they descend to land at Chongqing's Jiangbei Airport are the numerous mountains and hills surrounding this city. Terraced paddies contour the hills as farmers engage in multi-crop intensive agricultural activities primarily involving rice and wheat production. Once on the ground, one is struck by the near total absence of the ubiquitous bicycle found in many of China's other cities. Since this is a city of many hills and tunnels, bicycles are inappropriate for Chongqing's difficult terrain. Its many cars, motorcycles, and pedestrians clog the city's many two-lane streets. Indeed, expect to encounter numerous traffic jams in Chongqing's crowded downtown area.

This is definitely a working city with a vibrant economy and an envious urban industrial and commercial infrastructure. Known for its large-scale industrial and agricultural base, Chongqing and its surrounding area have developed one of China's most attractive integrated industrial complexes in the fields of energy, metallurgy, machinery, chemistry, textiles, electronics, and automobile and motorcycle production. In fact, it produces nearly 1 million automobiles and trucks and 2 million motorcycles each year. Numerous huge high-rise apartment complexes that house the city's industrial workers dot the city's ever-changing landscape. On the agricultural side, Chongqing's rural hinterland is famous for its grain production (rice, wheat, corn) and pig raising as well as for its agricultural processing industries. Indeed, three of Chongqing's counties are in the country's ten top counties for grain production. The city also boasts numerous universities and colleges as well as several scientific research institutes. Like many other cities in China, Chongqing has undergone a major economic transformation in recent years. It is destined to continue being one of China's most important industrial and agricultural cities as well as a major inland port for international trade. It is China's economic center for the upper reaches of the Yangtze River and the largest industrial and commercial city in southwest China. With the completion of the Three Gorges Dam, large commercial vessels will be able to reach Chongqing year around. It will become a true deep-water port.

Tourism makes up only a fraction of local economic activity. Approximately 130,000 overseas visitors come to Chongqing each year. The city has 23 hotels for foreign tourists, including two four-star hotels, and six three-star hotels. Another 79 hotels fall in the first, second, and third class categories.

THE VIEW

Like so many other cities in China, Chongqing is not a particularly beautiful city, at least not during the day. It's very much a utilitarian city developed for industrial production. But it can be a strikingly beautiful city at night as you view the city lights sparkling along the rivers and in the hills. The locals like to refer to their city at night as a glimmering palace floating on the water. Be sure to find a good vantage point at night to see the city lights, the two best being Goose Ridge and Loquot Hill.

WHERE TO STAY

And like other cities, Chongqing is crowded and somewhat chaotic despite the absence of bicycles that are often accused of being the culprit of chaos in other cities. If you really want to see the city, it's best to stay in a hotel near the city center (try the Chongqing Guest House) where you can walk to various places rather than commute through the heavy traffic from hotels on the outskirts of the city.

ARRIVAL

Chongqing is nearly a 2½ hour flight from Beijing, a 2 hour flight from Shanghai and Hong Kong, a 1½ hour flight from Guilin and Kunming, and a 1¼ hour flight from Xi'an and Guangzhou. The modern Jiangbei Airport is located 30 kilometers or about 40 minutes from downtown Chongqing. Buses and taxis regularly service the airport. Depending on the traffic situation, leave yourself at least one hour to get from downtown to the airport.

POPULATION

Many people are confused about the size of Chongqing's population, and for good reason. Its actual urban population is estimated to be more than 3 million. The problem with Chongqing's population figures is that they range from 1.9 million to 15 million. Officially the "city" population is 15 million. But this an administrative definition of the "city" which includes an area of 23,411 square kilometers, 9 districts, 9 counties, and 3 municipalities! It's what urbanologists call an extremely "overbounded" city that incorporates large segments of surrounding rural areas. The 3+ million urban population includes the immediate downtown population and nearby suburbs which house most of the industrial workers. It's what most people understand to be a true "urban area."

TRANSPORTATION AND TOURS

This is not a fun city to navigate on foot nor by bicycle. This is a hilly city where you constantly feel you are climbing a mini version of the Great Wall. The city has plenty of taxis and buses which tend to be overcrowded. You may want to contact the local CITS office to join an organized tour. They are located at the Renmin Hotel which is part of the People's Great Hall complex at the center of the city (Tel. 51449 or 53421, ext. 435). Alternatively, contact your hotel for information on their services, especially the overnight tour to the popular Dazu Stone Sculpture area which is located 168 kilometers northwest of the city.

WATER AND DRINKS

Like other cities in China, the water in Chongqing is not potable. You must use bottled water or the boiled water provided in the thermos in your hotel room. If you are downtown near Liberation Monument, you may want to visit the supermarket at the lower level of the New Century Department Store. They have an excellent selection of canned, bottled, and boxed drinks (sodas, milks, juices, beers) as well as bottled water.

SHOPPING

Shopping seems to be a favorite pastime for local residents who crowd the city's many department stores and street shops which are crammed with fashionable clothes and the latest in electronics. The major shopping area of the city centers around Liberation Monument, a convenient landmark for navigating the streets of downtown Chongqing. The main streets radiating from this monument house the city's major department stores and shops. Here you will find Chongqing's oldest and most popular department store, the **Chongqing Department Store**, that is reputed to offer the best quality and prices of all department stores in the city. In the next block is the newer and glitzier **New Century Department Store** with a fine supermarket at the lower level. The rest of the downtown area is of most interest to local shoppers. There's really not much here of interest to visitors other than the cultural experience of getting into the shopping crowds and occasionally making an inexpensive purchase from a street vendor and market stall.

While Chongqing is by no means a shopper's paradise, it does offer some surprising and attractive shopping options. The city is best known as a center for both traditional and contemporary art, especially paintings. Indeed, its Sichuan Fine Arts Institute has a fine reputation for being one of China's three top art schools. Many of China's most famous artists have been trained here and continue to produce some of the China's best art. If there is only one thing you shop for in Chongqing, make sure it is art. The quality is superb, especially after you have been subjected to so much tourist art in the shops of other cities.

If you arrive by air, be sure to stop at Chongqing's newest art gallery which is only 15 minutes from the airport—**Huare Contemporary Art Museum**. Opened in March 1996, this is China's first private art museum. This and other places in Chongqing to find quality art include the following:

❑ **Huare Contemporary Art Museum:** *Huixing District, Yubei, Chongqing, Tel. 0811-6801993.* Located 15 minutes from the airport on the right-hand side of the highway to the city, this is China's first private art museum. The stone building houses a spacious two-level gallery on the first floor (the large room on your left as you enter the front door) which displays numerous contemporary oil paintings and bronze sculptures. Many of the works on display are for sale, so don't hesitate to ask about prices. The main shopping area is in the basement where you will find several rooms filled with traditional Chinese paintings, contemporary oil paintings, antiques (ceramics), jade carvings, embroidery, unique lacquer paintings, tea pots, and a variety of handicrafts. It also includes a traditional Chinese painting demonstration area where you can see a local artists producing paintings using the traditional brushes, ink pads, and colored inks. The quality of paintings is excellent with most produced by local artists trained at the Sichuan Fine Arts Institute. Pricing here is very aggressive and requires exceptionally strong bargaining skills. Set aside the general rule that you should counter with 50 percent of the asking price. If you do, you'll be paying too much. The 50 percent rule is what the gallery's initial asking price should be. If a painting or carving is marked ¥4,000, divide that figure in half to get their real starting price, which should be ¥2,000. Begin with that price and start your traditional bargaining scenario. Paintings with a price tag of ¥4,000 can be purchased for as low as ¥1,300. Yes, you can get 60 to 70 percent discounts here! One senses the price tags are set up for Japanese tourists who are world-renowned for unsuspectingly paying excessively high prices. Whatever you do, don't start bargaining with more than 30 percent of the initial price.

❑ **Painter's Village:** *24 Hwa-Cun, Hualongqiao Street. Open daily from 9am to 4pm, if you want to meet the artists. Tel. 52177.* Somewhat difficult to find given the back streets and lanes you need to follow in order to locate the complex. If you visit only one place in Chongqing, make sure it's Painter's Village. Indeed, this could well be the highlight of your visit to Chongqing. A tranquil garden setting overlooking the Jialing River, Painter's Village is a famous artists-in-residence complex. Established in 1956 as a center for some of China's most renowned artists, today it includes 17 painters and their families who live and work in this compound. Most of the artists have won major awards and exhibited throughout China and abroad. Each artist has his or her own small studio/office in one of several buildings in the compound. Since the national economic reforms and the government's open policy, the Village has been opened to tourists who can now purchase the paintings. As a result, the director and his fellow artists have become somewhat entrepreneurial. They welcome tour groups and individual visitors. And they also welcome your cash, traveler's checks, or credit cards! When you visit the Village, you first enter a main room and gallery where you can view a representative sample of paintings produced by the resident artists. Scrapbooks/portfolios of each artist also are on a table, along with credit card machines, for your review and convenience. After visiting the gallery area, you can then visit the individual studios of the artists where you will have a chance to meet the artists, view their gallery collections, and make purchases directly from them. Here's one of the few chances you will have in China to meet famous artists and purchase directly from them. You'll immediately notice how many different mediums (ink, oils, water colors, block prints) and styles (traditional and contemporary) each artist works in. Each artist sets his or her own prices. Normally 60 percent of the proceeds go to support the Village, 30 percent goes to the artist, and 10 percent goes to the tax collector. But be careful here, just as you should be when shopping elsewhere in China. Prices are all over the place, from US$50 to US$30,000. You'll have to be your own judge about quality and value. Expect to find some of the best quality paintings here. The individual artists are known to discount anywhere from 50 percent on down, although any offer is appropriate since we do not sense the artists have any real feel for the market value of the art—whatever the market will bear, which is primarily the tourist market that goes through their doors; some artists may not bargain at all, claiming to have fixed prices. Whatever you do, make sure you bargain with the artists, and don't be shy. While we've seen some gorgeous art here from so-called "famous" artists, let's face it, this isn't Sotheby's where paintings should command US$15,000 price tags. This is Chongjing where artists may try to get what the market will bear. Who can blame them? But you may choose not to offer New York prices. Again, don't be timid able haggling over prices. We especially like the wonderful oils of Xu Kuang, many of which depict the people of Tibet, and the watercolors and block prints of Wu Qiannian.

❑ **Chongqing Oriental Artist Association:** Located on the grounds of the city zoo, this is actually a gallery and branch of the Sichuan Fine Arts Institute. It goes under the name of the **Eastern Institute of Paintings**. Once you enter the grounds of the zoo, you may want to first visit the four panda bears before proceeding on to this fine art gallery. You can't miss its large sweeping stone and silver glazed ceramic sculpture at the entrance to the gallery. Inside you'll find eight rooms, or 400 square meters of gallery space, filled with a large collection of traditional and contemporary Chinese and Western-style paintings, from inks to oils, as well as some antiques (ceramics) and handicrafts (rugs, batik, lacquer, stone and jade carvings). The quality here is excellent. Again, prices are subject to hard bargaining, and you should not be shy about making low offers. You won't hurt anyone's feelings. After all, you're dealing with some very savvy and entrepreneurial gallery personnel who also can be very aggressive. They know full well that their US$1,000 asking price for a painting should really command much less. But they will try to get what they can. After all, they've learned that some naive tourists will actually pay the first asking price!

❑ **Sichuan Fine Arts Institute:** Located in Huang Kuo Piing District, this is one of China's top art institutes. Today it has 1,000 students and 300 instructors who offer studies in seven major art fields. One of three major art institutes in China, the Sichuan Fine Arts Institute produces some of China's top artists, many of whom have settled in the Chongqing area and offer their paintings in local galleries. The Institute also includes a gallery where you can purchase top quality paintings. However, we prefer shopping at the more conveniently located branch gallery, Eastern Institute of Paintings, which is located at the zoo (see above).

❑ **Chongqing Municipal Museum shops:** So you think you're visiting a museum. Well, yes and no. This is one wild place for shoppers. This ostensible museum represents the extreme case of a public museum having discovered 19th century capitalism. The museum is basically a shopping center for arts and crafts rather than a typical museum displaying cultural artifacts. Shopping is found both inside and outside the main building. As you enter the first floor of the main building, turn to your right. At the end of the hall is a large shop offering locally-produced paintings, stone and jade carvings, and a large variety of handicrafts, from jade pillows to sandalwood fans. Upstairs you'll find several rooms devoted to selling a large selection of paintings, rubbings (from stone tablets on first floor), stone and jade carvings, fans, ink pads, chops, ceramics, and teapots as well as videos and CDs of the Yangtze River. Salespeople here are very aggressive with initial asking prices being ridiculously high. Quality appears good. But this is where the standard bargaining scenario goes awry. If you're interested in anything here, don't be shy about making an outrageous offer—20 percent of any quoted price. Our buying experience here is illustrative of what you can and should do if you're interested in making a purchase. We expressed interest in a ¥25,000 (US$3,000) painting. The final price given to us was US$220. In the end we didn't buy it because we didn't have a place for it in our home. But as we walked away, the vendor offered it to us for US$200, which represents a 93 percent discount! We've never encountered such wild pricing anywhere in the world we've shopped. Quite frankly, the printed prices are primarily designed for Japanese tourists who often, and unknowingly, pay such high prices as well as anyone else who thinks the price quoted necessarily reflects the value of the article. We did finally buy one item here, an antique wood carved piece, and it was discounted at 75 percent. Our rule of thumb for buying here is this: if you pay 50 percent or more of an asking price, chances are you probably paid too much. You will also find shops outside, leading to the front entrance of the museum. Look for the **Chongqing Antique Store** which is located at the bottom left side of the staircase leading to the entrance of the museum. This small shop includes oil paintings and ceramics. We trust they offer authentic antiques since most of their ceramics appear to have the official government red seal affixed.

❑ **People's Great Hall of Chongqing shops:** Located near the center of the city in a beautifully designed Chinese style building, this is another good example of entrepreneurism in public places. Consisting of a five-level amphitheater and the three-star Chongqing Renmin Hotel, the complex houses three arts and crafts shops. You'll find two small handicraft shops at the entrance of the People's Great Hall. However, the best shop is located just to the right of the entrance to the 4,000 seat auditorium. This large dusty shop is filled with paintings, antique ceramics, jade and stone carving, embroidery work, tea pots, and traditional Chinese medicine. But the good stuff is found at the back of the shop—on your right—which consists of a narrow walkway lined with paintings. This walkway, in turn, opens into four rooms filled with additional paintings. Some of the best quality art is found along the walkway and in these rooms. It's easy to miss the entrance to this area if you only browse around the main shop. If you have difficulty finding these additional rooms, be sure to ask. These rooms put a whole new face on what is essentially a typical tourist arts and crafts shop.

You may or may not be interested in Chongqing's many **department stores**, depending on your shopping needs. Catering primarily to local consumers, these places are handy for visitors who need to resupply themselves with important travel items, from suitcases and hardware to foods and drinks. Chongqing's two major department stores are located near each other, just off of Liberation Monument. **Chongqing Department Store** is the oldest and most popular one; it has 21 branches in the Chongqing area. The newer **New Century Department**

Store, complete with fountains and waterfalls (watch the slippery wet floor!), is found in the next block and includes a great supermarket at the basement level. Other department stores include the **Friendship Store**, which has nine branches in Chongqing, and the newer and more upmarket **Parkson Department Store, Chongqing Quying Purchasing Plaza**, and **Mega Department Store**.

SEEING THE SIGHTS

Despite its size, there's not a great deal to do in Chongqing other than visit a few historical sites and shop for arts and crafts. Two days in Chongqing should be sufficient to see the major sights and shop its major art galleries, unless you decide to go beyond Chongqing and visit additional historical and cultural sights located within 200 kilometers of the city. If you include these other areas, you should plan at least three, if not four, days for Chongqing.

You will find a few museums in Chongqing. But like museums in many other parts of China, the ones here have had to become more entrepreneurial as they receive fewer and fewer government subsidies to maintain their operations. China's economic reforms have required museums to raise more and more operating revenue on their own, from charging admission fees to developing shops and renting shop space. The result is often a museum operating like a bazaar. The Chongqing Municipal Museum is a perfect case in point. It has become so entrepreneurial that most of the museum is now devoted to selling arts and crafts. We kept looking for the museum displays and kept finding more shops! It is best characterized as an arts and crafts bazaar with a few exhibits of historical relevance. Some of Chongqing's major sights include:

❑ **Chongqing Municipal Museum:** This museum is more of a shopping center for arts and crafts than a museum with displays of artifacts much to offer visitors (see above). Its major displays are on the first floor, to your left as you enter. It includes numerous engraved stone tablets that are used to make rubbings. At the other end of the first floor is a display of ceramics and fans, just before you reach the arts and crafts shop.

❑ **People's Great Hall of Chongqing:** Completed in 1954, this beautiful landmark building designed in traditional ornate Chinese style is located near the center of the downtown area. It was modeled after Beijing's Temple of Heaven and parts of Tiananmen Square. Initially serving as the Great Auditorium for the Southwest China Administration Committee, today it is a five-level amphitheater with a seating capacity of 4,000 which is used for state meetings and theatrical and musical performances. The South and North Wings were converted into the three-star, 214 room Chongqing Renmin Hotel in 1981. The complex is another good example of how arts and crafts shops have a major presence at major historical sites (see above). It's an excellent place to shop for quality paintings and handcrafted items.

❑ **Loquat Hill:** Open 6:30am to 8pm. For a panoramic view of the city away from the hustle and bustle of Chongqing's streets, visit this highest point overlooking the city—also known as the Red Star Pavilion in Pipashan (Loquat) Hill Park, a former warlord's residence which includes gardens, ponds, and pavilions. Many visitors prefer going here at night for a spectacular view of the city lights.

❑ **Swan Ridge:** Another great place to get a good view of the city at night. The locals refer to this place as the "Kanshenglou" viewing tower in Eling Hill Park.

❑ **Nanshan Park:** Also known as South Mountain, this park is located on the south bank of the river. Once the residence of General George C. Marshall and Chiang Kai-shek, today it is the site of the General Joseph Stillwell Museum.

❑ **Cable Car Ride:** Operates from 6am to 11pm. This cable car line links the north and south banks of the Jialing River. Used primarily for local transportation, visitors may want to view the river and the Chaotianmen docks from this aerial vantage point. You can get on the cable car at the Cangbailu Station (Cangbailu Road) on the city side of the river or at the Jinshajie station on the other (north) side of the river.

❑ **Red Crag Village:** Also known as the Hongyancun Revolutionary Memorial Hall. Located in Hongyancun, this is the former residence and headquarters of Chou En-lai and the Communist's Eighth Route Army who between 1938 and 1945 played a key role in directing the Communist war effort against the Japanese and the Nationalist Chinese (Kuomintang) from Chongqing. The museum here includes photos and memorabilia from this important historical period.

❑ **Zoo:**   Located in Huang Kuo Piing District, the zoo is of most interest for its four panda bears, one of which is a giant panda. You can even have your photo taken with a panda. While here, be sure to visit the art gallery (Eastern Institute of Painting, Chongqing Oriental Artist Association) which is a branch of the Sichuan Fine Arts Institute (see above under "Shopping").

❑ **Chaotianmen Docks:** You can't miss these working docks if you are scheduled to take one of the Yangtze River cruise ships to Wuhan. The rather make-shift docks are being reconstructed with new tall embankments in anticipation of the rising water level created by the Yangtze River dam. Watch your step here. Everything is very rough. Tall steep cement stairways, which lack handrails and other safety devices, lead to the chaotic dock areas. Watch where you walk since much of the area is one big rock pile. You can easily fall or twist an ankle here. If you're carrying luggage from the road to a dock, it's best to hire one of the porters (a fancy term for your friendly local peasant with a bamboo pole and rope for carrying heavy loads) for 10 yuan (very high price but well worth the money!). A working dock area, a visit here will give you a good sense of the color and chaos of the river business along the Yangtze River. The whole area you see below you will be inundated by the waters of the Yangtze once the Three Gorges dam is completed.

ACCOMMODATIONS

❑ **Holiday Inn:** *15 Nan Ping Bei Lu, Chongqing, Tel. (08-11) 280-3380 or Fax (08-11) 280-0884. US$125 for a Standard room and US$195 for a Deluxe Suite. US$5.00 extra for riverview rooms.* Located on a hill overlooking the city and river in the Nan Ping Economic Development Zone, this is one of Chongqing's two four-star hotels but really it's the best hotel in the city. Initially built in 1979, the hotel retains excellent facilities and services. It includes 379 rooms of which 68 are suites, a Business

Centre, Health Club, meeting rooms, disco, tennis court, and swimming pool. The newly renovated rooms are well appointed and many have a river view. The hotel includes the Golden Monkey Coffee House, the Ba Ren Xiao Chi for Sichuan cuisine, the Golden Sand Chinese Restaurant for Sichuan and Cantonese cuisine, the 21st floor Sunset Grill for Western food, a Japanese restaurant, the German Bierstube, and a deli kiosk. A small shopping arcade includes shops offering a wide range of arts, crafts, and clothing, including a craftsman making personalized chops and an artist producing paintings. Not the best location for seeing the city; it lacks a city shuttle service. Once you're here, chances are you will stay in your hotel. If you like to walk around town at night, this is not the hotel for you.

❑ **Chongqing Guest Hotel:** *235 Minshen Road, Chongqing, Tel. (08-11) 384-5888 or Fax (08-11) 383-0643. US$68 for a double in the Jiabin Building or US$115 for a double in the VIP Building; US$200 for a Deluxe Suite in the Jiabin Building or US$335 for a Deluxe Suite in the VIP Building.* This is Chongqing's other four-star property. Located in the heart of downtown Chongqing, the location doesn't get much better. Famous for its traditional Chinese architectural style, the hotel has 267 guest rooms in its two sections—the less expensive Jiabin Building and the more expensive VIP Building. Includes an arts and crafts shop, Business Center, Apollo Night Club, Dragon and Phoenix Restaurant, Seafood Restaurant, and Hot Pot Restaurant. Nice lobby areas but worn rooms need major rehab, from carpets and beds to bath tubs and fixtures. Watch the electrical configurations if you plan to use appliances—more than one type per room (bring a set of adaptors). This hotel can be noisy with on-going construction. Officially designated a four-star property, but really not in the same class as the Holiday Inn. The staff tries hard but seems to be in chaos much of the time. The English of the staff is very rudimentary.

Chongqing has several three-star hotels. Most are located in the downtown area. However, don't approach these places with high expectations for facilities and service. They are at best "adequate" for short stays in Chongqing:

❑ **Renmin Hotel:** *173 Renmin Road 630015, Tel. (08-11) 385-1421 or Fax (08-11) 385-2076. Standard room begins* *at US$53; deluxe Suite goes for US$242.* Located in one wing of the beautiful People's Great Hall, this 213-room hotel is centrally located and includes the popular Palace Restaurant for seafood, Sichuan and Cantonese cuisine, the Yu Yuan Restaurant for Hot Pot, the Lark Cafe for Western food, and the Palace Night Club. Includes shops, meeting rooms, fitness center, sauna, massage, beauty parlor, billiard room, and game room.

❑ **Chongqing Hotel:** *41-43 Xin Hua Road 630011, Tel. (08-11) 384-9301 or Fax (08-11) 384-3085.* Built within the past 10 years, this hotel is conveniently located near the center of the city. Includes 200 rooms, a business center, and one of Chongqing's best Cantonese restaurants, the Chongqing.

Other three-star hotels worth considering are the **Wudu Hotel** (24 Shangzengjiayan, Tel. 08-11-385-1788 or Fax 08-11-385-0762), the **Chongqing Shaping Hotel** (84 New Xiaolongtann Street, Shaping District (Tel. 08-11-664-196 or Fax 0811-663-293), and the **Chongqing Milky-Way Hotel**.

RESTAURANTS

Chongqing is especially noted for its many spicy Sichuan dishes and especially for its popular hot pot. Most tourists dine in the major hotel restaurants. Three of Chongjing's best such restaurants are the two-storey **Chongqing** for excellent Cantonese cuisine (Chongqing Hotel, 41-43 Xinhua Road, Tel. 43996), the **Yangtze Restaurant** for Sichuan and Cantonese cuisine (within three minutes walking distance of the Holiday Inn), and the **Palace Restaurant** for excellent seafood, Sichuan, and Cantonese cuisine (Renmin Hotel, 173 Renmin Road, Tel. 385-1421). The restaurant just to the right of the entrance to the People's Great Hall is also very good.

BEYOND CHONGQING

Many visitors to this area use Chongqing as a base for visiting several other places. These include the following major sightseeing destinations:

❑ **Dazu Stone Sculptures:** Located 168 kilometers northwest of the city, the famous outdoor stone carvings of Dazu, dating from more than 1100 years ago, attract many visitors who are interested in exploring the rich history of this region. The stone carvings, which are mainly Buddhist sculptures, were produced during the later Tang (892 A.D.) and Song Dynasties, spanning a period of nearly 250 years. Altogether, this area claims more than 50,000 stone figures spread over 43 locations. You may be particularly interested in visiting the sites at Beishan, Fowan, Baodingshan, Xiaofowan, Dafowan, and Shimenshan. The most popular stone sculptures here are the "Thousand-Arm Goddess of Mercy" (1 mile north of Dazu town at Beishan or North Mountain or Dragon Mound Hill) and the 31-meter long "Sleeping Buddha" (7 miles north of Dazu town at Baoding). If you plan to stay overnight, the best place is the Dazu Guest House at Beishan (47 Gongmong Street, Longganzen 632-360, Tel. 721-888 or Fax 722-827). Expect to spend the whole day visiting this area as well as doing a lot of walking and climbing since most of the sites are accessible only by foot. You can arrange an overnight tour to this area through the CITS office in Chongqing.

❑ **Chengdu City:** Located approximately 340 kilometers by expressway northwest of Chongqing, this is an important historical and cultural city in southwest China. It is also the gateway city to Lhasa and Tibet.

❑ **South Hot Spring Park:** Located 18 kilometers from the city on the banks of the Yangtze River, this sulphur spring is a popular place to visit for the beauty and seclusion of the surrounding hills and mountains.

❑ **North Hot Spring Park:** Located 55 kilometers from the city, this scenic park includes four halls and three swimming pools.

❑ **Wangxiangtai Waterfall:** Located on Simian Mountain in Jiangjin County, this is China's highest waterfall at 152 meters. The surrounding area includes more than 100 waterfalls, ten lakes and ponds, forests, and wildlife areas.

❑ **The Yangtze River and Three Gorges Cruise:** Many visitors come to Chongqing primarily for the increasingly popular Yangtze River and Three Gorges cruises that either begin or end at Chongqing. The major cruise lines, such as Regal China Cruise and Victoria Cruises, cover the area between Chongqing and Wuhan. If you're booking one of these cruises (see the next section), you may want to plan an additional day or two in Chongqing, more if you plan to sightsee beyond the city, especially Dazu and Chengdu.

THE YANGTZE AND ITS THREE GORGES

To the Chinese it is known as the Long River or Changjiang. From its source in the high Tibetan range below the snow-capped peaks of the Himalayas, the world's third longest river starts its 3,900 mile journey to the East China Sea. To travelers from the West, it is known as the Yangtze. And travelers who want to cruise the Yangtze are being admonished to "go now," before the Three Gorges Dam changes forever the landscape along this magnificent river. As the water behind the new dam rises and the lower portion of the mountain walls become submerged, the visual height of the majestic walls which frame the river-banks will be lessened and many fear much of the beauty will be diminished as well.

There is still time. The river remains for now the lifeline it has been for centuries: a highway for commerce, the "fishing hole" for dinner, the fertile breadbasket that feeds one-third of China, and an inspiration for poets and painters who find its craggy mist shrouded peaks both magical and mystical.

❑ The Yangtze River is now the site for some of the world's most popular 4-7 day cruises.

❑ Once the dam is completed in 2009, Chongqing will become a major deep-water port.

❑ Most cruises operate between April and mid-November. But June and October are the most pleasant times to cruise the river. Avoid the July furnace!

❑ Most cruises take place between Chongqing and Wuhan. Cruising downstream from Chongqing to Wuhan takes one less day than the upstream trip.

❑ The Regal China Cruise Line represents the "best of the best" on the Yangtze.

Not to miss an opportunity, one overcast October morning we stood high above the river in Chongqing watching as the boat that would be our home for the next four days maneuvered an amazing docking procedure—literally moving sideways straight toward us to the landing. As it docked, this was the signal for the mass of humanity—passengers as well as porters who would heft two suitcases, one on either end of a pole which rested across their shoulders—to push forward toward the ship. Once on board Regal China Cruise's Princess Jeannie, we settled into comfort and put ourselves in the hands of its competent crew.

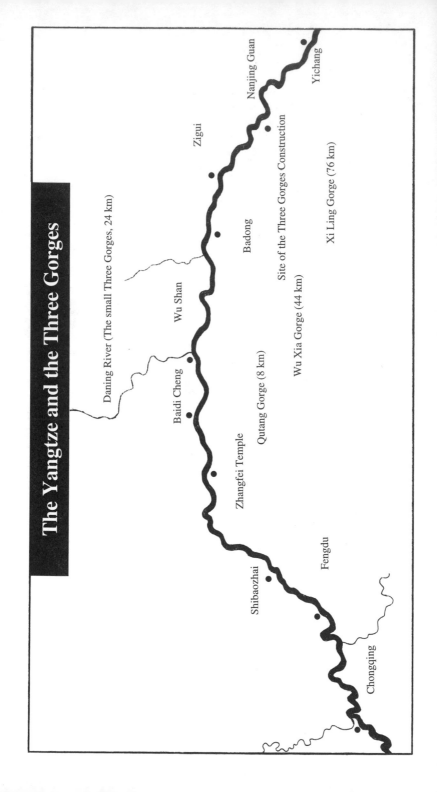

The Yangtze and the Three Gorges

Daning River (The small Three Gorges, 24 km)

Zigui

Nanjing Guan

Yichang

Badong

Wu Shan

Site of the Three Gorges Construction

Xi Ling Gorge (76 km)

Baidi Cheng

Wu Xia Gorge (44 km)

Qutang Gorge (8 km)

Zhangfei Temple

Shibaozhai

Fengdu

Chongqing

After a late departure from Chongqing, we sailed down-stream toward Fengdu—the 1300 year old Tang Dynasty city of ghosts. We arrived later than scheduled, just as darkness was about to envelop what according to literature, is the only city of ghosts in the world! We took the chair lift to the top of the hill to the ghost palace where clay figures are used in various dioramas including one that shows a vision of torture in hell—no doubt intended to be both entertaining and instructive.

Our crew anchored the boat in the river channel for the night. It is dangerous to navigate the river in darkness and the crew chooses to remain anchored until past daybreak so passengers can enjoy the views as we begin our journey through the first gorge—the Qutang. The Three Gorges are significant today for their beauty. But prior to the 1950's, when the government blasted the rocks in the gorges channel, the three gorges were also known for the danger they posed. With the submerged reefs blasted away and dangerous rapids calmed, the river now provides safe passage.

As the Princess Jeannie approaches the first gorge on the downriver journey, The Qutang Gorge, the river channel nar-rows and the volume of water that only minutes before had a wide berth between its banks is now forced into a much narrower area. Qutang Gorge is the smallest and perhaps the most dramatic. It is known as the Windbox to many westerners because the rock face of the walls has been carved by erosion into a shape some see as resembling a giant bellows. Only eight kilometers long, it takes only about twenty minutes and the Princess Jeannie is back out into the wider channel.

Between the first and second gorges we have the opportunity to take a smaller boat, a *wupan* that carries only 15-20 passen-gers into the Wushan Little Three Gorges on the Daning River. On the smaller boats one feels more a part of the river. Our guide pointed to the bridge high overhead. Once the new dam is completed and the water level rises to its projected 573 feet above sea level, that bridge would barely be above the water level we were told. Aside from the beauty of the lesser three gorges, it was interesting to see where holes had been chiseled high into the rock face of the canyon walls. They had supported poles that, in turn, had supported planks that formed a cantilevered walkway high above the river. In ancient times, these walkways attached to the nearly perpendicular walls above the river were the only land passage over the mountains and around the gorges. These gorges too, will see the water level rise and most all but the tops of the peaks will be submerged once the new dam is completed.

The Wu Gorge, the middle and most serene of the three is

44 kilometers long and we watch in fascination the changing mist on the jagged mountain peaks as the Princess Jeannie makes her way through the "Witches" gorge. The two hours sailing time through the Wu allows plenty of opportunity for camera buffs to shoot several rolls of film. By the time we reach the third gorge, the Xiling, which is 76 kilometers long, some passengers have nearly run out of film! After passing through the Xiling Gorge, the last of the gorges on the downstream route, night falls as the Princess Jeannie approaches the construction site of the new dam. Work goes on 24-hours a day, so it lights up the night sky. Shortly beyond loom the locks of the existing Gezhou Dam opened in 1989.

Even if you have traversed the locks of the Panama Canal, it is quite an experience as the water level in the lock slowly drains out lowering your large vessel along with other craft to the sea level of the Yangtze below the dam. As the huge doors of the locks parted, the Jeannie sailed out on the wide expanse of the Yangtze to continue our journey toward Wuhan where we would disembark. Between the dam and Wuhan the river banks were low, fairly flat and fertile. Along the banks of the Yangtze lies 25% of China's arable land. Although small towns with obvious industry dotted the river side, many of the villagers obviously were engaged in farming. The Yangtze flows on to Shanghai where it empties into the East China Sea.

The Chinese have a penchant for naming scenery—especially peaks—according to what they supposedly resemble: gathering cloud peak, climbing dragon peak, soaring dragon or flying phoenix peak. We found it difficult to discern most images. If you can visualize them it may add to your enjoyment, but if you too, have trouble seeing dragons in the mountain peaks, our advice is not to worry—just enjoy their beauty.

Although the highlight for most travelers along the Yangtze is the beauty of the often mist shrouded peaks along the three gorges, watching the everyday activities of the Chinese who both ply the river in their junks and live in villages along its banks provides hours of fascination. The fishermen dropping their nets into the water, children on the backs of water buffalo at work or play in the fields, women harvesting the crops—what is at once both quaint and picturesque to the traveler is daily life to the people of the Yangtze. Take along a novel by Pearl S. Buck to read before you turn in for the night, and you'll feel a part of China's ancient culture.

In October of 1997, the upstream cofferdam begun in 1994, was completed. The diversion canals were opened and the Yangtze redirected so work on the new dam could begin in earnest in the now dry riverbed. Once the new dam is completed—now projected to be in 2009—the city of Chongqing, where we had begun our journey, and situated thirteen hundred miles from the sea will become a major deep-water port. The increased water depth that will provide the deeper and wider channel necessary to handle ocean going vessels year around will submerge whole cities, archaeological sites and the vast bulk of the peaks of the Three Gorges. The "climbing dragon" peak may climb no more and may become "peeking from the water dragon." So the advice to "go now" is being heeded by thousands of tourists each year—determined to visit the Three Gorges before the channels become inundated, and visit the Little Three Gorges of the Daning before they literally disappear.

Most cruise lines operate on the Yangtze between April and mid-November. However, April and November can be cold and by early July the heat can be unbearable on deck—outside the air-conditioned confines of the ship. The early part of August is often rainy. June and October are generally considered the best months, however, in October everyone wants to visit so the boats operate at full capacity and some shore excursion areas may be crowded. If you want to beat the largest crowds, yet have a good chance of fine weather, consider the month of May or late August thru early September to travel the Yangtze. But there are no guarantees. We were on the Yangtze in late October and experienced cold and rainy weather which did interfere with our enjoyment of the cruise. However, we personally know people who traveled almost precisely one year earlier then we did and had absolutely wonderful weather. They hardly wore the sweaters they had taken for early mornings on deck and found themselves wearing shorts most of the time! So take suggestions as to the "best time of year" as indicators and factor it into selecting the date of your cruise, but don't let it be your only consideration.

Most cruises of the Yangtze Three Gorges are between Chongqing and Wuhan—the downstream route or Wuhan and Chongqing—the upstream route. Obviously downstream cruises are fewer days than upstream cruises. If your time is limited you may elect one of the downstream sailings. However, if you have more time than money and would enjoy being on the boat an additional day, you may prefer the upstream sailing. Upstream sailings generally cost slightly less even though passengers spend more days on the boat.

Several cruise lines offer trips of the Yangtze Three Gorges. The best ships are operated by **Regal China Cruise Line**. The Regal China Cruises was selected by *Travel & Leisure* magazine in 1996 as the best river cruise as well as by the Editor of *Conde*

Nast Traveler magazine in May 1996 as the best cruise on the Yangtze River. The *Princess Jeannie, Princess Sheena,* and the *Princess Elaine* have comfortable air-conditioned cabins, good food, closed-circuit television, and well-selected shore excursions. Regal China's cruise season begins in late April and ends in early November. Prices vary with the time of year and the size of the cabin—all are outside cabins. Regal China Cruises start at US$830 per person for a double stateroom on the upstream sailing for the shoulder season. The downstream per person price for a double in high season starts at US$980. If you want to splurge for a suite on a downstream high season sailing, it can be yours for US$2130 per person. For specifics, Regal China Cruise Line in the United States can be reached by phone at 1-800-808-3388 or by Fax at 212-768-4939.

Victoria Cruises has four spacious ships plying the Yangtze. Cabins have closed-circuit television and the ships are fully air-conditioned. The Victoria cruise season begins in mid-March and ends in early December. Upstream shoulder season cabins begin at US$620 per person and range to US$760 per person for the downstream high season sailings. Suites range from US$1130 per person for a junior suite to US$1890 per person for the Shangri-La suite. Victoria Cruises also offers 10-day cruises of the Yangtze that start or end at Shanghai rather than Wuhan. For specifics, Victoria Cruises can be reached in the U.S. at 1-800-348-8084 or by Fax at 212-818-9889.

10

Shanghai

Welcome to the New Shanghai, a city under construction and reconstruction from east to west! If you've been here before, you may be in for a shock—you probably won't recognize the place. If this is your first visit, you may be amazed how different Shanghai looks and feels from other cities in China. In fact, you may want to compare it to its major competitor to the south—entrepreneurial, capitalist, and high-rise Hong Kong—and to its powerful political overlord to the northwest—bureaucratic Beijing. Energetic, crowded, and blazing with neon lights at night, this city is hurling itself into the 21st century at an unprecedented rate. Above all, it's reclaiming its reputation as one of Asia's most dynamic, cosmopolitan, and materialistic cities. It's also China's closest thing to a shopper's paradise. If you're like us, you're going to love visiting and shopping the new Shanghai.

THE MATERIAL CITY AND ITS SATELLITE

There's a certain nostalgia these days, in both Shanghai and Hong Kong (try the Club Shanghai at the Regent Hotel in Hong Kong), for the Old Shanghai of the 1930s—the era of de-

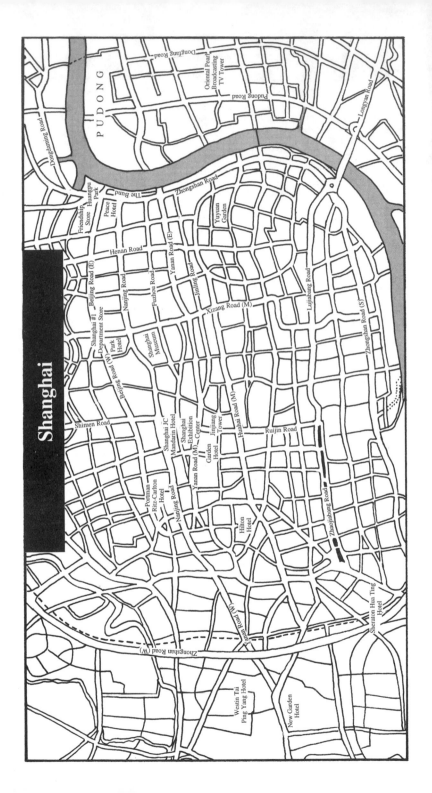

cadence, scandal, gaiety, grand ambience, big bands, late night carousing, and art deco. Much of Old Shanghai is back, and one senses it's party-time again. Despite decades of Beijing's cleansing of Shanghai's image and behavior, Shanghai once again is roaring ahead with both good and bad habits; it has an exuberant Western character and image like no other city in China, except for Hong Kong, and it can be a fun city for those with nostalgia for the Old Shanghai. It's literally re-inventing itself.

Like the old days, the New Shanghai may get itself into trouble as it over-expands while remaining shackled by a hybrid socialist/communist economy and becoming more dependent on the vicissitudes of international trade, commerce, and finance. If the recent meltdown of several Asian economies has any message to send, it is this word of caution: there may be much less here than what meets the eye. Indeed, for many foreign investors, the hype of the New Shanghai has translated into a kind of boom to bust economy—a lot of economic activity, but disappointing returns on investments. In the meantime, the New Shanghai continues expanding its infrastructure in spite of economic realities that strongly suggest there should be more long-term economic development than short-term real estate speculation and concrete, granite, and glass construction financed by dreams of future wealth. Having said that, most foreign inventors remain smitten by the notion that "we must be here at the reinvention." If not, they may loose out on some incredible opportunities that may yet arise. They're betting on a future in which nearly half of China's 1.2 billion consumers will do business via Shanghai. Sooner or later, this could all translate into some real money!

❑ Shanghai is reclaiming its reputation as one of Asia's most dynamic, cosmopolitan, and materialistic cities.

❑ The New Shanghai exhibits a curious form of boom and bust economy.

❑ While millions of dollars have been poured into making Pudong China's Wall Street, it may well become a high-tech ghost town.

❑ Shanghai is all about money—how to make it, how to spend it.

❑ Shanghai represents communism/socialism with its most extreme capitalist face.

In the aftermath of World War II, Shanghai remained dormant for over 40 years, having lost its once prominent international finance and trading roles. But during the past decade this city has risen like a phoenix at the head of the Yangtze River Basin. At least since 1990, this city has literally transformed itself every year. Return after twelve months and you may not recognize the place as more buildings are torn down, constructed, and renovated, or new expressways lace the city. The city is pouring billions of dollars into developing itself as China's new Hong Kong: new bridges, tunnels, expressways, a subway, light rail system, port facilities, an international airport, schools, offices, factories, apartments, parks, sewers, and water and electrical systems. Foreign investment and numerous joint ventures have fueled the raise of Pudong, Shanghai's new city of high-rise office buildings, hotels, and apartments located directly East and across the river from Shanghai's famous financial district, the Bund. Taking advantage of Shanghai's strategic location, its talented labor pool, and numerous tax breaks extended to joint ventures, foreign investors have poured billions of dollars into the future development of Shanghai and Pudong. Planned as China's Wall Street, Pudong has become a huge new city with lots of new buildings and infrastructure. At least since 1996, Pudong also has become China's new high-tech ghost town with a nearly 50 percent office vacancy rate. It may be a long time before this place becomes a functioning Wall Street. In the meantime, China's hybrid economy—not Mao, not Marxist, not communist, not socialist, not capitalist—continues to invest in the future of Pudong which is synonymous with the future of Shanghai and China. This could be China's new white elephant.

China's largest city and its center for commerce, finance, and trade, Shanghai has become the symbol of the new China with its numerous joint ventures, high-rise commercial buildings, five-star hotels, busy stock market, traffic jams, expressways, civic center, subway, tunnels, shopping centers, and growing, affluent middle class. But most symbolic of all is the imposing 1550-foot Oriental Pearl TV Tower in Shanghai's "new city" of Pudong on the east bank of the Huangpu River. As symbolic as Shanghai's revitalized Bund, Paris' Eiffel Tower, Sydney's Opera House, Rome's Colosseum, London's Big Ben, or New York's Empire State Building, the Tower dominates Shanghai's brash new skyline. Now Shanghai has two great symbols that face each other across the Huangpu River—the Bund represents its dynamic yet elegant past; the Tower represents its dynamic and brash future.

Whereas Beijing is all about politics, culture, and history, Shanghai is all about business, money, and shopping. You'll find some history and culture here, but you'll soon discover this city is all about people and money—how to make it, how to spend it. Put simply, these cities represent two very different cultures—one bureaucratic, where the pursuit of power dominates relationships (Beijing), and one entrepreneurial, where the pursuit of money and the good life dominates relationships (Shanghai). And the differences in outlook and behavior are none too subtle. New-found wealth, complete with millionaires and their conspicuous consumption of fancy cars, fashionable designer clothes, and night spots, add renewed color and contrasts to what had become a rather dull and colorless post-revolutionary city until the new economic reforms kicked in around 1990. Shanghai was once again given the green light to do what it does best—create wealth and pursue the materialistic good life.

Highly educated and Western in outlook, Shanghai also is known for its arrogance vis-a-vis other less cosmopolitan areas of China, especially Beijing. For many young Shanghainese, Communism is okay as long as you don't have too much of it Beijing-style and as long as you can have a good job and make good money in order to enjoy the new-found materialistic pleasures that have washed upon this city's bountiful shores. With such outlooks and its culture of materialism, Shanghai sets itself apart from the rest of China as the country's most un-Chinese city. Indeed, many Beijingers feel uncomfortable in Shanghai: it lacks the order and discipline attendant with the exercise of power and control that is so endemic to Beijing's political culture. This is a very fluid and unpredictable city, one prone to indulgences and excesses, characteristics that often make Beijing's political leaders very uncomfortable. But it's a really great city, one capable of moving products and money, which make Beijing's political leaders very happy much of the time. Accordingly, Beijing is somewhat ambivalent about this place. For right now, Shanghai is okay in Beijing.

A brash, confident, and dynamic Shanghai is nothing new. Shanghai has arisen once again as China's leading entrepreneur; it broadcasts to the world that it is open for as much business as the growing infrastructure can accommodate. And if it can't accommodate such businesses, it will build the necessary infra-structure to ensure it can, from roads to port facilities. Indeed, Shanghai has a long and infamous history of being China's commercial, financial, and trade center, simultaneously a cos-mopolitan, fashionable and decadent city. Beginning in 1842, with China's defeat in the First Opium War, Shanghai was one of five Treaty Ports opened to foreign trade and residence. The British, French, and Americans carved out their autonomous spheres of influence in a series of urban "settlements" and "concessions" that shaped the European architecture and congested traffic arteries that still dominate the city's central business district, especially along the Bund. Despite over 40 years of communist cleansing and retrenchment, during the past seven years Shanghai has come roaring back as if it were making up for lost time. For many old China hands, the so-called new Shanghai reminds them of the good 'ole days when Shanghai was rightly known as the "Pearl of the Orient" and the "Paris of the East." Just pop into the Jazz Bar of the landmark Peace Hotel along congested Nanjing Road any night between 8pm and 11pm and you can reminisce about Old Shanghai as the Old Jazz Band, composed of aging musicians who once played the cabarets and dance halls of the 1940s, still belt out the great tunes associated with Shanghai's former lifestyle.

A WESTERN, COSMOPOLITAN CITY

It's not quite Hong Kong, but give Shanghai a few years and it may well grow up to become another Hong Kong which is exactly what the ambitious and proud city fathers envision. This is a city of mixed architectural styles and startling contrasts, an interesting potpourri reflecting its strong post-1842 international influence and development. Old architectural masterpieces, reminiscent of a by-gone era of excessive Western involvement with this city, co-exist amongst some very dreary and unimaginative post-World War II commercial buildings, grandiose Soviet-inspired architecture, and modern high-rise, glass-walled office buildings adorned in granite and marble. New construction everywhere, crowded port facilities, teeming masses, streaming traffic, fine hotels and restaurants, nonstop shopping, and a vibrant nightlife awash with blazing city lights—despite power shortages—make this city one of Asia's most exciting places to be these days. It's China's most cosmopolitan and Western city, a model for what is hoped to be a new era of sustained economic development. If Deng Xiaoping's famous dictum *"To get rich is glorious"* has many true believers and practitioners, they certainly are found in Shanghai where they have learned to practice the art of getting rich, or at least consuming life's wealth of riches, to the fullest. Even though it has many characteristics of a Third World city—don't drink the water and watch out for the hoards of bicycles—Shanghai also

❏ To reminisce about the Old Shanghai, visit the Jazz Bar and its Old Jazz Band at the landmark Peace Hotel.

❏ Shanghai's waterfront, The Bund, is beautifully illuminated at night. While not exactly Paris, it is China's "city of lights."

❏ Pudong's 468-meter Oriental Pearl Tower is Shanghai's symbol of a new and entrepreneurial city destined to play a major international role in the future.

❏ Shanghai's major commercial waterway, the Huangpao River, slices through the city separating it into two major sections that are linked by two bridges and two tunnels.

has become extremely westernized, comfortable, and convenient. Of all cities you are likely to visit in China, Shanghai is the one you will feel most familiar with. It seems to make sense, at least a Western sense of how things should be organized. At times you can't believe you are still in China. But perhaps most important of all, Shanghai will give you an image of what the rest of China is likely to become in the coming decade. This is communism/socialism with its most extreme capitalist face. Not surprising, the political reverberations for this unprecedented form of communism/socialism are likely to be astounding in the not-too-distant future.

Welcome to Shanghai, a trip you won't soon forget. And if you are old enough to remember the Old Shanghai of pre-World War II, you'll remember it, too, was unforgettable—a special and adventuresome city of romantic lights along the river. While it's not quite Paris, it does have ambitions of becoming more than what it has been for nearly 50 years. Just where these ambitions will lead is anyone's guess.

SURPRISING NEW SHANGHAI

While Shanghai can date its history to more than 6,000 years, for all intents and purposes, this is a relatively young city that initially grew out of 19th century commercial and trade relations with the West that developed in the aftermath of China's defeat in the First Opium War in 1842. Shanghai quickly became the major gateway to China. Rather than colonize China, the British, French, Americans, and Japanese carved out spheres of influence in this gateway city. By 1920 the foreign community in Shanghai had grown to over 26,000 people.

The Old Shanghai of the pre-World War II era was an economic powerhouse, China's center for trade and commerce, and one of the world's most cosmopolitan cities. More than 100 banks located in and around the Bund where they financed much of the trade and development in China. Even then it surprised visitors who found Shanghai to be a vibrant and flamboyant city engaged in all kinds of hedonistic pursuits—a kind of Asian Sodom and Gomorrah.

All this came to an abrupt end with the Japanese capture of Shanghai in World War II and the subsequent communist assumption of power in 1949. Shanghai quietly closed its doors to the west as the Cold War dominated the post-revolutionary period. Shanghai retained its preeminent economic role in China but on a much diminished international scale.

GETTING TO KNOW YOU

Shanghai is a big city but one that is relatively easy to get oriented to given its grid structure and major landmarks. The first defining characteristic is the north-south **Huangpao River** that slices through the city. This is not to be confused with the Yangtze River which lies some 10 kilometers north of the city; the Huangpao River is one of its tributaries. The Old Shanghai, also known as **Puxi**, is on the west bank; the New Shanghai, or **Pudong**, is on the east bank. Crossed by two bridges and two tunnels, the busy river is Shanghai's lifeline to the international world of trade and commerce as ships ply its waters destined to discard and load their cargoes at the city's many port sites that line both sides of the river.

The city's second defining characteristic is the famous **Bund** which is now called Zhongshan Road. This is Shanghai's elegant promenade, a broad north-south walkway stretching from Huangpu Park in the north to Yanan Road in the south and bordering the west bank of the Huangpu River. One of its major defining characteristics is its sweeping backdrop of Western architectural masterpieces, major commercial and hotel buildings constructed in the pre-World War II period, many of which have symbolized the city for nearly a century. This string of buildings is separated from the boardwalk by a busy six-lane street but anchored to it by underground pedestrian tunnels that quickly connect the two areas. Recently renovated and elevated, this elegant, nicely landscaped, and well scrubbed marble boardwalk has become a major tourist attraction and a great outdoor area for lovers and strollers who come here to take pictures and admire each other, the city waterfront, the river traffic, and the emerging skyline of Pudong on the other side of the river. In many respects, the name Shanghai is synonymous with "The Bund." It's also a haven for early morning exercisers and singers and musicians who practice their skills in public. Here you'll see a delightful mixture of Western architectural styles (Victorian, neo-Grecian, neo-Classical) displayed in aging stone buildings noted for their clock towers, colonnades, marble pillars, turrets, and ornate designs. Once occupied by Western banks, trading companies, hotels, embassies, and private clubs, the buildings now house government agencies, banks, and businesses. A quick stroll along the Bund will give you an instant image of the Old Shanghai at its architecturally elegant best. Better still, visit the Shanghai Mansions just north of Huangpu Park for a view of the Bund. Built by the British in 1934 (Broadway Hotel), this building was subsequently occupied by the Japanese as their military headquarters during World War II and then served as a concentration camp. The Bund area still has class and remains one of our favorite stops in China.

The city's third defining characteristic is the imposing **Oriental Pearl Tower** in the new adjacent city of Pudong. Over 1500 feet (468 meters) tall, you can't miss it, even on a misty day. A combination TV tower, revolving restaurant, sky hotel, amusement park, and observatory, the tower is Shanghai's new city symbol, an icon to its future. But it's more than that. The tower also is an important signal to the world that Shanghai is on the move again, regaining its role as an economic powerhouse as its heads into the 21st century confident that it will play the lead role in shaping China's economic future. Connected to Shanghai by two modern bridges—the Nanpu (world's third largest double-tower cable-braced bridge) and Yangpu (world's largest suspension bridge)—and two tunnels, the Old and New Shanghai have increasingly embraced each other during the past few years as traffic between the two has increased exponentially.

The final defining characteristic of Shanghai is **Nanjing Road.** Running east and west midway off the Bund, this is Shanghai's extremely crowded and congested main shopping street. Here you will find Shanghai's most famous shops, department stores, hotels, and fast food restaurants. Foreign and local tourists along with local residents compete for scarce walking space along, and often in, this narrow road. Highly westernized with windows packed with the latest fashions and electronics, this also is the avenue for advertising wars between Coca Cola and Pepsi. It's also a wonderful street to people-watch as you absorb both the New Shanghai and New China where shopping for the good life is an officially sanctioned part of the Chinese way of "getting rich." Everything of commercial significance seems to happen along this well trodden non-stop shopping street. At night Nanjing Road becomes a colorful neon-blazing street with a constant flow of both human and vehicular traffic.

Shanghai has many other less obvious but also important defining characteristics. Many of them are in the making as the city continues to transform itself with ring roads and expressways. Its old buildings, parks, museums, exhibition center, and new commercial buildings constantly juxtapose the new and the old and give Shanghai a dynamic quality not found in other cities of China, with perhaps the exception of its sister, Hong Kong.

THE BASICS

CLIMATE AND WHEN TO VISIT

If you're planning to visit Beijing, chances are you already figured out the best time of the year to visit China. Since Shanghai is nearly 700 miles southeast of Beijing, you'll be in a subtropical area similar to northern and central Florida. That means it's hot, humid, and rainy during the summer months. Ideally you may want to plan your visit during a cooler and drier part of the year, especially October. Winter can get cold, with temperatures below freezing, but snow rarely falls in Shanghai. Spring is okay but the weather can be unpredictable with uncomfortable heat and humidity.

POPULATION AND PEOPLE

Shanghai may or may not be China's largest city, depending on how you both bound and count the people. Officially Shanghai has over 13 million people living in the greater Shanghai area, an over-bounded municipality of 5,800 square kilometers which incorporates several rural counties. Over 7 million people live in the city proper which we take as the real city population figure. The new city of Pudong boasts a population of nearly 3 million. Much of Shanghai's population lives in surrounding suburban communities.

❏ The best time to visit in terms of weather is October.

❏ Officially the population of Shanghai is over 13 million but in reality the urban area has just over 7 million.

❏ The people of Shanghai tend to be better educated than elsewhere in China—and it shows.

❏ Shanghai has a Christian population of 100,000 who attend the city's more than 40 churches.

❏ The Shanghainese are great collectors of antiques and memorabilia, more so than elsewhere in the country.

❏ Nearly 40 percent of all national imports and exports pass through Shanghai.

The people in Shanghai tend to be different from people in other areas of China you will visit. In general they tend to be more outgoing, personable, and business-oriented than those you meet in Beijing and many other cities in China. Things often get done in a logical and sensible manner, demonstrating a kind of entrepreneurial spirit lacking elsewhere in China. The people of Shanghai also tend to be much better educated then people elsewhere in China. Indeed, Shanghai is the center for more than 50 institutions of higher learning and the Shanghainese are reputed to have a higher educational achievement level than the people of Hong Kong. They also have the largest (100,000) Christian population in China of which 30,000 to 40,000 attend the city's more than 40 churches each week. The women in Shanghai are definitely the most fashionable in China. The Shanghainese also are great collectors of antiques and memorabilia. Parks are often crowded with stamp and card collectors. Many individuals offer private collections (family museums and exhibition rooms) of everything from watches, matchbox labels, and tea sets to old coins, chopsticks, and opera masks. Don't be surprised if you're approached by people who introduce themselves to you for the purpose of practicing their English.

TYPOGRAPHY

This is a flat city with lots of high-rise commercial buildings and expressways to vary its landscape. Bicyclers by the thousands (6 million) love this city's stressless typography. Accordingly, you'll need to watch out for the many bicycles that crowd Shanghai's narrow streets. Regulated by barriers or prohibited on the most crowded streets, bicycles can creep upon you quietly and unexpectedly.

ECONOMY

Strategically located at the head of the Yangtze River basin, Shanghai stands to benefit enormously from the overall economic development of the Yangtze River. As one of China's special economic zones, outside of Hong Kong, Shanghai has become China's major manufacturing, trading, and financial center. Nearly 40 percent of all national imports and exports pass through Shanghai. The city also is noted for its automotive industry which produces 300,000 Volkswagens each year—the major reason visitors see so many Volkswagen Santanas on the streets of Shanghai. Joint venture investment in Shanghai is the highest of any city in China. Much of the manufacturing, trade, and commerce is centered in the new city of Pudong which houses either the main or branch offices of all major international players involved in investment and trade with China.

Pollution is still a major problem in Shanghai due to its heavy industrial character. However, most of Shanghai's old polluting industries have been moved out of the city proper and either relocated in nearby rural areas or closed or dismantled altogether. Many of the old pre-Revolution plants still remain, especially on the Pudong side of the Huangpu River, crumbling from age or being razed for new high-rise buildings.

GETTING THERE

Shanghai is easily accessible by plane, train, boat, and road. Most visitors arrive by plane. You can fly directly into Shanghai from several destinations in North America, Europe, and Asia on such major carriers as Northwest Airlines, United Airlines, Singapore Airlines, Thai International, SAS, Japan Airlines, Lufthansa, Korean Air, Dragonair, Canadian Airlines International, Air France, All Nipon Airways, Aeroflot, and China's national carrier, China Eastern Airlines. Flights between Hong Kong and Shanghai, Guangzhou and Shanghai, and Beijing and Shanghai take about 2 hours.

If you take one of the downstream Yangtze cruises that originates in Chongqing, it's most convenient to disembark at Wuhan and then take a flight from Wuhan to Shanghai. Otherwise, the boat trip from Wuhan to Shanghai takes 3 days and is relatively unremarkable.

Shanghai can be easily reached by rail from most major cities in China. However, expect some long journeys. For example, the train takes 26 hours to go from Beijing to Shanghai and 36 hours to go from Guangzhou to Shanghai.

AIRPORT

The airport is located about 30 minutes west of the city center. It's a relatively modern facility with several convenient services for visitors. If you arrive without a hotel reservation, go directly to the hotel reservation booth to make arrangements.

GETTING AROUND

While Shanghai is a very large city, most places you will want to visit are located within easy walking distance or a short taxi, bus, or metro ride. You may want to hire a car and driver to take you around the city. Contact your hotel concierge, tour desk, or front desk for information on such rentals as well as how to use the bus and metro system. Three main bus numbers will take you to most of the major destinations: 20, 505, and 911. Signs in the metro are in both English and Chinese. Check at your hotel or go directly to the Garden Hotel to see if the Jin Jiang City Tour bus still operates—a special city tour bus service begun in May 1996. This is the first such service in China. Operating between the hours of 9am and 9pm, the bus starts from in front of the Garden Hotel. Running every half hour, it makes more than 10 stops along the way. You can purchase a ticket (20 yuan) on board from the tour guide. You can get off at any time and pick up any subsequent buses by showing your ticket. But do check to make sure this service is still operating. There is some question whether or not it will continue, depending on the level of demand for the service. It initially got off to a very slow, and unprofitable, start.

Be sure to pick up the latest edition of the "Shanghai Official Tourist Map" which is published by the Shanghai Municipal Tourism Administration and is available at most hotels. The map includes detailed sections of three major shopping areas: Nanjing Road, Huaihai Road, and Yu Garden and Yuyuan Bazaar. The municipality also publishes an informative newspaper for tourists, "Shanghai," and a tourist booklet, "Shanghai: Official Visitors Guide."

TOURS

More than 50 tour companies provides services to tourists both in and around Shanghai. Highly competitive, most of them will arrange tours to other areas of China. One of our favorite tour groups is **Shanghai Jin Jiang Tours** (191 Chang Le Road, Shanghai 200020, Tel. (86-21) 6472-0500 or Fax (86-21) 6466-2297 (ask for Mr. Ying Guo Hong). They are a full service tour company that operates throughout China.

PRECAUTIONS

There are only two things you really need to watch out for in Shanghai: don't drink the tap water and be careful when crossing the street or walking in the street—you can easily get run over by a bicycle!

SHOPPING

Shanghai is where the shopping action in China is concentrated. This is a relatively sophisticated, fashionable, and wealthy city where shopping seems to be a favorite pastime. Hundreds of stores line Shanghai's two main shopping streets, Nanjing and Huaihai, drawing thousands of shoppers to their doors each day. New department stores, most of which are joint ventures and which primarily cater to Western tastes, sprout through the densely populated central business district. Human waves of shoppers crowd the streets as well as Shanghai's popular markets.

The large concentration of shops in Shanghai does not

necessarily mean business is booming for everyone. The number of window shoppers far out-number actual buyers. Indeed, Shanghai has more shops than the local economy can presently support. Many shops in Shanghai, especially joint venture, are open simply because the owners believe they have to have a retail presence in Shanghai since it is such an important developing city.

FOUR SHOPPING CULTURES

You may immediately notice four shopping cultures operating in Shanghai. The first shopping culture is youthful, reflecting the new-found wealth of young people in their 20s and 30s who seem to have lots of disposable income which they readily spend on clothes and accessories. Indeed, a fashion conscious city with lots of young people making good salaries as employees of joint venture firms means lots of young shoppers crowding the department and clothing stores along Nanjing Road and the more fashionable nearby Huaihai Road. You may or may not wish to follow the shopping habits of this crowd since its styles and quality tend to be very "local." Along Nanjing Road you'll find lots of very cheap clothing stores that tend to cater to local tourists from the rural areas. Yes, here you can buy a suit for US$20, but you probably don't have a place you want to be seen wearing it! It looks as cheap as it costs.

❑ Shanghai has two major shopping streets—Nanjing and Huaihai roads—and four distinct shopping cultures.

❑ Most new department stores are joint venture operations which have given the older stores stiff competition.

❑ Shanghai's major shoppers tend to be young people who love window-shopping and spending money on clothes and accessories.

The second shopping culture relates to what many older Shanghai residents love to do—collect antiques and memorabilia. You'll find many of these people in the parks and near the Bund selling and trading stamps and cards. Others are found in the antique and flea markets selling a large range of collectibles, everything from watches and porcelain to Cultural Revolution posters and furniture. Others operate their own private museums and exhibition halls where they offer unique collections of antiques and memorabilia. These people fuel Shanghai's antiques market. They represent much of what is old in the new Shanghai. If you love antiques and enjoy poking around flea markets, Shanghai may well become your favorite city. It has lots of unique things to offer visitors who are interested in the last 100 years of Shanghai. You can even find a list of these collectors on the following

Internet site: *http://www.sh.com/play/museums1.htm*

A third shopping culture represented in Shanghai is similar to one you will find in many other cities—lots of department and Friendship Stores offering a wide range of typical arts and crafts. You've probably seen it before in great abundance, and it's here again in Shanghai in even greater abundance. One wonders who buys all the stuff, especially since it all looks the same after a while. Like so many other products in China, the arts and crafts seem to be over-produced.

The fourth shopping culture is well represented in the upscale shops found in five-star hotels and shopping centers that primarily cater to the new local rich and foreigners who seek imported name-brand goods. In Shanghai you'll see more of this shopping culture operating because of the greater wealth found in this city. Expensive European designer label clothes and accessories, such as Versace, Escada, Cerruti 1881, and Ferragamo, are well represented in Shanghai. If you are from North America or Europe, chances are you will not be interested in this shopping culture since it is very expensive (more so than back home) and sizes may be inappropriate.

WHAT TO BUY

Except for antiques and special collectibles reflecting the history of Shanghai, most shopping items available in Shanghai are also found in other major cities of China—lacquerware, embroideries, carpets, jade, carvings, cloisonne, paintings, needlepoint tapestries, filigree jewelry, and clothing. These items just seem to be in greater abundance in Shanghai than in other cities.

Most antiques available in Shanghai date from the late Qing Dynasty. If you are interested in old porcelain, the shops and market stalls have much to offer collectors. Good collections are found at the Duoyunxuan Painting and Calligraphy Shop (422 Nanjing Dong Lu), Wenfang Sibao (Four Treasures of the Studio, in Jinjiang compound), Shanghai Chahangjiang Seal Carving Factory (722 Huaihai Zhong Lu), and Chuangxin Old Wares Shops (1297 Hihai Lu). Also try the official antiques market on Dongtai Lu; a Sunday morning antiques market in Fuyou Lu near the Yu Garden; and the Yu Garden Bazaar (area within the Old City).

MAJOR SHOPPING STREETS

Most shopping in Shanghai is confined to two major streets, one more upscale (Huaihai Road) than the other (Nanjing Road). If you spend most of your time walking these two streets, you will cover at least 90 percent of the shopping opportunities offered in Shanghai. You'll also be up to your elbows in a new cultural experience as you maneuver through crowds of young people enjoying Shanghai's new consumer life. The other streets offer a few shopping opportunities but nothing on the scale of Nanjing and Huaihai roads. In fact, except for the streets with antique shops, you may want to skip most of these other streets altogether since they will likely disappoint you. The major shopping streets include:

❑ **Nanjing Road:** This is Shanghai's most famous shopping street. Divided into East and West sections, it's long and can be exhausting. Depending on your interests, it may be more of a cultural experience than an adventure in quality shopping. The good news is that you can skip 90 percent of what you encounter along this street (local stuff for local residents and local tourists) and thus quickly complete what initially appears to be a formidable day-long task. Nearly 10 kilometers in length, Nanjing Road stretches west from the Bund to Jing-an Temple. Starting at the Bund and moving west (begin at the Peace Hotel at the corner of Nanjing Road and Zhongshan Road), the first four kilometers of this street are extremely crowded and overwhelming with waves of people, bicycles, cars, and buses assaulting the casual window shopper. In fact, this is China's most dense shopping street. Once the city's greatest shopping street, today Nanjing Road looks worn; it's primarily of interest to locals and out-of-towners looking for inexpensive clothes (want to pick up a US$20 suit before returning home?). For tourists, it's a great place to do serious people-watching and pick up a few cheap souvenirs (try #496 for unique and inexpensive knives and scissors). There is little available here for shoppers in search of quality treasures. Nonetheless, the street is undergoing transformation as more joint venture department stores and shops move in and offer a combination of imported and joint venture produced goods. Indeed, one of Old Shanghai's noted department stores has reestablished itself here—**Sincere Department Store**. The street also is home for the city's largest store, **Shanghai Number One Department Store**, which reportedly services over 100,000 customers each day! Be sure to stop at the famous art deco **Peace Hotel** (has two nice clothing shops, Dawson and Emi's). Some of the most famous shops along this street include **Guan**

Long Photographic Co.; **Shanghai Philatelic Corporation** (#244, great for stamp collectors), **Hendali Watch & Clock Co.** (#262), **Duoyun Art Gallery** (specializes in calligraphy supplies and paintings), **Shanghai Arts & Crafts Jewelry & Jade** (#438), **Zhang Xiao Quan Knives and Scissors** (#496, offers 300 kinds of scissors, knives and meat cleavers), **Guo Hua Chinaware Stores** (#550, 2nd floor for foreigners), and **Hua Lian Commercial Building** (used to be the famous Shanghai #10 Department Store). Further west along Nanjing Road you'll come to the back side of the huge **Shanghai Exhibition Centre** (the front entrance is located at 1000 Yanan Road) as well as two of Shanghai's top hotels which also include small upscale shopping arcades: **Portman Ritz-Carlton** (#1376) and **Shanghai JC Mandarin** (#1225).

❑ **Huaihai Road:** Located four blocks south of Nanjing Road in and around where the Jinjiang and Garden hotels are located (between Shimen and Pu'an roads and including Moaming Man Lane adjacent to the Garden Hotel), this street was formerly known as Avenue Joffe. It's considered Shanghai's Fifth Avenue because of its better quality and fashionable clothing stores. The best quality shopping here is found in the upscale **Jin Jiang Dickson Center**, a three-storey red brick building across the street from the Jin Jiang Hotel. Its granite interior with fountain and escalators house such name-brand shops as Polo Ralph Lauren, Charles Jourdan, Guy Laroche, Versace, Escada, Cerruti 1881, Mondi, Perry Ellis, and Gieves and Hawkes. The famous Hong Kong shirt maker, Ascot Chang, also has a shop here. Across the street is the five-star **Jin Jiang Tower Hotel** with its two-storey shopping arcade with designer label shops such as Versace, Bally, Givenchy, Versus, and Ermenegildo Zegner. The street also has several major department stores and shopping centers, such as Isetan, Shanghai Shui Hing, Time International, and Maison Mode.

❑ **Jinling Road:** Being renovated to became a "mini-Nanjing Road."

❑ **Sichuan Road:** Intersects with Nanjing Road near the river front. Clothes and household goods.

❑ **Fuzhou Street:** At one time Shanghai's infamous street of noted bordellos, today Fuzhou Street is famous for its bookstores. Unless you read Chinese, don't expect to find much of interest here.

❑ **Beijing Road:** Primarily noted for the well stocked six-storey **Shanghai Friendship Store** which is located near the Bund and within a few minutes from the Peace Hotel.

❑ **Shimen Road:** Off of Nanjing Road near the Shanghai Exhibition Center. Known for its clothing shops.

❑ **Jiujiang Road:** Known for its clothing shops.

❑ **Huating Road:** Known for its clothing shops.

❑ **Jiangyin Street:** Has shops selling fish and flowers.

❑ **Liuhe Road:** Look for antique shops.

❑ **Dongtai Road:** Look for antique shops.

❑ **Taiyuan Road:** Noted for shops and stalls selling stamps, notes, and tickets.

HOTEL SHOPPING ARCADES

Some of the best shopping for visitors will be found in the shopping arcades of the major hotels. Most hotels have good quality arts and crafts shops and clothing boutiques of interest to both visitors and wealthy local residents. Some hotels host special art and furniture exhibitions. The best hotel shopping arcades include:

❑ **Portman Ritz-Carlton:** *1376 Nanjing Road West.* Offers Shanghai's largest hotel shopping arcade, a two-level shopping and office complex along with hotel shops. Within the hotel, look for **ShangART**, Shanghai's first professional gallery of contemporary Chinese art. Ferragamo, Cerreti, and Cartier also are located here. In the shopping arcade, look for **Gold Stone** for arts, crafts and jewelry; and shops offering clothes and accessories. The area also includes a small supermarket and department store.

❑ **Westin Tai Ping Yang:** *5 Qun Yi Nan Road*. Excellent quality arts and crafts shops on second floor. Offers some old wood screens and decorative pieces. Occasionally has special furniture exhibits.

❑ **Sheraton Hua Ting:** *1200 Caoxi Road*. Includes lots of small shops, organized like a bazaar, offering a wide selection of carpets, handicrafts, furniture, clothes, ceramics, leather bags, luggage, and jade carvings.

❑ **Jin Jiang Tower:** *161 Changle Road*. Includes a two-storey shopping arcade with name-brand clothing and accessory shops such as Versace, Bally, Givenchy, Versus, and Ermenegildo Zegna. Includes a small branch of the Friendship Store and one shop specializing in antiques only.

❑ **Shanghai Hilton:** *250 Hua Shan Road*. Offers two fashionable lobby clothing and accessory shops, including a Fendi shop. Also has a small shopping arcade with an arts and crafts shop offering a good selection of ceramics and paintings.

DEPARTMENT STORES

Not surprising, Shanghai boasts the largest number of department stores in China. Most are relatively new and are joint ventures offering a large variety of locally produced and imported products. Some are upscale and cater primarily to the growing upper classes. Within the past few years, the older department stores have experienced heavy competition from the newer ones which offer a more exciting retail environment and more interested products. Not surprising, the older stores are noted for their lower quality products and old fashioned displays.

You may or may not find much of interest in these department stores except for some arts, crafts, and food products organized in separate sections for tourists. Most department stores cater to the consumer needs of local residents, especially domestic tourists on a limited budget. Accordingly, you may find visiting department stores to be more of a cultural experience than an exercise in good shopping.

Department stores are especially well represented along Nanjing Road and Huahai Road. Some of the major ones include:

❑ **Shanghai #1 Department Store:** *830 Nanjing Road East, Tel. 6322-3344.* This is one of Shanghai's oldest, largest, and most popular department stores. Includes six floors plus a basement of products, and offers everything from food and clothes to arts and crafts. It boasts 36,000 products, 100,000 visitors a day, and 3,000 salespeople. However, it's also facing fierce competition from the newer more upscale department stores springing up at this intersection. If you want to see Shanghai's department store past, this is the place to come. It won't last much longer in this condition. Displays tend to be old fashioned and products lack quality and class. If you go to the second floor, you can exit onto the overhead walkway which connects to the newer Shanghai New World department store as well as new department stores being built at other corners of this intersection. You'll also get one of the best overhead views of all the street traffic below. Also includes two other branches located at 523 Huaihai Road (Shop 2 which is part of the Shanghai International Shopping Center adjacent to Isetan Department Store) and 99-105 Bao Shan Road (Shop 3).

❑ **Shanghai New World:** Across the street from the Shanghai #1 Department Store. Very upscale seven-storey department store (a joint venture with Hong Kong New World) with central atrium and lots of imported and joint venture products. Fourth floor has a good selection of handicrafts. Includes separate floors for amusements and foods.

❑ **Hua Lian Commercial Building:** *Nanjing Road.* Built in the 1920s and previously known as the Shanghai #10 Department Store. Located next door to the Overseas Chinese Store. Shanghai's fourth largest department store with three and a half floors of typical department store goods.

❑ **The Friendship Store:** *40 Beijing Road East, Tel. 6329-4600.* Somewhat off the beaten shopping path but only a few minutes walk from the Bund, this is Shanghai's oldest and largest friendship store. It's also one of the best Friendship stores we've encountered. The six floor department store section includes a small bookstore on the first floor and a huge arts and crafts area on the fourth floor. Look for excellent quality carved jade and agate and one of the best selections of fans. The fifth floor includes carpets, antiques (mainly porcelain), furniture, Tiffany lamps, screens and terra cotta soldiers. A second building, across the parking lot and next to the Friendship Supermarket, specializes in quality paintings and antique ceramics. Nice displays throughout this store. You'll also find branches of the Friendship Store in other locations in Shanghai, including one specializing in antiques at the Jin Jiang Hotel. Also look for a new branch of this store across the street from the New Century Hotel and Westin Hotel.

❏ **Shanghai Exhibition Center:** You can't miss this imposing building—the Soviet Union's great contribution to monolithic (some might say tacky wedding cake) architecture in Shanghai. Located at 1000 Yanan Road (the backside of this compound extends to Nanjing Road, near the five-star Portman Ritz-Carlton and Shanghai JC Mandarin hotels), this complex used to house Shanghai's premier Friendship Store—where all the tour buses stopped so foreigners could do their one-stop shopping. Those days are over. While this center still has lots to offer in the arts and crafts departments, it has seen better days. Somewhat worn and facing strong competition from the more upscale shops and departments stores closer to the Bund on Nanjing and Huaihai roads, this area is still worth visiting, especially if you are in the market for huge carvings, bronzes, cloisonne, and other arts and crafts. The compound is divided into two major shopping areas. The best section is found in the building on the left and is operated as the **Shanghai Arts and Crafts Trading Corporation**, one of the largest arts and crafts emporiums in Shanghai. Here you will encounter a huge inventory of arts and crafts—ceramics, embroidery, cloisonne, ivory, jade, carpets, paintings, silk fabrics, lacquer, furniture, screens, jewelry, cashmere sweaters, clothes, and foods. The second shopping area is just to the right of this first building, at the front door of the main building. Here you will find the **China Tourist Souvenir Corporation**. While many of the same arts and crafts are found here (paintings, rugs, ink slabs, chops, jade and stone carvings, embroidery, clothes, lacquer screens), you'll also find more tourist kitsch, including T-shirts. The quality is not as nearly as nice as the first shop in this compound.

❑ **Nextage (Yaohan):** *501 Zhangyang Road, Pudong New District, Shanghai, Tel. 6573-0111.* If you have only time to visit one department store in Shanghai, make sure it's this place. Located in the commercial center of Pudong area, this is Shanghai's, China's, and Asia's largest department store. It's big and it's really nice, all 140,000 square meters of floor space. Popularly known as "Yaohan" and China's first joint venture involving a department store (between the Japanese Yaohan group and the Chinese government), the building and sign tell you this is the Nextage Shopping Center. Walk in the front entrance and you immediately get a sense of the new Shanghai: cosmetic counters and a large car dealership with numerous new cars on display, from BMWs to Buicks. The seven floors of this complex are jam-packed with the latest fashions, accessories, electronics, and household goods. But it's really the fifth floor we highly recommended. This is China's finest arts and crafts emporium found in a department store. Here you'll find top quality paintings, jewelry, furniture, screens, jade and stone carvings, calligraphy supplies, cloisonne, rugs, fans, ivory, ceramics, dough figures, embroidery, cashmere sweaters, agate bowls, and pearls. It even has an excellent antique section (authorized) with a good collection of ceramics, lacquer boxes, and walking sticks. Everything is nicely displayed and the service is excellent. The only problem here is that not many tourists know about this shopping center and the fifth floor. It's a bit off the beaten tourist path and no signs, including the floor directory, are in English. Some signs are in Japanese. You can easily get here if you take the city tour bus (Jin Jiang City Tour) which includes this department store as one of its six stops. This Yaohan store is significant in another way: in July 1996 the Yaohan Group moved its international headquarters from Victoria Bay, Hong Kong, to this site. It now oversees Yaohan's 450 branches in 16 countries and regions around the world.

❑ **Shanghai Overseas Chinese Store:** *627 Nanjing Road East, Tel. 6322-5508.* Once only open to Overseas Chinese, today it's open to anyone who passes through its doors. Includes four floors of clothes and household goods. Fifth floor includes coffee shop and bowling alley.

❑ **Shanghai Arts and Crafts Sales Service Center:** *190-208 Nanjing Road West, Tel. 7327-5264.* Housed in an aging building with equally aging displays on four floors, this is a long-established arts and crafts store offering a wide range of typical tourist-oriented products: cloisonne, jewelry, jade products, furniture, needlepoint pictures, inlaid screens porcelain, pottery, lacquer and enamel wares, paintings, calligraphy supplies, embroidered clothes, silk tapestries, woolen carpets, sandalwood fans, lamps, table clothes, cashmere sweaters, and knitwear. Look for their selection of unique hand painted T-shirts on third floor (¥60) and wooden model boats on fourth floor (model of the Mayflower costs ¥5400).

❑ **Printemps Shanghai:** *939-947 Huaihai Road at Shanxi Nan Road, Tel. 6431-0118.* An elegant joint venture department store (Hong Kong's Top Form International and Shanghai Yimin) with an imposing Art Deco facade. Includes six floors of name-brand boutiques offering the latest in men and women's fashion and casual wear.

❑ **Isetan:** *527 Huaihai Road East, Tel. 6375-1111.* Located on the first four floors of the East end of International Shopping Center (the Huaihai branch of the Shanghai #1 Department Store occupies the other half), this is a joint venture department store with Japan. Indeed, most signs are in either Chinese or Japanese. Like more Isetan department stores found in Asia, this is a popular and fashionable upscale store offering many imported name brand products, especially for clothes and accessories (Benetton, Puma, Elle, Cerruti 1881, Nautica, Yves Saint Laurent, Episode, Esprit, Levi's).

❑ **Shanghai Shui Hing Department Store:** *830 Huaihua East, Tel. 6358-9636.* Located in the Huaihua Commercial Center, this is a joint venture with Hong Kong. Offers a wide range of upscale products.

❑ **Wing's Department Store:** *869 Nanjing Road West, Tel. 6258-2688.* A joint venture with Hong Kong, this classy six-story department store offers numerous upscale products. The first floor is primarily devoted to international brand name clothes and accessories, such as Gieves and Hawkes, Jessica, Bally, Burberry, and Dunhill. The third floor includes a Hong Kong designer's gallery. Other floors include cosmetics, kitchenware, gifts, bedding, leather goods, and jewelry.

❏ **Sincere:** *479 Nanjing Road East, Tel. 6322-1953.* Recently relocated to Shanghai after several years absence, this is another new upscale joint venture department store with investment from Hong Kong. Consists of five-levels. Expensive but nothing of particular note here.

❏ **Mosta:** *889 Nanjing Road West, Tel. 6217-5076.* A joint venture with Taiwan, this is another popular department store offering a wide range of standard to upscale department store goods.

You'll also find numerous other department stores throughout Shanghai. Not surprising, you may feel the city is saturated with such shopping places.

SHOPPING CENTERS

In China it's sometimes difficult to separate department stores from shopping centers. Nonetheless, in Shanghai you'll find several places that clearly fit into the western notion of a shopping center—a well defined area composed of separate shops under the same management. Most of these shopping centers either offer exclusive European name-brand goods or products of China's many joint venture companies. Most cater to the growing middle and upper classes.

❏ **Maison Mode:** *1312 Huaihai Road West at Changchu Road.* Shopping in Shanghai will never be the same after this place opened in 1995. The beautiful granite and marble building exudes the class associated with men's and women's suits selling for more than ¥1000 each. This is unquestionably Shanghai's most elegant shopping center. It's where many of the top name European designers have opened shop in Shanghai. It definitely caters to Shanghai's rich, especially those who see the finest in Italian and French clothes and accessories. The indoor part of the complex includes shops such as Bally, Prada, Christian Dior, Louis Feraud, GBR, Cartier, Kenzo, Alfred Dunhill, Hugo Boss, and Modial. The outdoor section includes elegant shops fronting on the street which are not accessible from inside: Salvatore Ferragamo, Mandarina Duck, and Yves Saint Laurent.

❏ **Jin Jiang Dickson Center:** *Corner of Changle Road and Maoming Road* (across from the Jin Jiang Hotel). This three-storey upscale shopping center, complete with fountain and escalators, offers the latest in European fashion. Look for Polo Ralph Lauren, Charles Jourdan, Guy Laroche, Versace, Escada, Cerruti 1881, Mondi, Perry Ellis, Broadway Fur, Bogner, and Gieves and Hawkes. The famous Hong Kong shirt maker, Ascot Chang, also has a shop here.

❑ **Times International:** *550 Huaihai Road.* Located directly across from Isetan Department Store, you can't miss this eye-catching building: it has a huge Omega clock with a four-story pendulum on its front. The only shopping in this five-story building is on the first floor. It consists of the Lane Crawford Designer Shops, a collection of name-brand clothing and footwear boutiques for men: Canali, Hugo Boss, Ferre, Lanvin Missoni, Longchamp, Pal Zilner, and Bruno Magli. There's not much here except for the Lane Crawford name which hopes for further expansion in Shanghai.

❑ **Magnolia Underground Shopping Center:** This is the mystery shopping center for most people who claim to have seen Shanghai! They missed out on one of the most interesting shopping finds in China because they were preoccupied shopping and sightseeing above-ground. If ever there was a symbol of the ending of both the Cold War and the Sino-Soviet conflict, as well as the rise of a new pragmatic and entrepreneurial China, this is it: an underground bomb shelter converted into an upscale shopping mall! Perhaps we should call this "Mao's Mall" since Mao Zedong was responsible for digging such underground infrastructures in China's major cities. But he would probably turn in his grave (mausoleum on Beijing's Tiananmen Square) if he saw such a conversion. This is one of China's most interesting shopping centers and one worth a look just for its uniqueness and a cultural experience. You can easily miss it if you don't know about it or fail to look for it. Our recommendation: visit it while you are visiting the Shanghai Museum; it's only a pleasant three minute walk from the museum entrance or exit. It will give you a totally different impression of above-ground Shanghai. Completed within the past three years and consisting of nearly 200 joint venture shops, it's located underground at the subway entrances and exists on People's Square (between the Municipal Building and Shanghai Museum), the shopping complex actually consists of two shopping centers:

The Hong Kong Shopping Center and the DMall Shopping Center. Both are quite impressive. You can enter the complex from three different subway entrances and exits. As you descend into the underground, you feel you're entering a five-star hotel with its beautiful granite floors and walls. These are some of the most beautiful and well appointed subway entrances and exits we have ever encountered! The **Hong Kong Shopping Center** consists of nearly 80 upscale shops lining a long wide hallway primarily offering fashionable clothes, accessories, and jewelry. Here you'll find an Elle shop for fashion and Paris Enterprise Ltd. for a nice collection of geodes, neck pieces, and jewelry. You'll also find the Pepsi Specialty Store, just in case you want to join the cola wars in Shanghai by advertising your cola preference on Pepsi-monogrammed clothes and accessories. If you need to resupply drinks and snacks, be sure to stop at the Park'N Shop convenience store. As you exit from the Hong Kong Shopping Center, just a few meters outside and to your left is the **DMall Shopping Center**. Consisting of over 100 upscale shops, this is a much more expansive shopping area with a central staircase and several hallways branching out from the center. The theme here again is fashion and accessories. However, you'll also find jewelry stores, a bank, optical shop, food court, coffee shop, and a tea shop in this area. If you're interested in different varieties of tea, be sure to stop at Ten Fu's Tea which is located adjacent to the exit or entrance, depending on how you enter or exit the DMall complex.

❑ **Shanghai International Shopping Center:** *523-527 Huaihai Road.* "International Shopping Center" may be somewhat of a misnomer since it consists of two department stores (the second shop of Shanghai #1 Department Store and Isetan Department Store) and a sixth floor shopping center which includes jewelry, a small foreign language bookstore, and a department store offering furniture, clothes, and bicycles.

❑ **Manhattan Plaza:** *Nanjing Road East near Sofitel Hotel.* This four-storey mall includes lots of shops offering the latest in watches, perfumes, jewelry, and clothes, including casual wear from Benetton and Esprit.

OLD CITY AND YU YUAN MARKET AREA

One of the highlights of shopping in Shanghai is a visit to the Old City which is called **Yu Yuan** or Jade Garden. This is one of the "must visit" sections of the city for tourists as well as locals. Tourists come here to shop, eat, and sightsee; locals come here primarily for the pleasant gardens (Yu Yuan Garden). It's a colorful and fun place to visit, one that can be very crowded on weekends. You can easily spend two to three hours shopping and eating your way through this delightful area.

Located in the southeastern section of the city, you enter the area at Fuyou Road. You'll see a big tourist map and sign on the corner of Li Shui and Fuyou roads which will give you a quick orientation to this rather large and expansive area. If you come here early (around 6am)on a Sunday morning, you can shop the popular **Fuyou Flea Market** which is filled with antiques, collectibles, and junk. Be sure to bargain hard. If you proceed left of the sign along Fuyou Road, turn right a Yu Yuan Xin Road to enter the area (look for Lao Mao Gold Shop on the corner; if you come to KFC on your right, you've come too far). Once you enter this area, you'll probably be impressed with the traditional Chinese architecture, the gardens, the temple, the traditional tea house, the artisans demonstrating their crafts, and over 100 shops and restaurants as well as numerous street vendors. The whole area invites you to explore its many shops. Some of the most popular shops include **Tong Han Chun Tang**, a famous Chinese pharmacy; **Wanli Walking Stick Shop** for a collection of old walking sticks; **Wang Sin Kee Fan Shop**; **Zhang Xiaoquan Scissors Shop**; and **Theater Costume Shop**.

But the real shopping highlight for many visitors is the basement of the **Huabao Building** which houses the "Old Arts and Crafts Market of Shanghai Old Town God Temple." This area consists of a maze of over 100 antique and curio dealers who display their collectibles in small shops. The quality here is good and you may be lucky in finding a rare treasure, from ceramics to snuff bottles.

If time permits, try one of the three excellent restaurants in this area: Nan Xiang (across from the teahouse and great for dumplings); Lakewide Gourmet Restaurant (known for its steamed bread with beat juice); and Green Wave Restaurant (great *dim sum* but you'll need a translator since everything here is in Chinese)

ANTIQUE AND COLLECTIBLE MARKETS

Shanghai has two markets that specialize in antiques and collectibles. For many visitors, these are the highlights of their Shanghai shopping experience. Both markets are filled with a large assortment of goods that reflect the strong "collectible" character of Shanghai. These are fun places to shop. Be sure to bargain hard for everything you purchase.

❑ **Dong Tai Market:** Located at the intersection of Dong Tai Road and Liu He Kou Road, this is Shanghai's largest antique and curio market. Open from 10am to 5pm daily. Hundreds of shops and stalls offer a staggering array of large to small antiques, arts, crafts, bric-a-brac, collectibles, and furniture. If you start at the intersection of Dong Tai Road and Liu He Kou Road, you'll be standing in front of one of Shanghai's best antique furniture and lacquerware shops—**Chine Antiques** (38 Liu He Kou Road, Tel. 6270-1023). This is actually a branch shop of the main shop and warehouse which is located at 1160 Hong Qiao Road. This shop has a very nice collection of antique Chinese furniture, especially wardrobes and chests, and lacquer boxes. Most of the furniture comes from the countryside and is restored at the warehouse. The restoration work is some of the best we found in China. While this is a small branch shop, you can get a good sense of their current inventory, which is very large, by viewing several albums of photos. Be sure to ask to see the photos. Don't worry about shipping—they are experienced in shipping furniture all over the world. If you bargain well, you should be able to get discounts ranging from 20 to 55 percent. Large antique Chinese chests that may sell for US$2,000 to $5,000 in Hong Kong, Singapore, or New York will go for US$400 to $700 here.

Since you are at the intersection, take a short walk along Liu He Kou Road until you come to a few furniture and accessory shops. In particular, on your right look for **G.E. Tang Antique and Curio Co.** at 50 Liu He Kou Road (Tel. 6328-8240). This shop has two floors of very nice furniture, including carved doors, screens, and roof ridges. Across the street is **Shanghai Hai-Chin Industry and Trading Co.** which offers a good selection of small carved items and paintings.

Returning to Dong Tai Road, turn right or left and you'll enter the heart of this market. Most of the shops are on the right, but don't forget to explore the area on the left. This is treasure hunting territory for tourists, expats, and locals alike. You can easily spend two to three hours, or even more, browsing through the many small antique and curio shops and stalls that line both sides of the streets. Each place is crammed with it's own unique collection of antiques, curios, and collectibles. While you may come across some flea market junk, the quality here is generally good and serious for collectors. Porcelain is especially prevalent in many of the shops and stalls, but also look for clocks, baskets, carvings, old tea pots, furniture, boxes, posters, photographs, radios, walking sticks, typewriters, rugs, and small embroidered shoes. The list goes on and on. The shops are open every day except Sunday when vendors take over the street (see below).

❑ **Fuyou Flea Market:** As noted above, this Sunday-only flea market is located along Fuyou Road at the Old City or Yu Yuan Gardens area. Starting at 6am on Sunday mornings, vendors spread out their antiques and assorted collectibles on the ground for potential buyers who haggle over quality and prices. If you're visiting Shanghai on a Sunday, you may want to join other tourists and expatriates who frequent this market and discover an occasional treasure.

FAMILY MUSEUMS AND EXHIBITION HOUSES

Shanghai's reputation for antiques and collectibles is uniquely represented in the presence of several family museums and exhibition houses. Each tends to specialize in a particular type of collectible. Serious collectors and shoppers should seek out these places, some of which may be difficult to find on your own. Several are located in suburban and nearby rural areas. The major such museums and houses include:

❑ **Shanghai Folk Collection Exhibition House**
   1551 Zhongshan Road South

❑ **Bao Wanrong Theatrical Costumes Exhibition**
   No. 11, Lane 138, Rushan Road, Pudong

❑ **Chen Baoci's Butterfly Exhibition**
   No. 2, Lane 77, Zichang Road, Pudong

❑ **Chen Baoding Calculation Instruments Exhibition**
No. 8, Lane 378, Jianguo Road West

❑ **Chen Yutang's Collection of Ancient Jars**
326 Xizang Road South

❑ **Du Baojun's Collection of Rain Flower Stones**
No. 268, Caoyang Village 5

❑ **Fang Binghai Family Collection of Ancient Cases**
F/3, No. 4, Building 10, Honglu Sub-area

❑ **Huang Guodong's Collection of Paper Fan Coverings**
No. 1, Lane 47, Ninghe Road, Nanshi District

❑ **Hu Renfu's Collection of Root Sculptures**
No. 13, Lane 470, Loushanguan Road

❑ **Peng Tianmin's Collection of Natural Models**
No. 23, Lane 60, Linyin Road

❑ **Xi Binjie's Collection of Boat Models**
No. 131, Lane 1143, East Yuhang Road

❑ **Huang Genbao's Collection of Miniature Musical Instruments**
No. 6, Lane 41, Daling Road and Pailou Road

❑ **Wang Xianbao's Collection of Nine Dragon Fans**
No. 1125, Wayu Matou Street

❑ **Wei Zhi'an's Museum of Agates**
No. 6, Lane 21, Balin Road

❑ **Xu Sihai's House of Tea Art**
No. 332 Xingguo Road

❑ **Yu Liuliang's Numismatic Collection**
267 Hongzhen Laojie

❑ **Zheng Genhai's Collection of Rare Shells**
No. 42, Laoshan Village 2, Pudong

❑ **Zhao Jinzhi's Museum of Golden Keys**
11 Xueye Road, Pudong

For more information on private collectors, including names, addresses, and specialty items, we recommend visiting the following Web site which includes a current listing of private collections: *http://www.sh.com/play/museums1.htm*. If you're in the market for old clocks, watches, matchbox labels, abacuses, tea sets, boat models, chopsticks, porcelain, opera masks, cameras, sculptures, water containers, coins, and lots of knick knacks, these are the people to visit. You're also likely to have a cultural experience meeting new people with such specialized interests.

SPECIAL SHOPS AND SHOPPING OPPORTUNITIES

Shanghai offers several other special shopping opportunities you may be interested in pursuing. Some of our favorites include:

❑ **Shanghai Arts and Crafts Institute:** *79 Fengyang Road, Tel. 6437-3454.* If you enjoy meeting artists, seeing arts and crafts demonstrations, and making purchases at the point of production, and especially in the ambience of an old mansion, this is a "must see" place for any visitor to Shanghai. This Institute may well be one of the highlights of your visit to Shanghai. Housed in an old mansion that was converted and opened in 1956 to become the present-day Institute, today this place consists of 19 studios producing more than 30 different types of arts and crafts as well as three shop areas offering a variety of handicrafts, souvenirs, antiques, and curios. The purpose of the Institute is to create new arts and crafts themes and develop designs that can be disseminated elsewhere in China. You can visit each studio where you can meet the artisans and see them at work producing various arts and crafts: lacquerware, inlaid screens, oil paintings, lanterns, jade and ink-stone carvings, dough figurines, micro carvings (on porcelain, bamboo, and ivory), woolen needlepoint, silk embroidery, silk flower making, paper cutting, and T-shirt painting (for ¥90 you can have your name printed on a T-shirt). Since the Institute is partially self-supporting, everything here is for sale, including what's being produced in each of the studios (cashier at the top of the stairs on second floor). You also can commission works to your specifications. However, most visitors do their shopping in the three rooms set aside on the first floor as the Institute's shop. As you enter the building, the room on the right includes antique ceramics, most of which are being re-sold from other antique shops. The antiques are certified with the government's red-wax seal affixed. The room in the middle specializes in ceramics and screens. The room on the left includes lacquer boxes, embroidery, snuff bottles, clothes, and rugs. The Institute provides packing and shipping services.

❑ **Shanghai Museum Shops:** *201 Renmin Da Dao, Tel. 6372-3500.* Located at People's Square (same area as the new Municipal Hall and Performing Arts Center), this relatively new museum is one of the great prides of China and one of the best museums we've ever encountered. Shaped like a giant *ding* (food vessel), the granite building houses two shops well worth visiting. The shop to the left of the entrance specializes in books, paintings, cards, CDS, videos, paper cuts, chops, and calligraphy supplies. The shop to the right, the Shanghai Museum Shop, offers a good selection of antique reproductions (ceramics, bronzes, paintings, and calligraphy found in the museum's collection) as well as jewelry, jade carvings, cloisonne, scarves, postcards, and T-shirts. Both shops have a lot more meaning after you visit the exquisite displays in this outstanding museum.

❑ **Foreign Language Bookstore:** 390 Fuzhou Street. This is the largest foreign language bookstore in Shanghai. The first floor includes CDS, audiocassettes, pens, and English language books for foreigners. It includes a small section of English books on Shanghai. It also includes some books in Japanese and French. The second floor includes foreign language books for locals, especially students studying English.

❑ **Shanghai Philatelic Corporation:** *244 Nanjing Road East.* This famous stamp company is a "must visit" place for serious stamp collectors.

❑ **Hengdali Watch and Clock Company:** *262 Nanjing Road East.* Well known and reliable watch company. Represents Rolex, Rado, Longine, Omega, and Tudor.

❑ **Duoyun Art Gallery:** *422 Nanjing Road East, Tel. 6322-3410.* Serious artists and art collectors visit this well known shop (operating for nearly 90 years) that specializes in calligraphy supplies, paintings, antiques, and books. The first floor is primarily devoted to calligraphy supplies and handicrafts. The really good stuff, however, is found on the second (paintings) and third (antiques) floors. The higher you walk up the flights of stairs, the better the quality of art and antiques. We especially like the selections on third floor (antiques, fans, and small ceramics). The quality here is outstanding which is also reflected in the very high prices. For serious collectors with serious money.

❑ **Shanghai Jingdezhen Porcelain Artware Company:** *1175-1183 Nanjing Road West.* Located near the Shanghai JC Mandarin and Portman Ritz-Carlton Hotels, this long established and reputable corner shop ("Model Unit") offers two rooms of porcelain, from dishes and figurines to collectible antique porcelain vases. Also includes a collection of tea pots, jade, and wood boats. Commissioned to sell antiques.

❑ **Changxin Old Ware Store:** *1297 Huaihai Road.* Located across the street from the exclusive Maison Mode shopping center, this is an old, well established shop offering two small rooms of quality antiques: furniture, lacquer boxes, and ceramics. We discovered one of the most gorgeous antique ceramic pots here, but the ¥35,000 price tag was not in our budget!

❑ **Zhang Xiao Quan Knives and Scissors:** *496 Nanjing Road East.* Interesting old shop that offers over 300 kinds of locally produced scissors, knives, and meat cleavers in all sizes and shapes. Not great quality but the prices are real cheap and the shop is somewhat of a cultural experience. US$.50 to $2.00 will get you a cute but somewhat crudely made Shanghai scissors to meet your travel needs as well as serve as an inexpensive souvenir.

❑ **Chine Antiques:** *38 Liu He Kou Road* (small shop in Dong Tai Market) *and 1660 Hong Qiao Road* (large shop), *Tel. 6270-1023.* Excellent quality antique Chinese furniture and lacquer boxes. Huge inventory of chests and cabinets. Does excellent restoration work. Will ship worldwide.

❑ **Shanghai Carpet General Factory (T&D Arts Plaza):** This is reputed to be Shanghai's largest carpet factory (it has only three). At the same time, this is a 2-in-1 factory and shop complex. The first two floors are devoted to arts and crafts. The third floor is a carpet factory and shop. Most visitors start at the third floor where they can see artisans weaving wool tapestries and trimming wool carpets. The tapestry room is especially interesting. Here you'll see young men and women weaving tapestries from photos. If you're interested in having a tapestry made from your favorite photo, here's the place to commission one. They price the tapestries by the desired density of the weave (knots per foot). At the other end of the hall is a large carpet shop where you can purchase different qualities and designs of both wool and silk carpets. The labeled prices seem high, but that's not unusual for a carpet shop anywhere in the world (think in terms of your friendly mattress shop back home where mattresses are always on sale!). We recommend going for at least a 50 percent discount, if not more, for most of these carpets. However, you may not be impressed with the quality, designs, and colors. Some are really dreadful, destined for someone else's culture! The handicraft shops on first and second floors have a wide range of typical "Friendship Shop" goods for tourists. The second floor shop is primarily devoted to embroidered products, clothes, silk scarves, and neckties. The expansive first floor shop includes wood carvings, embroidery, cloisonne, jewelry, paintings, dough figurines, chops, and luggage (Louis Vuitton knock-offs) as well as purses (Chanel knock-offs at US$100 to $380, depending on your bargaining skills—but definitely not in the Chanel league for quality).

ACCOMMODATIONS

Shanghai offers some of the best accommodations in all of China. It boasts several five-star hotels as well as many four-star hotels. Most of these are joint venture hotels that are managed according to international service standards. Most boast excellent facilities, from restaurants, discos, and bars to business centers, shopping arcades, health centers, and conference centers. Many host special events and exhibitions.

FIVE-STAR

❑ **Shanghai Hilton:** *250 Hua Shan Road, Shanghai 200-040, Tel. (86-21) 6248-0000 or Fax (86-21) 6248-3848.* Located in the commercial center of Shanghai, this is one of the best located hotels for access to Shanghai's major shopping area, especially to the shops along upscale Huai Hua Road. It's also the city's first joint venture hotel. The Hilton's 775 rooms and suites offer true five-star luxury in the area that was once the French Quarter. From here it is a short stroll to Nanjing Road which leads to the Bund. The gleaming marble lobby is filled with light from the Atrium Cafe, and the walls are tastefully decorated with Chinese tapestries, screens, and prints. Four Executive Floors feature up-graded rooms and suites and an executive lounge with complimentary American breakfast, afternoon tea and pre-dinner cocktails. Nine restaurants offering a range of Continental as well as Asian cuisines assure the guests will be well-fed. There is also the Gourmet Corner which offers a tempting array of take-out specialities from the pastry and butcher shops. A fully-equipped gym, sauna, streamroom, whirlpool, tennis court and indoor pool are open to hotel guests. A full-service business center caters to business travelers. Two lobby clothing and accessory shops, including Fendi, and a small shopping arcade are found at the lobby level. A fleet of chauffeur-driven limousines is available and there is a scheduled shuttle to the airport.

❏ **Westin Tai Ping Yang:** *5 Qun Yi Nan Road, Shanghai 200335, Tel. (86-21) 6275-8888 or Fax (86-21) 6275-5420.* The Westin is located midway between the international airport (7 kilometers) and downtown (6 kilometers) and next door to the Shanghai International Trade Center, the International Exhibition Center, and the Shanghaimart which opened in mid-1997. It's also located adjacent to the four-star Yangtze New World Hotel which is directly across the street from a new branch of the Friendship Store (has a good supermarket on first floor). The lobby feels spacious with its high ceiling and is tastefully decorated with large wall hangings of a modern Eastern motif. The Westin has 578 guestrooms including 39 suites and four floors of Executive Club rooms. Now in its sixth year of operation, the Westin has just completed a refurbishment of all guestrooms and public areas. Computers are provided in the Executive Suites. Five restaurants offer a choice of Continental or Asian cuisines including the Compass Rose buffet which serves Mediterranean fare with a small selection of Asian dishes in an elegant European-country style setting. A fully-equipped Business Center, limousine service, and fitness center are available. Guests also are offered direct access to the Shanghai International Country Club, an 18-hole golf course designed by Robert Trent-Jones Jr., located 45 minutes from the hotel. The shopping arcade on the second floor features several nice shops selling furniture, porcelain and other quality Chinese arts and crafts.

❑ **Portman Ritz-Carlton:** *1376 Nanjing Xi Lu, Shanghai 200040, Tel. (86-21) 6279-8888 or Fax (86-21) 6279-8887.* Located in the Shanghai Centre, this imposing 48-story hotel is located opposite the Shanghai Exhibition Centre; many business, shopping, and entertainment facilities are found within the complex. Formerly known as the Portman Shangri-La, this impressive property recently became part of the Ritz-Carlton chain. The enclosed drive-up is impressive with its powerful columns and open exterior area make for a grand entry way. Entrance into the hotel is via an enclosed bridge walkway which opens onto a lobby decorated with two massive stone lions and two large terra cotta horse replicas stand at the entry to Zhou's Bar. The 600 rooms and suites are some of the most spacious in the city. The Ritz-Carlton Club rooms and suites provide extra pampering for both business and leisure travelers. Guests enjoy personalized concierge service, private 24-hour check-in and late check-out, special in-room amenities, one-time complimentary pressing service, exclusive butler service and a private lounge serving five complimentary food and beverage presentations daily. Four restaurants offer a range of Continental and Asian cuisines. The Chinese Restaurant serves seafood, Cantonese delicacies and Shanghainese village dishes. The Japanese Restaurant features a sushi bar and teppanyaki grill. The Grill serves hearty American grilled fare and The Café is open 24-hours daily serving a range of Oriental and Western cuisine in a relaxed setting. Full business services and a comprehensive health club and spa offer exercise equipment, aerobics room, sauna, indoor and outdoor pools, squash, racket ball and tennis courts. The second level of the hotel has a small bookstore and a gift shop which sells art, furniture, and lacquer baskets as well as a few knick-knacks. Other shopping facilities include a supermarket, a few name-brand import shops, and a stone art shop which are in the shopping complex attached to the hotel. Several major airlines, such as Northwest, All Nippon, Singapore, Thai, and Dragonair, maintain their offices in the shopping complex.

Shanghai's other five-star hotels well worth considering for accommodations, dining, and shopping include:

❑ **Garden Hotel Shanghai**
58 Maoming Road South
Tel. (86-21) 6415-1111

❑ **Jinjiang Tower**
161 Changle Road
Tel. (86-21) 6415-1188

❑ **Shanghai JC Mandarin Hotel**
1225 Nanjing Road West
Tel. (86-21) 6279-1888

❑ **Sheraton Hua Ting Hotel & Tower Shanghai**
1200 Caoxi Road North
Tel. (86-21) 6439-1000

FOUR-STAR

❑ **Galaxy Hotel**
888 Zhingshan Road
Tel. (86-21) 7275-5888

❑ **Holiday Inn Crowne Plaza**
388 Panyu Road
Tel. (86-21) 6252-8888

❑ **Hotel Nikko Longhai Shanghai**
2451 Hongqiao Road
Tel. (86-21) 6268-9111

❑ **International Equatorial Hotel**
65 Yanan Road West
Tel. (86-21) 6248-1688

❑ **Jianguo Hotel**
439 Caoxi Road North
Tel. (86-21) 6439-9299

❑ **Jinjiang Hotel**
59 Maoming Road South
Tel. (86-21) 6258-2582

❑ **Peace Hotel**
20 Nanjing Road East
Tel. (86-21) 6321-6888

❑ **Rainbow Hotel**
2000 Yanan Road West
Tel. (86-21) 6275-3388

❑ **Radisson SAS Lansheng Hotel**
1000 Quyang Road
Tel. (86-21) 6542-8000

❑ **Sofitel Hyland Shanghai Hotel**
505 Nanjing Road East
Tel. (86-21) 6351-5888

❑ **Yangtze New World Hotel**
2099 Yanan Road West
Tel. (86-21) 6275-0000

RESTAURANTS

Reflecting Shanghai's cosmopolitan nature, the food in Shanghai is an interesting blend of Chinese and Western cuisines. Fresh vegetables and seafood, especially the popular Shanghai crab, take center stage in both Chinese and Western restaurants. Look for lots of dumplings and noodles as well as rice.

Shanghai dishes tend to be sauteed, fried, grilled, braised, and steamed with the heavy use of sugar, oil, ginger, Shaoxing wine, and soy. Many Chinese from other regions note that Shanghai dishes are too oily and sweet for their more refined tastes.

Shanghai has several famous old restaurants: **Lao Fandina** in the old city and the **Dragon and Phoenix** in the Peace Hotel.

Look for some of the city's best restaurants in the major joint venture hotels. More and more international chefs are operating the kitchens of these hotels.

CHINESE—Beijing

❑ **Ge Yuan, Yu Yuan, Tao Yuan**
Rainbow Hotel
2000 Yanan Road West
Tel. 6275-3388
11:30am - 2:00pm; 5:30pm - 11:30pm

❑ **Shanghai Jinjiang Shangri-La Restaurant**
2/F, Union Building
100 Yanan Road East
Tel. 6326-5381
11:30am - midnight

❑ **Yan Yun Lou Restaurant**
755 Nanjing Road East
Tel. 6322-3298
11:00am - 10:30pm

CHINESE—Cantonese

❑ **Bai Yu Lan Chinese Restaurant**
Garden Hotel
58 Maoming Road
Tel. 6433-1111
7:00am - 9:30am; 11:30am - 2:30pm; 5:30pm - 10:00pm

❑ **Dynasty Restaurant**
Yangtze New World Hotel
2099 Yanan Road West
Tel. 6275-0000
11:00am - 12:30pm; 6:00pm - 10:30pm

❑ **Emerald Garden**
Westin Tai Ping Yang Hotel
5 Zungi Road
Tel. 6275-8888
11:30am - 2:30pm; 5:30pm - 10:00pm

❑ **Golden Phoenix**
Hotel Equatorial Shanghai
65 Yanan Road
Tel. 6248-1688
11:30am - 2:00pm; 5:00pm - 1:00pm

❑ **Guan Yue Tai**
Sheraton Hua Ting
1200 Caoxi Road North
Tel. 6439-1000
11:30am - 2:00pm; 5:30pm - 10:00pm

❑ **Hai Yue Ting Cantonese Restaurant**
Hotel Sofitel Hyland Shanghai
5/F, 505 Nanjing Road East
Tel. 6351-5888
6:00am - 9:00am; 11:30am - 2:30pm;
5:30pm - 10:30pm

❑ **Jinjiang Food Street Restaurant**
Jinjiang Hotel
59 Maoming Road South
Tel. 6258-2582, Ext. 791
8:00am - 2:30pm; 5:00pm - 11:30pm

❑ **Peach Garden**
Shanghai JC Mandarin
1225 Nanjing Road West
Tel. 6279-1888
11:30am - 2:30pm; 5:30pm - 10:30pm

❑ **Sui Yuan**
Shanghai Hilton
250 Huashan Road
Tel. 6248-0000; 11:30am - 2:00pm;
6:00pm - 10:30pm

❑ **Tian Yuan**
Holiday Inn Crowne Plaza
388 Panyu Road
Tel. 6252-8888, Ext. 12023
6:00am - 10:00am; 11:30am - 2:30pm;
5:30pm - 10:30pm

❑ **White Cloud**
Jianguo Hotel Shanghai
439 Cao Xi Road North
Tel. 6439-9299, Ext. 3315
6:30am - 10:00am; 11:00am - 4:00pm;
5:00pm - 10:00pm

CHINESE—Chaozhou

❏ **Chao Zhou Garden**
Yangtze New World Hotel
2099 Yanan Road West
Tel. 6275-0000
11:00am - 2:30pm; 5:30pm - 10:30pm

❏ **Five Grand Wonders**
Jiang Guo Hotel Shanghai
439 Cao Xi Road North
Tel. 6439-9299
10:30am - 2:00pm; 6:00pm - 9:00pm

❏ **Fortune Rim Nam**
Hotel Equatorial Shanghai
65 Yanan Road West
Tel. 6248-1688

CHINESE—Shanghainese

❏ **Gui Hua Restaurant**
110 Yu Yuan Road
Tel. 6373-2119
8:30am - 10:00pm

❏ **Hai Yu Lan Ge Shanghainese Restaurant**
Hotel Sofitel Hyland Shanghai
3/F, 505 Nanjing Road East
Tel. 6351-5888
11:30am - 10:30pm

❏ **Pearl Garden Restaurant**
Regent Club
1/F, 556 Fuzhou Road
Tel. 6320-5496
11:30am - 4:00am

❏ **Shanghai Old Town Restaurant**
(Lao Fan Dian)
242 Fuyou Road
Tel. 6328-9850
11:00am - 2:00pm; 5:00pm - 10:00pm

CHINESE—Sichuan

❏ **Bamboo Garden Jinjiang Tower**
161 Chang Le Road
Tel. 6433-4488
7:00am - 10:00am; 11:30am - 2:00pm; 5:30pm - 10:00pm

❏ **Fu Rong Zhen**
Holiday Inn Crowne Plaza
388 Panyu Road
Tel. 6252-8888, Ext. 12007
11:30am - 2:30pm; 5:30pm - 10:30pm

❏ **Sichuan Court**
Shanghai Hilton
250 Huashan Road
Tel. 6248-0000
6:00pm - 10:30pm

CONTINENTAL

❏ **The Belvedere**
Hotel Equatorial Shanghai
65 Yanan Road West
Tel. 6248-1688
11:30am - 2:30pm; 6:30pm - 10:30pm

❏ **Brasserie Tatler**
Shanghai JC Mandarin
1225 Nanjing Road West
Tel. 6279-1888
24 hours

❏ **Cafe Bistro**
Westin Tai Ping Yang
5 Zunyi Road South
Tel. 6275-8888
24 hours

❏ **Cheers**
Holiday Inn Crown Plaza Shanghai
388 Panyu Road
Tel. 6252-8888, Ext. 13010
5:00pm - 1:00am

❑ **Compass Rose**
Westin Tai Ping Yang
5 Zunyi Road South
Tel. 6275-8888
6:00pm - 10:30pm

❑ **Continental Room**
Garden Room
58 Maoming Road South
Tel. 6433-1111
11:30am - 2:30pm; 5:30pm - 10:00pm

❑ **Salle d'Elegance**
Rainbow Hotel
2000 Yanan Road West
Tel. 6275-3388
11:30am - 2:00pm; 5:30pm - 9:30pm

FRENCH

❑ **Brasserie Orientale**
Hotel Sofitel Hyland Shanghai
505 Nanjing Road East
Tel. 6351-5888
6:000am - midnight

❑ **The Bund**
Jinjiang Tower
161 Chang Le Road
Tel. 6433-4488
6:30am - 10:30pm

❑ **L'iris Grill**
Jianguo Hotel
439 Cao Xi Road North
Tel. 6439-9299, Ext. 3398
6:00am - 10:30pm

❑ **Tappan Grill**
Shanghai Hilton
250 Huashan Road
Tel. 6248-0000
11:30am - 2:00pm (Mon.-Fri.); 6:00pm - 10:30pm (Sat.)

INDIAN

❑ **Tandoor Indian Restaurant**
Jinjiang Hotel, New South Building
59 Mao Ming Road South
Tel. 6258-2582, Ext. 9301
11:00am - 2:30pm; 5:30pm - 11:00pm

ITALIAN

❑ **DaVinci's**
Shanghai Hilton
250 Huashan Road
Tel. 6248-0000, Ext. 8622
Noon - 2:00pm; 6:00pm - 10:30pm

❑ **Giovanni's**
Westin Tai Ping Yang
5 Zunyi Road South
Tel. 6275-8888
6:00pm - 10:30pm

❑ **Luigi's**
Sheraton Hua Ting
1200 Cao Xi Road North
Tel. 6439-1000
5:30pm - 10:30pm

JAPANESE

❑ **Benkay**
Hotel Nikko Longbai
2451 Hongqiao Road
Tel. 6255-9111
11:30am - 2:30pm; 6:00pm - 10:00pm

❑ **Ginza Restaurant & Karaoke Bar**
Jinjiang Hotel
59 Maoming Road South
Tel. 6258-2582, Ext. 792
11:00am - 2:30pm; 5:00pm - 11:30pm

❑ **Inagiku**
Westin Tai Ping Yang Hotel
5 Zunyi Road South
Tel. 6275-8888
6:30am - 8:30am; 11:30am - 2:00pm; 5:30pm - 10:00pm

WESTERN

❑ **Blue Heaven Revolving Restaurant**
Jinjiang Tower
161 Changle Road
Tel. 6415-1188
Tel. 7:00am - 10:00am; 6:00pm - 10:00pm

❑ **Hard Rock Cafe**
A05 & 110, Retail Plaza, Shanghai Centre
1376 Nanjing Road West
Tel. 6279-8133
11:00am - 2:00am (Sun.-Thurs.)
11:00am - 3:00am (Fri.-Sat.)

❑ **Rose**
Garden Hotel
58 Maoming Road South
Tel. 6415-1111
7:00am - 9:30am; 11:30am - 2:30pm; 5:30pm - 10:00pm

❑ **Tony Roma's A Place For Ribs**
109, Retail Plaza, Shanghai Centre
1376 Nanjing Road West
Tel. 6279-7129

SEEING THE SIGHTS

Shanghai abounds with sites of interest to visitors. While it can date its history to more than 6,000 years, except for one fabulous museum, this history is not well preserved for sightseeing. Unlike many other cities that offer numerous historical sites from earlier centuries and dynasties, Shanghai's sites tend to be more recent, reflecting its 19th and 20th century European architectural heritage as well as more recent joint venture initiatives and infrastructure projects. After all, this is a relatively new city—developed in response to post-1842 political developments—compared to many other major cities in China. You'll find, for example, over 300 Western-style homes, commercial buildings, and churches dating from this period. Many of them are included on a walking architectural tour of Shanghai. Much of Shanghai's sightseeing also centers around shopping, especially its colorful markets.

You may want to take advantage of the new **Jin Jiang City Tour**. This is an air-conditioned bus tour that runs every one-half hour. Departing in front of the Garden Hotel, it's a two-hour guided city tour that enables you to get off at various stops whenever you like and then pick up other buses at a later time. This flexible city tour costs only 20 yuan. The tour buses run from 9am to 9pm, and tickets are good for the whole day. This is only such city tour available in China. Be sure to check if it is still operating since it may suspend operations.

Shanghai's major sightseeing attractions and activities include the following;

❑ **Shanghai Museum:** *201 Renmin Da Dao, Tel. 6372-3500.* Put this museum at the very top of your "must see in China and Shanghai" list. Shanghai and its friends have poured tons of money into making this one of the world's finest museums. It's located on the south side of People's Square. Constructed in gray granite and occupying 10,000 square meters of exhibition space, this beautiful new museum is shaped like a *ding* (food vessel). You may not be prepared for this museum. It's awesome. If you visit only one museum in all of China, make sure it's this one. It's unlike any other museum you'll encounter in China. Extremely user-friendly with multi-language audios keyed to many displays, a multi-media computer tour guide, and lecture rooms with a spontaneous interpretation system, this is one of the best museums we've ever encountered anywhere. Wonderful displays, terrific audio explanations, and truly a first-class operation. Opened in December 1995, its eleven permanent galleries display over 120,000 Chinese cultural relics: bronzes, ceramics, sculptures, paintings, calligraphy, furniture, jades, seals, coins, and minority arts. It also includes three temporary exhibition halls and hosts special exhibits from abroad. You can easily spend hours here exploring Chinese history and culture. You'll walk away from this museum much more knowledgeable about Chinese history and a renewed appreciation for what a truly outstanding museum is and can be. Our only regrets—we should have stopped here early in our visit to Shanghai, and we should have set aside a full day to really cover all of the museum. And, as mentioned earlier, don't forget to stop at the two shops on the first floor. There's great shopping here, too!

❑ **The Bund:** *Zhongshan Road.* A showcase of Shanghai's architectural heritage of beautiful old buildings in a variety of architectural styles, this famous and attractive boardwalk along the west bank of the Huangpu River has been recently reconstructed, elevated, and landscaped. A great place to stroll day and night to people watch, hold hands, or just enjoy the ambience of the river and architecture. Be sure to see The Bund at night when the buildings are illuminated and Shanghai literally becomes a "city of lights" along the Huangpu River.

❑ **Dr. Sun Yat-sen Residence:** *7 Xiangshan Lu.* This is the 1918 to 1924 residence of Dr. Sun Yat-sen who lead the 1911 revolution that ended dynastic rule in China. Converted to a museum, the home includes his library of 2,700 books and numerous photos and memorabilia.

❑ **First National Congress of the Chinese Communist Party Meeting Site:** *76 Xingye Lu.* The Chinese Communist Party was officially founded in Shanghai on July 23, 1921 at the home of one of its founders which is located in the former French Concession. Visit this historic site where you can see photos of the revolutionaries, a first copy of Marx's Communist Manifesto translated into Chinese, and a room with a table and 12 stools used by Mao Zedong and his comrades for their initial meetings.

❑ **Huangpu River Cruise:** *Zhongshan Road.* Take a pleasant cruise along the Huangpu River. The round-trip covers 60 kilometers between The Bund and the Yangtze River. Great way to see the bustling and rapidly expanding port facilities that contribute to making Shanghai one of the most important cities in China's overall economic development.

❑ **The Old City and Yu Garden:** *132 Anren Road.* Originally built in the 14th century to secure the community against Japanese pirates, the walls of the Old City are still evident in this well defined commercial and residential community located in the southeast section of the city. The shophouses that define this charming yet crowded area have been restored to their traditional Ming-style architecture. The area boasts a popular

Sunday morning street bazaar (Fuyou Flea Market), shops jam-packed with products of interest to locals and visitors alike, some great restaurants, the city's popular Yu Garden (Yu Yuan), a delightful teahouse, and an ancient temple (Old Town God Temple). The gardens actually lie to north of the Old Town area behind high walls. The five acres (2 hectares) of charming Suzhou-style gardens, complete with ponds filled with colorful carp and lotus, 30 pavilions, stone dragons, flowers, and arching trees, draw numerous visitors who come here to enjoy the ambience and explore the nearby restaurants, shops, and temple. The beautiful old two-storey Huxin-ting Teahouse, which is built over a pond at the entrance to Yu Garden and connected by the zig-zagging Bridge of Nine Turns, is especially popular with workers and retired people who stop here for refreshments, watch people, and enjoy the ambience of the area.

❏ **Great World Entertainment Centre:** *1 Xizhang Road.* China's largest cultural and entertainment center for opera, magic shows, acrobatics, and concerts.

❏ **People's Square:** Formerly a horse racing track, this large square is anchored by the Municipal Government Office, the new Performing Arts Center, and the Shanghai Museum. Includes attractive landscaping and fountains. If you go underground, you'll discover one of Shanghai's best kept shopping secrets—what we earlier called "Mao's Malls," two elegant shopping centers with over 200 joint venture shops.

❏ **Oriental Pearl Broadcasting & TV Tower:** Located in the new city of Pudong on the east side of the Huangpu River, this imposing 468-meter tower is the third tallest in the world and the tallest in Asia. In addition to being a television and radio tower, its a multi-functional structure offering entertainment, accommodations, a restaurant, and an observation tower.

❏ **Jade Buddha Temple:** *170 Anyuan Road.* Includes two white-jade statues of Buddha as well as 7,000 volumes of block-printed teachings from the Qing Dynasty.

❏ **Jin'an Temple:** *1686 Nanjing Road West.* Nearly 1,700 year old, this is a working Buddhist monastery and temple.

❑ **Shanghai Art Gallery:** *456 Nanjing Road West.* Exhibits the works of Shanghai artists. Can purchase what you see and like.

❑ **Shanghai Zoo:** *2381 Hongqiao Road.* Closed on Tuesday. Covers an area of 100 acres. Displays over 350 species, including the giant panda, golden-haired monkey, and Chinese Tiger.

❑ **Christian Churches:** Shanghai's community of 100,000 Christians attend several of the cities many churches. If you visit Shanghai during the Christmas season, you may want to attend one of the city's many Christian services. Some of the most interesting church structures of interest to tourists include:

- **Community Church:** *53 Hengshan Road.* Built in 1925, this British countryside building is used for services of Shanghai's Protestant denominations. City's largest Protestant church.

- **Xijiahua Cathedral:** *158 Puxi Road.* Originally constructed in 1837 and significantly expanded in 1906, today this Mediaeval Roman building seats 3,000 people. It's the main cathedral for Shanghai's Roman Catholic community.

ENTERTAINMENT

There's lots to do in Shanghai in addition to shopping and sightseeing. Given the strong business orientation of this city, you'll find many bars, discos, and nightclubs along with more traditional Chinese opera, ballet, acrobatics, classical and jazz concerts, and theaters. In many respects, Shanghai is China's cultural and entertainment capital. It boasts 15 professional performing groups (opera, ballet, music, comedy, acrobatics) and over 40 specialist companies. Always check with your hotel concierge or the local newspapers (*Wenhuibao* and the *Shanghai Evening News* are in Chinese and the *Shanghai Star* is in English) for the latest information on what's going on in Shanghai's entertainment world. Entertainment highlights include:

❑ **Old Jazz Band:** *Peace Hotel, 20 Nanjing Road East.* Individuals in search of entertainment associated with the Old Shanghai should plan an evening drinking and dancing at the famous art deco Peace Hotel and its Tudor-style bar. Consisting of aging musicians who played here in the pre-revolutionary period (and reportedly practiced in secret during the Cultural Revolution), this band continues to delight crowds by belting out the old tunes nightly from 8:00pm to 2:00am. The cover charge is ¥42.

❑ **Shanghai Centre Theatre:** *1376 Nanjing Road West, Tel. 6279-8600.* This 1001-seat, multi-purpose theater is the center for numerous operas, ballets, concerts, dramas, and films. Check in the local newspaper or with your hotel concierge to find out what's playing during your visit to Shanghai. If you're staying at the Portman Ritz-Carlton Hotel, you're lucky. The theater is located within this huge hotel, office, and residential complex.

❑ **Shanghai Concert Hall:** *523 Yanan Road East, Tel. 6327-4383.* China's best symphony orchestra, the Shanghai Symphony Orchestra, gives frequent concerts here as does the Shanghai Philharmonic Orchestra and the Shanghai Ballet Troupe.

❑ **Shanghai Acrobatic Theatre:** *400 Nanjing Road West, Tel. 6327-3574.* This popular acrobatics and circus theater in the round puts on spectacular performances complete with tigers, monkeys, and dogs.

❑ **Discos:** Shanghai has plenty of discos, most of which are attached to major hotels. All have cover charges and the usual set-up of disk jockey, loud music, and blazing lights:

- **JJ Disco:** 1127 Yanan Road East (near the Hilton)
- **Reading Room:** Shanghai JC Mandarin
- **Passion Disco:** Galazy Hotel
- **Nicole's:** Sheraton Hua Ting
- **Casablanca:** Hongqiao Hotel
- **Starlight:** Yangtze New World
- **The Talk of the Town:** Hotel Equatorial

❑ **Bars and Lounges:** Like discos, most of these establishments are attached to the major joint venture hotels:

- **Penthouse Bar and Lounge:** Hilton
- **Judy's Place:** 176 MaoMing Lu

- **Charlie's:** Holiday Inn Crowne Plaza
- **Trader's Pub:** Shanghai JC Mandarin
- **Top Ten:** Portman Shangri-La
- **Oasis Lounge:** Garden Hotel
- **Brewery:** Sofitel Hyland
- **Chelsea Bar:** Westin Tai Ping Yang
- **Hollywood Bar:** Radisson SAS Lansheng

BEYOND SHANGHAI

Many visitors enjoy visiting several places within a one to three hour drive of Shanghai. Most of these places are renowned for their beautiful scenery and ambience, from canals to gardens. Some of the most interesting and popular destinations include:

❑ **Hangzhou:** Located nearly four hours from Shanghai by train or a half hour by plane, Hangzhou's West Lake is one of China's most beautiful areas—lovely landscapes, arched stone bridges, and tree-lined streets. Visitors come here to enjoy the scenery and fresh air. If you plan to stay over, which is a good idea, the two best hotels operated by the New World Hotels International include the 388-room **Shangri-La Hotel** (78 Beishan Lu) and the 549-room **Dragon Hotel** (Shuguang Lu).

❑ **Suzhou:** Located within two hours driving distance from Shanghai, this is China's most famous garden and canal city. This small city has nearly 100 gardens that both local and foreign tourists come to photograph. The canal setting of the city has helped retain the traditional architecture of Suzhou since, like Venice, the structure of the city cannot be easily altered by development given the extensive networks of canals, bridges, and narrow tree-lined streets and walkways. Except for the hordes of tourists that descend on this city, this is one of the most charming cities to visit in China. It's also one of China's most scenic cities for artists who come here to paint pictures of it's bridges, canals, and homes. You'll find lots of opportunities here to shop for arts and crafts. The best part of Suzhou is just walking its streets and bridges to enjoy the ambience of the canals and white-washed homes. It has real character, unlike many other cities. It is also known for its silk. If you decide to say overnight, the two best hotels are **Bamboo Grove Hotel** (108 Zhu Hui Lu) and the **Suzhou Hotel** (115 Shi Quan Lu).

❑ **Zhou Zhuang:** Located approximately 70 kilometers west of Shanghai, this is a relatively new tourist site with a town atmosphere similar to more crowded Suzhou. Built around canals with picturesque bridges, this ancient town was designated in 1993 as one of Jiangsu Province's major historical and cultural towns. With a history dating more than 1000 years, the town includes the famous stone Key Bridge (Double Bridge), Yuan Bridge (Bridge of Wealth and Peace), and Zhengfeng Bridge that date to the Yuan, Ming, and Qing dynasties. It also includes two historical meeting halls and other residents which are open to tourists. Be sure to tour the largest of the meeting halls—Zhang Ting. Once consisting of more than 100 rooms, this residence includes interesting displays on the second floor, including a traditional kitchen. It also contains two shops—one offering embroidered silk screens and the other a large collection of paintings. Relatively close to Shanghai, Zhou Zhuang is a relatively pleasant canal town to stroll around its narrow walkways, see students painting the famous bridges, enjoy the ambience of an historical town, take a canal ride on a local version of a Venitian gondola, shop the town's many antique and souvenir shops, and enjoy a meal at one of the town's many canal-side restaurants. While Zhou Zhuang does not have as much to offer as Suzhou, it does have the advantages of being closer to Shanghai and having fewer tourists crowding its streets and walkways. The town remains relatively untouched by foreign tourists who primarily go with tour groups to Suzhou. The major visitors at this time are local tourists. This will probably change in the future as more and more tour groups discover the pleasures of Zhou Zhuang.

❑ **Wuxi:** Located two hours by train from Shanghai, this is another picturesque canal city and a popular resort area around Lake Tai, one of China's five largest fresh-water lakes. The city also is an important center for silk production. You can take an interesting four-hour cruise via the Grand Canal from Wuxi to Suzhou. Along the way you'll witness the business commerce talking place along this channel, complete with barges, warehouses, and factories.

Guangzhou

Until recently China's most important window to the
outside world, Guangzhou today has settled in as
South China's largest and most prosperous city which
ironically hosts numerous foreign visitors but claims
fewer and fewer tourists each year. Also known as Canton, this
city of 4 million people (6.3 million in larger rural area) serves
as the capital of booming Guangdong Province. It's the economic development center for the rapidly developing Pearl
River Delta which incorporates Hong Kong, Macau, the Special
Economic Zones of Shenzhen and Zhuhai, and the cities of
Dongguan, Panyu, Shiunde, and Nanhai. It's the city of the
very entrepreneurial Cantonese and the home to thousands of
Overseas Chinese who have played key roles in the economic
and political development of China.

GETTING TO KNOW YOU

Located just 182 kilometers north of Hong Kong, Guangzhou
is one of China's most prosperous cities. Its close proximity to
Hong Kong and its entrepot role vis-a-vis the rest of South
China has resulted in turning this city into China's economic
powerhouse. It's a very modern and Western city, second only
to neighboring Hong Kong.

Until just a few years ago, Guangzhou also was one of
China's major tourist destinations. Located only 30 minutes by
plane or 2½ hours by train from Hong Kong, most individuals

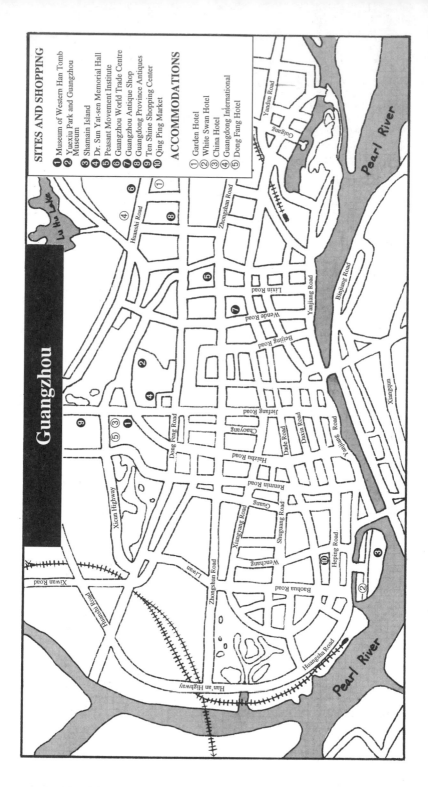

and tour groups entering China via Hong Kong normally began their China adventure in Guangzhou. Indeed, foreign tourism in China was largely centralized in Guangzhou. As China's major gateway city to other destinations in China, Guangzhou benefited immensely from the thousands of tourists who were forced to stop there en route to other places. Hotels, restaurants, shops, and transportation services catering to tourists grew accordingly.

But no more. As China increasingly opened itself to the outside world in recent years, it offered several gateway cities to tourists. As a result, many individuals and tour groups now bypass Guangzhou altogether, flying directly into Beijing, Shanghai, Guilin, Xi'an, and even Chongqing. The impact of these destination changes and new international routings have been enormous on Guangzhou. No longer do large numbers of tourists come to this city to visit its many sites, shops, restaurants, and hotels. Other more interesting cities in China now attract tourists.

❑ Guangzhou is South China's largest and most prosperous city outside of Hong Kong.

❑ The city is extremely crowded during the semi-annual trade fairs in April and October.

❑ This is China's garden city because of its many flowers, trees, tropical vegetation, and landscaped streets.

❑ The city's young people tend to be very Westernized in terms of spending habits.

❑ English is widely spoken in Guangzhou, more so than other cities in China.

❑ Given Guangzhou's subtropical climate, the best times to visit are October to March.

Guangzhou has become a kind of tourist backwater in recent years. It seems to offer little of interest to tourists who would rather first go to Beijing, Shanghai, Xi'an, Guilin, and the Yangtze River area. They visit Guangzhou only as a fifth or sixth city choice.

For all intents and purposes, Guangzhou has settled in as a major destination for businesspeople who come here to attend the popular international trade fairs and invest in the rapidly developing Pearl River Delta economy. Indeed, the province of Guangdong receives over 35 million visitors each year, most of whom come from Hong Kong, Macau, and Taiwan. The city of Guangzhou is a major beneficiary of such Pearl River Delta traffic. The city is extremely crowded during the semi-annual trade fairs in April and October. Thousands of businesspeople from all over the world crowd into Guangzhou to attend the two-week long event that showcases Chinese export products. If you plan to visit Guangzhou during these two months in the hopes of snapping up some shopping bargains, be sure to make hotel reservations several months in advance. Even then, expect hotels to be fully booked and room prices to double during these periods. If you decide to attend a trade fair, be prepared to endure lots of traffic jams, crowded restaurants and shops, and exorbitant prices. But you will get to do lots of shopping, which may be exactly what you want to do. As we'll see later, smart shoppers know when to best attend these fairs to save money and avoid the crowds.

Despite its loss in popularity with tour groups, Guangzhou still has a lot to offer visitors. It's a very modern city with well developed tourist facilities. It's rich in history since it played important political roles in recent Chinese history. Known as China's garden city because of its many flowers, trees, tropical vegetation, and landscaped streets, Guangzhou is filled with important historical sites, and it remains a non-stop shopping and dining city. Despite its vegetation, it's not a particularly beautiful city. Like so many other rapidly developing Chinese cities, its a utilitarian city of concrete streets, expressways, and bridges and towering steel and glass buildings reminding one that Guangzhou is indeed close to the architectural talent of Hong Kong.

As a major development center, Guangzhou has extremes of wealth and poverty as well as a rapidly developing middle class tied to joint venture operations. The city also attracts thousands of unskilled young people who migrate from villages and towns in search of low wage labor in Guangzhou's many factories and service industries. Indeed, the pavement around the city's railway station serves as a temporary home for hundreds of newly arrived migrants who have no where to go. Sitting on newspapers and looking like country bumpkins, most are destined to remain jobless since the economic boom in Guangzhou is all but over. Indicative of new social dislocation attendant with China's new capitalist economy, many of these young people eventually return home having failed to find work. Others get into trouble as pickpockets and burglars. Nonetheless, Guangzhou's reputation as an economic mecca coupled with the government's more open policy on migration to help deal with Guangzhou's labor shortages has contributed to this problem. The sight of so many homeless people arriving in the promised land of Guangzhou serves as testimony to the economic drawing power of this city. To many Chinese, Guangzhou continues to mean new opportunity and wealth.

Guangzhou today is largely defined by its new economics which are very Western in content. While the city offers several sightseeing opportunities, this is a city of many restaurants, hotels, shops, and night spots. The city's young people, many in their twenties who earn good wages working for joint ventures, are very Westernized in terms of spending habits. Crowding shopping centers, restaurants, and discos at night, they spend a great deal on shopping, dining, and entertainment, thus giving this city a very cosmopolitan, Western character. English also is widely spoken in Guangzhou, more so than other cities in China. Consequently, you may feel more at home in Guangzhou enjoying the pleasures of this city.

While Guangzhou probably will not be at the top of your travel list as a "must see" city and it will most likely not become your most exciting travel destination, nevertheless, it is worth visiting if your schedule permits. And if your schedule only permits a few days in China, you may want to concentrate on visiting Hong Kong, Shenzhen, and Guangzhou. In close proximity to each other, these three cities can pack a powerful "China experience" into only a few days. They will give you a quick overview of the "New China" where economics play a central role in the overall development of the country. You'll discover the very entrepreneurial and talented southern Chinese who, despite Beijing's politics and government bureaucracy, are leading China economically into the 21st century. And you'll be impressed by what is becoming one of Asia's great powerhouses of economic development, the Pearl River Delta that includes Guangzhou and its satellite cities along with Shenzhen, Hong Kong, and the soon (1999) to be acquired Macau. Much of the Overseas Chinese money that has flowed into the development of China since 1979 has been centered in this area, and it shows more than in any other place in China.

But if you have two or four weeks to visit China, you'll probably want to put Guangzhou in a different perspective vis-a-vis other popular destinations in China. Like other visitors to China who must set priorities, we put Beijing, Shanghai, Xi'an, and the Yangtze River ahead of Guangzhou. But we still visit Guangzhou and the nearby new city of Shenzhen because it exhibits a very different China, one that will continue to transform the rest of the country.

THE BASICS

WHEN TO GO

Like Hong Kong, Guangzhou boasts a subtropical climate with summers often being very hot and humid. The rainy season runs from April to September, with typhoons affecting the city during August and September. The best times to visit Guangzhou are October to March.

However, weather should not be your only consideration in visiting Guangzhou. If you fail to look at the city's calendar for festivals and conventions, you could be in for some unpleasant surprises. First, try to avoid the extremely busy lunar New Year in January when thousands of Overseas Chinese invade the city as they return to visit their birthplace. Second, you may want to avoid the semi-annual trade shows during April 15-25 and October 15-30 when crowds become oppressive and prices can double on hotel rooms. On the other hand, if you are a dealer or if you want to do some serious shopping at the fair, these may be the best times for you to visit Guangzhou. Good bargains can be found during the last four days of the fair when vendors begin unloading their excess inventory at deeply discounted prices.

GETTING THERE

Guangzhou is conveniently located near Hong Kong. Numerous daily flights, which take only a half hour, connect Hong Kong with Guangzhou. Several other flights connect Guangzhou with Macau, Bangkok, Jakarta, Surabaya, Kuala Lumpur, Penang, Osaka, Seoul, Vientiane, Hanoi, Ho Chi Minh City, Singapore, Manila, Melbourne, and Sydney. Alternatively, you may want to take the express train from Hong Kong which makes the 182-kilometer trip in 2½ hours. Regularly scheduled tour buses also connect Hong Kong, Macau, and Shenzhen with Guangzhou. The Hong Kong to Guangzhou route takes about 3½ hours. From Macau it takes about five hours. From Shenzhen its about a three-hour trip.

Connections to Guangzhou from other major cities in China are very good, especially if your come by air. Regularly scheduled flights connect Guangzhou to Beijing, Shanghai, and Xi'an.

You can also reach Guangzhou from Hong Kong by boat: jetcats and overnight ferries. The jetcat takes about 3½ hours. An overnight ferry also connects Macau with Guangzhou.

AIRPORT TO CITY

Guangzhou has one of the most conveniently located airports in China. Baiyun Airport is only 12 kilometers from the city. From the time you leave the airport until the time you reach your hotel may be only 10 minutes, depending on the traffic situation. The recent widening of the airport to city road has made this a relatively quick and easy trip to the city.

The airport is connected to the city by buses and metered

taxis. Given the relatively inexpensive taxis and short distance to the city, we recommend taking a taxi.

GETTING AROUND

Getting around Guangzhou can be difficult given its notorious traffic congestion. Since the city is very spread out, encompassing an area of 60 square kilometers, getting around on foot is impractical. You'll need to use the new subway, buses, minibuses, taxis, or a bicycle to get around in the city. Taxis are widely available and can be hired on an hourly or daily basis in addition to their regular single trip metered rates. While other forms of transportation are cheaper, you really need to know where you're going to make them work. Since taxis are relatively inexpensive, we prefer taking them and avoiding the headaches of trying to figure out the local subway and bus transportation systems. This is not a great city to bicycle in given the traffic congestion. It's also not a city we wish to get lost in and thus waste valuable travel time.

THE CITY

Variously known as Wuyangcheng (the Five Goat City), Suicheng (the City of Rice Ears), Huacheng (Flower City), and Canton, Guangzhou has been at the center of history in South China. While its origins are ancient, as you will quickly see when visiting the relatively new Museum of Western Han Tomb of the Nanyue King, it's perhaps best known as a trading center, a city that has played an important role in the opening of China to the West. In fact, Guangzhou has played a very important role in Chinese trade and commerce for more than 16 centuries. It was the starting point for the Silk Road of the Sea in the third century. Its strategic downstream location on the Pearl River meant all trade and commerce from most of South China passed by its shores where it was processed for export.

 From the 16th century on, Western powers expanded their trade and commerce with Guangzhou. By the 19th century, Western powers, especially the British, were clamoring for greater shares of the "China trade" as they extracted concessions through unequal treaties, corrupted China with opium, fought and won two Opium Wars, and eventually (1860s) settled in on Shamian Island with warehouses, factories, and houses protected from riotous locals. Much of the island was expanded through reclaimed land. Firmly in control but fearing the worst, the foreign community of English and French divided the island into the British enclave (western four-fifths) and French enclave (eastern one-fifth).

Closed to the Chinese, the fortress-like island became an economic, political, and social oasis connected to the city by two gated bridges that were closed at night. The island developed its own social and religious worlds complete with beautiful villas, tree-lined streets, schools, tennis courts, churches, and a sailing club. Today this island retains much of its European colonial character and is the site for one of Guangzhou's best hotels, the White Swan. Any visit to Guangzhou must include a visit to Shamian Island and this particular hotel.

Guangzhou also played important roles in both the nationalist and communist revolutions of the 20th century. Dissatisfaction with foreign influence, as apparent in Guangzhou's foreign enclaves, and corrupt Chinese imperial rule gave rise to revolutionary movements centered in Guangzhou. Much of the republican activity, for example, that led to the fall of the Qing Dynasty in 1911 was centered in Guangzhou. Sun Yat-sen, the republic's first president, was from this area and he headed the Nationalist Party (Kuomintang) in Guangzhou. In 1925 the Communist Party leadership established the National Peasant Movement in Guangzhou as well as trained many of its leaders here. Overall, Guangzhou justly deserved its reputation as a hotbed for revolutionary activity. And even in the eyes of Beijing's rulers today, Guangzhou is viewed as potentially a political problem if not controlled properly. As in the past, it has the potential to pursue its own radical path.

❑ Good bargains are found during the last four days of the trade fairs when vendors unload their excess inventories at deeply discounted prices.

❑ Shamian Island retains much of its European colonial character.

❑ Guangzhou has a justly deserved reputation as being a hotbed for revolutionary activity.

❑ This city boasts the largest number of cars and motorcycles per capita of any city in China.

❑ Guangzhou is well known for its pickpockets who frequently prey on tourists.

Located along the Pearl River (Zhu Jiang), today Guangzhou is a hotbed of economic activity, a business city primarily oriented toward businesspeople rather than tourists. The city has been virtually transformed during the past 15 years by a booming business sector. In many respects, it is a new city of busy expressways, shopping centers, hotels, and commercial buildings juxtaposed to old parks, markets, and residential areas. Given its excellent transportation, education, and financial infrastructure as well as its close proximity to Hong Kong, foreign investment in Guangzhou and the surrounding Pearl River Delta area is extremely high, more so than any other area in China. The city is often viewed as a competitor to Shanghai because of its booming economy and its "most favored city" status in the eyes of the central government in Beijing. However, Guangzhou has a considerable head start on Shanghai and its economic infrastructure is solidly rooted in real trade and commerce rather than government subsidized projects which are so apparent in creating a new and sometimes false economy for Shanghai.

Underlying Guangzhou's new found wealth are centuries of traditional trade and commerce and an infrastructure that supports both a new and old city. The city's budding skyline of attractive high-rise hotels and office buildings overlook dingy buildings that are decades old. The city bustles with cars, motorcycles, and people, all of which are seemingly involved in nonstop shopping and nightlife. Bicycles have been replaced by pollution belching motorcycles and cars. In fact, Guangzhou has the largest number of cars and motorcycles per capita of any city in China. Not surprising, the city also is very noisy and often reeks with heavy doses of air pollution. Like Shanghai, there is sufficient evidence that the old decadent China now has new clothes; it's entertaining both locals and outsiders who represent China's new affluence.

The major areas of the city of interest to visitors lie north and east of the Pearl River and Shamian Island. Here you'll find the major markets, shops, and hotels, especially along Beijing Road, Zhongshan Road, Wende Road, Dongfeng Road, and Liuhua Road.

SHOPPING TREASURES

There are more shopping opportunities in Guangzhou than in most cities of China. However, much of the shopping is oriented toward the export market for clothes and accessories which may or may not be of interest to you. Even if you like shopping for such products, the sizes, styles, and fabrics may be inappropriate for you. But there are lots of other shopping treasures in Guangzhou awaiting those who know what to look for and where to shop.

WATCH YOUR WALLET

Given Guangzhou's booming economy and disproportionate number of poor people living outside its go-go economy, crime is a recurring problem in Guangzhou. Regardless of what you learned in other parts of China concerning personal safety, be especially careful with your wallet or purse wherever you visit, but especially in the city's crowded shopping centers and markets. Guangzhou is well known for its pickpockets who frequently prey on tourists.

WHAT TO BUY

There's lots of shopping available in Guangzhou. The days when tourists headed for the ubiquitous Friendship Store or a ivory carving factory to do all of their shopping are gone. In the past few years Guangzhou has been transformed into one big shopping mall, from well appointed department stores to up-scale hotel shopping arcades. But the city also retains many of its traditional shops and markets.

Guangzhou's department stores and hotel shopping arcades are filled with fashionable clothes and accessories. Its factories, shops, and markets offer a wide range of jewelry, art, carvings, embroidery, painted porcelain, antiques, and souvenirs. If you visit Guangzhou during the trade fairs in April and October, you'll have a chance to survey a huge variety of products, from textiles, rugs and furniture to the latest in cotton, silk, leather, and fur fashion. An estimated 40,000 products are displayed during these fairs.

WHERE TO SHOP

If you want to shop Guangzhou right, you'll need to travel to several different shopping areas. The city's major shopping areas are found in and around the major hotels, exhibition center, museums, and Beijing, Zhongshan, Wende, Huanshi, and Daihe Roads.

SEMI-ANNUAL TRADE FAIRS

This is the big trade event in China and the ultimate bonanza for shoppers. Held twice a year, during April and October, thousands of international traders visit the enormous trade grounds which are located in the northern section of the city at the intersection of Liuhua and Renmin Roads (117 Liuhua Road), across the street from the Dong Fang Hotel and Liuhua Park. Known as the **Chinese Export Commodities Fair**, hundreds of Chinese companies showcase their products and offer good buys on most everything on display. The retail shops on the fair grounds are open to the public, not just registered international traders. If you really want to get some great buys on everything from furniture to furs—which might help offset the inflated hotel prices—attend the fair during the last four days. During this time vendors sell their floor samples at excellent prices (it's either that or cart everything back to their home base). If you plan to attend the trade fair at the very beginning, you'll need to book your hotel reservations at least two months in advance. Since many people leave the trade fair after a few days, you should have less problem getting a room toward the end of the fair. But the key to buying is to attend during the final four days.

Once the trade fair ends, you can still shop at the permanent retail section which presents itself as an upscale department store (by local standards) complete with marble floors. Recently renamed the **Ten Shine Shopping Center** (previously known as the Chinese Community Import-Export Trade Shopping Fair), this expansive shopping center primarily offers clothes, cosmetics, watches, pens, leather goods, cigarettes, and liquor. You'll find familiar labels such as Esprit, Elle, Arrow, Jagger, G. Verdi, Arnold Palmer, and Rolex.

SHOPPING STREETS

Several streets in Guangzhou are favorites for shoppers. However, you may have difficulty finding shops by their names and addresses since few have signs. You'll have to identify shops by other distinguishing characteristics. The most popular streets include:

❑ **Beijing Road:** While this is a very popular shopping street for locals, don't expect to do much shopping here. The small shops lining this street are an interesting cultural experience for tourists, a cut above a street market. Located just off Zhongshan Road near Wende Road, this street is lined with numerous private shops offering lots of inexpensive clothes. If you have limited time, you can find much better places to visit in Guangzhou, especially the many shops in the next major street to the east, Wende Road. Beijing Road also has two popular department stores, Guangzhou Department Store (next to the night market) and Xinta Xin Department Store (at corner of Zhongshan and Beijing Roads).

❑ **Wende Road:** This is one of our favorite shopping streets because of its large concentration of art and antique shops. However, the street is in transition as buildings are being torn down and replaced with new properties. Just off of Zhongshan Road and parallel to Beijing Road, both sides of this street yield numerous shops offering antiques, paintings, handicrafts, jewelry, and books. The Ming style building at the northern section of this street, across the street from the Municipal Library, offers two floors of paintings from all over China. The adjacent **Guangzhou Antique Shop**, also owned by the municipality, is one of the oldest and best shops on this street. It offers two floors of excellent quality arts and antiques, including ceramics, teapots, ivory, snuff bottles, jewelry, and jade. Be sure to go to the second floor (stairs found behind the first floor counter or main entrance through the music store next door) which really has the best quality items. Look for numerous antiques with the official red or brown wax seals, ceramics (huge selection in back room), carved gold panels, ivory, lacquer boxes, chops, ink blocks, wood carvings, paintings, and calligraphy supplies. You'll also find a shipping desk which will handle your large purchases. Further south and on the right hand side of the street is a long and narrow shop (**Writer's Bookstore** or **Feng Lin Shan**, but has no sign!) offering an excellent selection of watercolors and oils from all over South China as well as Hong Kong and Taiwan Be sure to go to the back of the shop where most of paintings are found. Further south along this sign of the street is the popular **Art Mall**, a unique shopping center filled with more than 50 small art and framing stalls. You can't miss this place since the nine shops facing the street look like they are part of a shopping complex. Here you'll find both Chinese and Western style paintings. The remainder of this street includes several small shops which you may or may not find of particular interest. For something different, stop in the small alley across from the Art Mall to watch the small bird and fish market.

❑ **Huanshi Dong Road:** Concentrated in a two block area across the street from the five-star Garden Hotel, this is a very popular shopping and dining area for young people and upscale shoppers. The main shopping center here is the **Guangzhou World Trade Centre Complex** which consists of two multi-floor shopping centers, the North Tower and South Tower. This is one of Guangzhou's most modern and expensive shopping centers, complementing but by no means competing with the very upscale shops across the street in the shopping arcade of the Garden Hotel (see "Hotel Shopping Arcades" section that follows). It's especially popular with local young people who appear to have lots of disposable income. Chances are you won't find many things here to add to your collection of Chinese shopping treasures. Nonetheless, it's well worth visiting this shopping complex just to see what's on the local market and observe all the determined local shoppers in pursuit of name brand goods. The **South Tower** consists of several small upscale boutiques offering clothes, shoes, and handbags, such as Benetton, Mondial, Jessica, and Gallery with such international name brand goods such as Nina Ricci, Lancel, Dunhill, Cartier, Chloé, Givenchy, Christian Dior, and Yves Saint Laurent. Laid out with lots of narrow curving hallways, this shopping arcade is somewhat confusing and confining. At the second floor it is joined to the North Tower by an enclosed walkover. The **North Tower** is actually the **Guangzhou Friendship Store**, one of the most upscale department stores in all of China! Consisting of six floors, it's jam-packed with excellent quality products. The first floor includes a nice supermarket as well as eyeglasses, cosmetics, and designer label clothes for men from Valentino, Alfred Dunhill, Yves Saint Laurent, and Givenchy, all of which are produced in China under licensing agreements. The second floor includes silk fabric, blouses, scarves, and dresses. The third floor is devoted to shoes, coats, suits, sweaters, and shirts. The fourth floor displays a large selection of cameras, watches, electronics, computers, and kitchen items. The fifth floor is especially popular with tourists because it offers the more traditional "Friendship Store" items—jewelry, handicrafts, rugs, glassware, cloisonne, ceramics, tapestries, paintings, calligraphy supplies, and embroidery screens. The sixth floor is primarily devoted to furniture.

❑ **Dishipu Street:** Located at the end of the fish and aquarium section of the popular Qing Ping Market, this 1 kilometer street is closed for pedestrians from 1:00pm to 9:30pm on Saturdays and Sundays. Especially popular with locals, numerous shops line both sides of this street offering inexpensive clothes, shoes, food, CDs, and tapes. Another cultural experience but one that might yield a few inexpensive CDs of popular Western and Asian artists. The street also includes several popular restaurants.

❑ **Dong Feng Road East:** Only one shop worth visiting here, **Guangdong Province Antiques Company**. Located at 555 Dong Feng Road East (previously located at 696 Renmin Road), this is one of the city's best quality antique stores for jade jewelry, ceramics, embroidery, and paintings. Much smaller than the municipal antique store on Wende Road and somewhat isolated from the city's main shopping areas (take a taxi to get here), nonetheless, it has lots to offer collectors and few tourists come here. We especially like the selection of old embroidery pieces that served as collars and pillow ends. The store offers a 5% discount on cash purchases but does take credit cards.

MARKETS

Guangzhou has several markets offering a wide range of foods and household goods. Its night markets tend to be very popular and crowded. However, chances are you will not find many things of interest in these markets. Most are interesting cultural experiences. Nonetheless, you may want to venture into the following markets for some very interesting cultural experiences:

❑ **Qing Ping Market:** Wow, what an in-your-face market! Located within a 15 minute walk directly north of the White Swan Hotel, this is one of Guangzhou's oldest and largest traditional markets famous for its live animals and spices. It's open from 6:30am to 6:30pm. This is definitely a cultural experience if you want to see the transformation of live animals into raw meat. Watch the locals pick out the cute live bunny rabbit, cat, dog, or duck and within a few minutes it comes back wrapped for dinner. This experience could turn you into a dedicated vegetarian. The market primarily consists of fruits, vegetables, meats, live animals, and herbs and spices. Its covered walkways tend to be extremely crowded. With so much activity going on, the place also tends to be trashy. The live animal section consists of turtles, prawns, and eels piled high in large tubs and caged chickens, ducks, rabbits, dogs, and cats. As you will quickly see by observing the butchers, this is not the pet section. There is a large pet section but it consists of tropical fish, aquariums, and supplies and is located just outside this area in an open lane. You may be fascinated with the herb and spice section which consists of several small stalls selling a large variety of herbs and spices. The market also includes a small antiques and collectibles section with vendors offering ceramics, pots, carvings, pipes, coins, and snuff bottles from small stalls. If you only have time to visit one market in Guangzhou, make it this one. A great place for photo opportunities.

❑ **Daihe Road**: This narrow walkway is a street market consisting of several small private owned shops and stalls offering a large selection of antiques, jade, arts, and handicrafts. This essentially is Guangzhou's jade market. Each shop and stall tends to specialize in a particular item. Look for pottery, teapots, carved stones, coins, pearls, clocks, porcelain, hair pins, embroidered pillow covers and collars, and lots of jade carvings, bracelets, and beads. This is great market for all types of collectibles.

HOTEL SHOPPING ARCADES

Given the business and trade fair orientation of Guangzhou as well as the city's close proximity to the shopping culture of Hong Kong, more hotels in Guangzhou have shopping arcades than hotels in other cities of China. If you missed out on good quality hotel shops in other cities, you're in for a change here in Guangzhou. Several hotels offer shopping arcades:

❑ **Garden Hotel**: *368 Huanshi Doug Road*. Located directly across the street from the Guangzhou World Trade Centre and the Guangdong International Hotel, this is Guangzhou's top five-star hotel. And it has a large upscale shopping arcade to complement its fine reputations. Located to both the right and left of the dramatic and expansive lobby, the shopping arcade includes numerous designer boutiques and jewelry shops such as Max Mara, Lanvin, Mondi, Valentino, Hugo Boss, Gieves and Hawkes, Bally, Rene Derhy, Banrie, Stefanel, Cerruti 1881, and Philippe Charrio. For quality arts and crafts, visit the Treasure Palace and Times Art Gallery. As might be expected, everything here is very expensive. While upscale and interesting, this particular hotel shopping arcade yields few Chinese treasures. This is not our type of shopping for China.

❏ **White Swan Hotel:** Located on Shamian Island and facing the Pearl River, this five-star hotel has one of the best shopping arcades for tourists interested in quality arts and crafts. The attractive lobby area with its cascading waterfall, bridge, and gold fish pond flows into the lower level shopping arcade with its upscale boutiques, jewelry stores, and arts and crafts shops. You'll find several shops offering good quality lacquer furniture, large carvings, paintings, ceramics, and jars. Since prices tend to be a bit high, be sure to bargain in these shops. Peasant paintings that sell for 200 yuan should be bargained down to 120 yuan. Don't worry about buying large items since a shipping office is available at the end of the arcade (next to the art galleries) to handle large purchases.

❏ **China Hotel:** *Liuhua Road.* Located near the trade fair exhibition center, this hotel includes its own shopping arcade, the **China Hotel Shopping Arcade**, as well as the attached **F&F Shopping Plaza** which also belongs to the hotel. Includes some name brand shops such as Ermenegildo, Alfred Dunhill, and Vasto for clothing and accessories. Jewelry and Goldsmith is a good quality jewelry shop. The F&F Shopping Plaza includes lots of upscale clothing shops, shoe stores, leather shops, and a good quality arts and crafts shop for ceramics, paintings, and jewelry (Guangdong Collection House of Arts and Crafts Treasures on 2nd floor).

❏ **Dong Fang Hotel:** *120 Liuhua Road.* Located across the street from the trade fair exhibition center, part of this huge Russian style hotel complex has been converted into a newly completed shopping arcade, Dong Fang Times Square. Shops offer lots of clothes and accessories that especially appeal to trade fair buyers who stay as this conveniently located hotel.

❏ **Guangdong International Hotel:** *339 Huanshi Dong Road.* Formerly known as the Gitic Plaza Hotel, this imposing 63-story hotel includes a second floor shopping arcade with clothes, accessory, and arts and crafts shops. Very quiet compared to other hotel shopping arcades. Attached to McDonald's and includes a Dan Ryan's.

DEPARTMENT STORES

Guangzhou has several department stores. However, the ultimate department store is the Guangzhou Friendship Store at the Guangzhou World Trade Centre Complex on Huanshi Dong Road (See "Shopping Streets" above). After visiting this fashionable one, all others are downhill, catering more to local tourists seeking inexpensive and less fashionable items. Other major department stores include: **Nan Fang Da Sha** at 49 Yanjiang Road; **Guangzhou Department Store** on Beijing Road next to the night market; and **Xinta Xin Department Store** at the corner of Zhongshang Roads. And don't forget the **Ten Shine Shopping Center** at the exhibition center on Liuhua Road (see "Semi-Annual Trade Fairs" above).

MUSEUM SHOPS

Guangzhou's two major museums also have shops that offer a good range of arts and crafts. **The Museum of Western Han Tomb of the Nanyue King** includes a nice collection of paintings, jade, sandlewood fans, ceramics, carvings, tea pots, necklaces, snuff bottles, and embroidery. **The Municipal Museum** in Yuexiu Park includes several small shops on the fifth floor of the major building offering ceramics, tea, traditional medicines, books, and T-shirts. But the main shop is in the building through which you exit the museum grounds. This large shop is filled with arts and crafts, including paintings, jade, cloisonne, rugs, sandlewood fans, and antique ceramics as well as a huge porcelain collection from the famous town of Foshan. Prices tend to be on the high side, so be sure to bargain hard. Vendors just outside this building and across the street offer better starting prices on several souvenir items.

UNDERGROUND SHOPPING CENTER

Like Shanghai and Beijing, Guangzhou also has its underground shopping center. Built in the 1970s in response to the Sino-Soviet threat, this converted bomb shelter is located in front of the railroad station. It approximates a flea market. You enter the shopping center in the parking lot near the main road and adjacent to the taxi stand. The red granite stairs lead to numerous small private shops and stalls that look like one big underground bazaar offering clothes, luggage, bags, and accessories. At times very crowded, this shopping area is popular with young people from the provinces in search of inexpensive clothes and accessories which they can pack in their newly acquired bags and luggage just before leaving on the train. You may find this to be more of a cultural experience than a place to do quality shopping. It's certainly not the quality of Shanghai's underground shopping center. Word of caution: watch your wallet and purse in the narrow and crowded lanes that separate the stalls. Pickpockets are known to frequent this area.

ACCOMMODATIONS

Hosting millions of visitors each year, Guangzhou has thousands of hotel rooms and several excellent quality hotels. Except during the trade fair weeks in April and October when hotels are fully booked, you should have no problem finding accommodations during the rest of the year when many hotels have low vacancy rates. Reflecting its primary clientele—businesspeople—most of these hotels are very large business hotels offering a good range of restaurants, health facilities, business centers, conference facilities, and entertainment, including nightclubs, discos, and karaoke lounges. The city's best hotels include these five-star properties:

❑ **Garden Hotel:** *368 Huanshi Dong Road, 510064. Tel. (86-20) 8333-8989 or Fax (86-20) 8332-4534. In US, Tel. 1-800-44U-TELL.* This 30-storey hotel includes over 1,038 rooms and an impressive lobby with a picture of the Red Chamber in the back of the reception area. This is considered Guangzhou's best five-star hotel. Includes the city's most upscale hotel shopping arcade. Conveniently lo-cated across the street from the Guangzhou World Trade Center and the Guangdong International Hotel.

❑ **White Swan Hotel:** *1 Southern Street, Shamian Island, 510133. Tel. (86-20) 8188-6968 or Fax (86-20) 8186-1188.* Nicely located on the quaint and quiet Shamian Island and facing the busy Pearl River, this hotel is a member of the Leading Hotels of the World and the favorite of tourists. Originally built in 1983, it has been well maintained and is an excellent choice for anyone visiting Guangzhou. It especially appeals to tourists who enjoy the ambience of the area and who do not have pressing business in the city. Includes an excellent hotel shopping arcade offering a wide range of local products. While located outside the city center in blissful isolation, it's only a 15 minute walk from the hotel to the interesting Qing Ping Market. We liked this hotel when we stayed here in 1984 and we still like it today.

❑ **China Hotel:** *Liuhua Road, 510015. Tel. (86-20) 8666-6888 or Fax (86-20) 8667-7014. From US, Tel. 1-800-44UTELL.* This 18-storey hotel offers 1017 rooms. Conveniently located near the exhibition center and the Dong Fang Hotel complex. Includes five restaurants, three lounges, and upscale shops. Pleasant orchestra plays in the lobby every evening. Attached to the F&F Shopping Plaza. Hard Rock Cafe located next door.

❑ **Guangdong International Hotel:** *339 Huanshi Dong Road, 510098. Tel. (86-20) 8331-1888 or Fax (86-20) 8331-3490.* This 63-storey hotel with 702 rooms is the tallest building in Guangzhou. Staying on one of the top floors will give you a spectacular view of the city and surrounding area. Includes 14 restaurants and lounges, helicopter landing pad, conference facilities, and a shopping arcade with McDonald's attached.

❑ **Dong Fang Hotel:** *120 Liuhua Road, 10016. Tel. (86-20) 8666-9900 or Fax (86-20) 8666-2775. In US, Tel. 1-800-44UTELL.* This huge Russian-style and government operated hotel is conveniently located across the street from the exhibition center. New lobby area joins two buildings, one of which is the Tung-Fang Hotel. Newly opened "Dong Fang Times Square" shopping arcade has reduced the total number of guest rooms which used to number 1300. McDonald's located in front of hotel. Rated a five-star property but tends to deliver two-star service, especially at the front desk. Not a good choice if you're expecting five-star service. Needs to have a few stars removed from its name!

Other places to consider include:

❑ **Holiday Inn City Center:** *Huan Shi Dong Road, 28 Guangmin Road, Overseas Chinese Village. Tel. (86-20) 8776-6999 or Fax (86-20) 8775-3126.* 24 stories with 400 rooms. Four-star property.

❑ **Landmark Hotel:** *8 Qiao Guang Road, Haizhu Square, 510115. Tel. (86-20) 8335-5988 or Fax (86-20) 8333-6197.* 39 stories with 730 rooms. Four-star property.

❏ **Central Hotel:** *33 Ji Chang Lu, Sanyuanli. Tel. (86-20) 8667-8331 or Fax (86-20) 8667-8331.* Part of the exhibition center. A 6-storey, four-star property with 234 rooms.

❏ **Aiqun Hotel:** *113 Yanjiang Road West, Tel. (86-20) 8666-1445 or Fax (86-20) 8888-3519.* A 300-room property located along the Pearl River. Three-star property.

❏ **Bai Yun Hotel:** *367 Huanshi Dong Road, 51160, Tel. (86-20) 8333-3998 or Fax (86-20) 8333-6498.* Three-star hotel located next to the Friendship Store. 34-storey property with 700+ rooms.

❏ **Equatorial Hotel:** *931 Renmin Road, Tel. (86-20) 8667-2888 or Fax (86-20) 8667-2582.* 300 room property. Three-star property.

RESTAURANTS

Guangzhou is the mecca for Cantonese food which tends to be lighter and fresher than other Chinese cuisines. The rice in Guangzhou is also reputed to be tastier and less sticky than rice from other parts of the country. The city abounds with restaurants serving seafood and popular Cantonese dishes. It also abounds with popular evening food markets and stalls that serve excellent dishes under questionable sanitary conditions. Unless you want to play Russian roulette with the local street dishes, we highly recommend dining in the major hotel restaurants or trusted fast food restaurants. However, several of the following restaurants also would be good choices:

❏ **Ban Xi (or Pan Xi) Restaurant:** *151 Xiang Yang Road 1, Tel. 8888-5655 or 8888-8706.* This old but still popular lakeside restaurant is famous for its large variety of dim sum—nearly 1000 different types. Seating more than 3000 people in a series of teahouses set in gardens and overlooking the lake, the teahouses are connected by a series of bridges and walkways that zigzag through bamboo groves and tropical foliage. Very pleasant surroundings as well as excellent food. Popular for VIPs.

❏ **Datong Restaurant:** *63 Yanjiangzi Rd., Tel. 8188-8441.* Offers more than 1000 dishes. Famous for its crispy-skin chicken, roast suckling pig, cactus with chicken wings, Xi

Shi duck, and dim sum. Nice view of the Pearl River from the terrace of this high-rise restaurant.

❏ **Quangzhou Restaurant:** *2 Wenchangnan Rd., Tel. 8188-7840.* Operating since 1936, this rambling two-storey teahouse restaurant is famous for its maotai chicken, sliced chicken with liver and ham, kapok duck, shark's fin, fragrant perch ball, roast goose, eight treasures, and turtle casserole.

❏ **Nanyuan Restaurant:** *120 Henan Qianjin Road, Tel. 8444-8380.* Located outside the city center in beautiful landscaped grounds, this popular Chaozhou restaurant is known for its seafood, roast goose, chicken in bean sauce, embroidery-ball cabbage, braised chicken wings, and chicken vegetable soup.

❏ **Dongjiang Restaurant:** 337 Zhongshansi Road, Tel. 8333-5568. Centrally located, this restaurant specializes in Dongjiang cuisine. Popular dishes include salt-roast chicken, stuffed beancurd, steamed pork with salted, dried mustard cabbage, and eight-treasure duck.

❏ **Snake Food Restaurant:** *41 Jianglan Road, Tel. 8188-2317.* Great restaurant for young people who love the exotic character of the restaurant and food. Operating for more than 80 years, this popular two-storey restaurant includes live snakes in cages on the first floor on the way to the kitchen. Serves great snake dishes. Includes over 100 unique dishes, such as dragon, tiger and phoenix with chrysanthemum, two dragons playing with a pearl, fried snake, stewed snake slices with chicken liver, five-color fried snake shreds, and four-treasure fried snake. Start your meal with snake wine!

❏ **Dasanyuan Restaurant:** *260 Changdi Road, Tel. 8188-3277.* One of Guangzhou's famous restaurants for stewed shark's fins in soya sauce and tea chicken.

The Chinese restaurants at the Dong Fang (Jade Palace), China (**Chaozhou Garden** and **Four Seasons**), Guangdong International (**Imperial Garden**) and White Swan (**Jade River**) Hotels are excellent choices. Try the **Food Street** at the China Hotel on Liuhua Road with its open kitchens preparing Cantonese, hot pot, and other kinds of food at reasonable prices. Similar food markets can be found at the Garden Hotel

(**Laiwan Market**) and the Holiday Inn (**Dai Pai Dong Food Alley**). And you'll have no problem finding the ubiquitous Western fast food outlets, such as McDonald's, Pizza Hut, and KFC, and such theme restaurants as the Hard Rock Cafe.

MAJOR ATTRACTIONS

While Guangzhou is not Beijing and Xi'an when it comes to historical sites, nonetheless, it has a lot to offer visitors interested in the history of South China and the Pearl River Delta. Guangzhou has two excellent museums well worth visiting:

❑ **Museum of Western Han Tomb of the Nanyue King:** Located in the northern section of the city on Liberation Road and near the railroad station and the China Hotel. Constructed in 1988 next to a relic-rich tomb discovered in 1983, this relatively new museum provides an excellent overview of the ancient history of the city (203BC to the first century AD). This is actually a surprisingly good museum. Visit the excavated tomb chambers at the top of the museum and then visit the exhibition hall after seeing an English language video in the first floor book and stamp shop. Highlights of this fine museum include a burial suit encased in jade on the first floor and a terrific ceramic pillow collection on the second floor. The third floor includes "Cultural Relics of the Five Goats City" which includes numerous ceramics and bronzes. On a hot day this can be a stifling museum since it is not air-conditioned.

❑ **Yuexiu Park and Guangzhou (Municipal) Museum:** Located in the Central District's Jiefang North Road, this is the largest park in Guangzhou. It includes several historical sites, including The Five Goat Statue (symbol of the city), Sifang Battery, Dr. Sun Yat-sen Monument, and the Zhenhai Tower. The Tower, an attractive five-storey red lacquer Ming-style building, has been converted into the municipal museum which covers Guangzhou's more than 2200 years of history. Includes a large model of the city and numerous photos and articles representing both ancient and modern Guangzhou history. Often crowded with school children on museum field trips. Includes shopping on the fifth floor as well as in a separate building through which you exit the museum grounds.

❑ **Shamian Island:** Located in the southern part of the city at the confluence of the Pearl River, this is the old enclave of the British and French traders. Now the site for the five-star Swan Hotel and the old Victory Hotel, Shamian Island still exudes a colonial ambiance with its European buildings and tree-lined streets. Compared to the rest of Guangzhou, the island is relatively quiet and peaceful, a nice place to stroll along the streets and contemplate what Guangzhou used to be like during the past century or two.

❑ **Dr. Sun Yat-sen Memorial Hall:** A beautiful blue ceramic roofed building located at the foot of Yuexiu Mountain. Dr. Sun Yat-sen looms large in the history of Guangzhou and China. This revolutionary of the early 20th century helped shape the post-imperial history of China. This memorial hall, which served as Dr. Sun Yat-sen's residence when he became president of the Republic of China in 1912, records much of his political career. Consists of a huge octagon-shaped hall capable of seating over 4,500.

❑ **Peasant Movement Institute:** Located at 42 Zhonghan Silu. Once a Confucian temple, it served as a peasant training institute for the Communist movement during the 1920s. Somewhat of an architectural masterpiece, visitors are especially drawn to the beautiful roof with its glazed ceramic animals.

❑ **Exhibition Hall of the Revolution:** Located next to the Peasant Movement Institute, this building displays historical photos and documents of the Communist revolution with special emphasis on the key roles of Mao Zedong and Zhou Enlai in Guangzhou.

❑ **Zhen Family Temple/Guangdong Folk Arts and Crafts Center:** Located at 7 Zhonghan Road (and Liwan Road), Tel. 81841559. Constructed in the 1890s by the Zhen clan, this building variously served as a Confucian school, a family temple for ancestral worship, and a protected army office during the Cultural Revolution. It now functions as the Guangdong Folk Arts and Crafts Center. Lavishly decorated in ornate Confucian style with lots of intricate carvings and sculptures. Includes an arts and crafts shop with good buys on linens.

Other worthwhile sites include several memorials to revolutionary martyrs (**Mausoleum of the 72 Martyrs** and the **Monument to the Guangzhou Uprising**), temples (**Guangxiao** and **Six Banyan Trees**), the oldest mosque in China (**Huaisheng**), and a cathedral (**Shisbhi or Cathedral of the Sacred Heart**). Guangzhou also has some lovely gardens and parks such as the **South China Botanical Garden, Orchid Garden, Xi Yuan, Liuhua Park,** and **Guangzhou Cultural Park.**

ENTERTAINMENT

Beijing and Shanghai have a much more active nightlife than Guangzhou. But Guangzhou is increasingly coming of age as it responds to the entertainment needs of the many thousands of business people who visit the city each day.

While shopping and eating seem to be the favorite evening activities for thousands of local residents and visitors, Guangzhou also has a vibrant nightlife centering around bars, discos, and nightclubs. In fact, the city has seen a virtual explosion of discos in the past five years, with many DJs coming in from Hong Kong. Some of the most popular discos include **JJ's** (18 Jiao Chang West Road) which is a Hong Kong transplant; **Fa Fi** (17 Zhongshan Road, 1st Building, 1-3) with its underwater theme and go-go dancers; **Boxing Disco** (corner of Huanshi Dong Lu and Luhu Road) with its boxing ring where you can test your boxing skills with a partner; and the **One Love Reggae Bar** (801-15 East Dong Feng Road) which offers some of the best music in the city.

Some of the most popular bars outside hotels include the **Hill Bar** (367 Huanshi Dong Lu), **42nd Street** (399 Huanshi Dong Lu), **U King's** (668 Remin Bei Road), **Lucy's** (5-7 Sha Mian Yi Street, Shamian Island), **Kathleen's** (60 Tao Jin Lu), and **Green Island** (North Gate, Liuhua Park). Popular hotel bars include **Corner Bar** (China Hotel), **The Inn Bar** (Holiday Inn), **Atrium Lounge** (Guangdong International Hotel), and **Hare & Moon** (White Swan Hotel).

If you like karaoke, you'll be in karaoke heaven with the numerous karaoke bars found in hotels and elsewhere in the city.

You'll also find plenty of evening cultural events to attend, from traditional Chinese opera and musical concerts to famous acrobatic and magician shows. Check with your hotel concierge for particular times and places.

Shenzhen and
Hong Kong

S henzhen is China's most successful new city, an incredible monument to Beijing's post-1979 new economic
policy that encouraged *"socialism with Chinese characteristics."* Shenzhen seems to be all capitalism with few socialist characteristics, a go-go economic phenomenon that even
surprises its Chinese architects. Such capitalism really hap-
pened in a very big way in Shenzhen as hundreds of joint
venture factories located here during the past 15 years and
hundreds of thousands of young people migrated here to start
new lives in China's rapidly emerging export-oriented economy.
Today, they produce millions of dollars of toys, electronics,
footwear, and garments for export via Hong Kong.

At the same time, Shenzhen has become a major tourist
destination hosting more than 35 million visitors each year.
Little known to many Western visitors to China, including their
travel agents and tour groups who recommend destinations, it's
a city with two tales, one of which should persuade you to
definitely include Shenzhen in your travel plans. Indeed, we
recommend that you put it on your "must see" list.

GETTING TO KNOW YOU

Shenzhen is a magnet for both business and tourism, a gigantic
factory town as well as a huge resort complex. About 20 years
ago this area was a quiet town with only two intersecting roads

located within one hour by highway from Hong Kong. But since 1979 Shenzhen has risen like a phoenix to become one of China's great economic stars. As foreign investment from Hong Kong created numerous joint ventures to produce toys, electronics, footwear, and garments for export, Shenzhen quickly experienced phenomenal growth. Designated by Beijing as one of China's Special Economic Zones to attract Overseas Chinese industrial investment, today Shenzhen is a very modern city of over 2 million inhabitants. Hundreds of factories and dormitories line the roads around Shenzhen, giving evidence to the fact that this is one of China's most important industrial areas.

But there is a tale of two cities here that you should understand before including Shenzhen on your travel calendar. Shenzhen is much more than just a new factory community. The first Shenzhen is the rapidly developing business city of over 2 million people. This is the city of factories, dormitories, high-rise apartment buildings, offices, and hotels. It's a relatively planned city with orderly streets and white washed buildings. It's also a very crowded and heavily polluted commercial and residential city. Everything about this place tells you it is new and oriented toward business. Thousands of businesspeople visit this city each year to do what they do best—conduct more business. Unless you have business to do in Shenzhen, you probably will not be interested in visiting such a utilitarian city. As might be expected, this city is a concrete jungle of commercial buildings, hotels, and high-rise apartment buildings. There's nothing particularly worthwhile to recommend in the first Shenzhen, other than the five-star Shangri-la Hotel which is located near the railway station.

- ❑ Shenzhen hosts over 35 million visitors each year.

- ❑ Shenzhen is both a gigantic factory as well as a huge resort complex.

- ❑ OCT Shenzhen is a wonderful oasis in the midst of exuberant industrialization.

- ❑ Shenzhen is easily accessible by road, train, or plane from Hong Kong and Guangzhou.

- ❑ If you're visiting Hong Kong, you can get a special 72-hour visa to visit Shenzhen.

- ❑ Hong Kong dollars can be used interchangeably with the local currency.

The second Shenzhen is all about culture, entertainment, and resort accommodations. Located within five miles of the first Shenzhen, this area is officially called **OCT Shenzhen** which stands for the Overseas Chinese Town of Shenzhen. Located in the shadow of its neighboring industrial giant, OCT Shenzhen is a wonderful oasis in the midst of exuberant industrialization. It occupies an area of only 5 square kilometers and boasts a population of 40,000. Established in 1985 with Hong Kong investment dollars, OCT Shenzhen is primarily concerned with tourism. It's a training center for developing the Chinese industry as well as an attractive resort destination. Until recently, most of its visitors were Overseas Chinese. It has three major theme parks that attract thousands of visitors each day:

- Miniature of Splendid China
- Folk Culture Villages
- Window of the World

It's also in the process of planning a fourth theme park that may be developed in cooperation, or as a joint venture, with Disney World. Combining a bit of Disneyland with Hollywood as well as incorporating the Chinese flair for large and colorful dramatic productions, these three theme parks draw millions of visitors to OCT Shenzhen each year. They should be your major reasons for visiting Shenzhen.

A PLACE FOR EVERYONE

We normally would not visit such a place because of its "staged" nature, plus we've often been disappointed visiting cultural villages in other countries (not another dance performance!). However, OCT Shenzhen is very different from your run-of-the-mill "country in miniature" theme parks. This place is a first-class operation developed and managed by talented personnel who put on first-class productions. While it may seem designed for individuals who have little time to visit China and thus only want a quick overview and sampling of the country, OCT Shenzhen is different. It has both depth and drama. The government corporation (OCT Economic Development Company) in charge of developing OCT has pulled out all stops to make this a real quality destination for first-time visitors to China as well as for those who want to enjoy a pleasant resort. Even seasoned travelers to China will find this place well worth visiting. If you're traveling with children, chances are this place will be a real "hit" with them. It's a great place to either start or end your China adventure.

What's nice about OCT Shenzhen is its proximity to Hong Kong and relative ease of entering and exiting for short stays. If your main destination is Hong Kong but you still wish to visit some of Greater China, we highly recommend a day trip to OCT Shenzhen. Better still, plan to stay overnight there and perhaps go on to Guangzhou for another day or two. Combining Shenzhen with Guangzhou will give you an excellent overview of what lies ahead in Greater China.

THE BASICS

WHEN TO GO

Like Hong Kong and Guangzhou, Shenzhen boasts a subtropical climate which during the summers can be very hot and humid. The rainy season runs from April to September. Since much of your activities in OCT Shenzhen will be outdoors and involve a great deal of walking, although trams are available, ideally you should try to visit here sometime between October and March.

GETTING THERE

Shenzhen is easily accessible by road, train, or plane from Hong Kong or Guangzhou. Depending on where you originate, you may want to take a train or plane to Guangzhou and then go by bus or car to OCT Shenzhen. The relatively new six-lane expressway (toll-road) connecting Guangzhou with Shenzhen is excellent and takes only two hours. From Hong Kong, you can easily reach OCT Shenzhen by tour bus within an hour and a half.

VISAS AND ENTRY

China treats OCT Shenzhen as a very special place it wants to promote to visitors and thus showcase the best of Chinese history, culture, and entertainment. Here you can condense what might have been a 30-day trip to China into one long day of spectacular sightseeing and entertainment. Encouraging millions of Overseas Chinese and foreign visitors to sample this unique "China in Miniature," the government does not require a regular visa to enter China at this border crossing with Hong Kong. You will need a special 72-hour visa which can be easily obtained within 12 to 24 hours through any travel agency in Hong Kong. If you arrange to go to OCT Shenzhen from Hong Kong by tour bus, the tour company will take care of your visa as part of the tour package.

If you plan to visit OCT Shenzhen from Guangzhou, all you need is your regular visa. Since Shenzhen is a Special Economic Zone, it has its own border crossing and Immigration officials that function similarly to border crossings to a foreign country. Even local Chinese must have proper documentation and special passes to enter this area. Population movement in and out of Shenzhen is strictly controlled by authorities as you will quickly notice at the border check points. To go on to Guangzhou, if you have come from Hong Kong, requires a different type of visa.

GETTING AROUND

Assuming your major destination is OCT Shenzhen, once you arrive by bus or car, the whole 5 square kilometer area is easily accessible on foot. Most of the hotels are located in and around the three theme parks. Within the theme parks you can get around on foot or by trams. You may want a guide which are some of the best guides we encountered in China. And for good reason. Shenzhen is a major center for tourism training in China. It attracts some of the best young people who speak excellent English.

If you plan to visit Shenzhen or go beyond this city, you'll need a car and driver. Remember, if you enter Shenzhen on a special visa, you are only permitted to visit Shenzhen and the border crossings in and out of Shenzhen are strictly controlled. Guangzhou and other cities in the Pearl River Delta will not be in your future on this particular visa.

MONEY

Because so many visitors come from Hong Kong on day trips, the Hong Kong dollar can be used interchangeably with the local currency, the Yuan. Therefore, you need not change your Hong Kong dollars into Yuan. But prices are slightly higher when you pay in Hong Kong dollars.

VISITING THE THREE SITES

OCT Shenzhen is China's finest window for the outside world. It's organized to educate and entertain those who have little time to visit all of China. Essentially a resort community modeled in part on Disney World, OCT Shenzhen is developed around three outdoor theme parks that offer hundreds of interesting attractions and lots of shops, restaurants, and entertainment. Approximately 20,000 people visit the three parks each day. During holidays the number can swell to 100,000. Heavily promoted amongst Overseas Chinese, the majority of visitors come from Hong Kong, Macao, and Taiwan. At present only a few visitors come from Europe and North America, although the numbers are increasing as more and more people from these regions learn about the treasures and pleasures of OCT Shenzhen.

Since each of the three theme parts are located adjacent to one another, they are easily accessible. Each has a separate admission fee which for foreigners is a little more than twice the fee for locals. Each theme park will take two to five hours to complete, depending on how fast you move. If you plan to visit all three theme parks, which really is not necessary, plan two full days of park touring. Our recommendation is to visit the first two parks: Splendid China and Folk Culture Villages. The third park, Window of the World, primarily appeals to locals or to Overseas Chinese who have little travel experience in Europe and North America.

SPLENDID CHINA

This park provides a wonderful overview of China's famous historical monuments, scenic spots, and major tourist attractions. Built in miniature on a 1:15 scale, it includes everything from the Great Wall and terracotta warriors of Xi'an to Beijing's Forbidden City and the Potala Palace in Lhasa. It even includes a miniature of the Three Gorges of the Yangtze River. If you don't have time to visit these sites in China, this is the closest you'll get to the real thing. And if you have visited many of these representative sites, you'll probably enjoy the miniatures which are done in remarkable detail. Chances are many of the miniatures will spark your interest in visiting the real sites in the future.

CHINA FOLK CULTURE VILLAGE

Located next door to Splendid China, this is China's major cultural park that emphasizes the important role of minorities. It demonstrates the country's unique folk arts, culture, and architecture. Altogether, the government recognizes 56 nationalities. This theme park showcases 21 minorities in 24 model village settings. Each village puts on regularly scheduled cultural performances (folk dances, music, singing, and even a popular knife pole climbing) throughout the day. Many also include demonstrations of arts and crafts as well as have small shops selling their products (one of the best is in the large mosque) and food. This theme park also has its own commercial street with 30 arts and crafts shops offering silk embroidery, sugar paintings, pottery, and carvings as well as food stalls. Look for Huizhou Street, Tian Yi Ge, Food Street, and Seaside Street for shopping and food. But the highlights of this theme park are the two spectacular cultural performances held in the evening (see Entertainment section) as well as the main restaurant where you may want to dine before the 7:30pm cultural performance which is held in the auditorium. This is the favorite theme park for many visitors.

WINDOW TO THE WORLD

This theme park is designed to showcase major historical sites, scenic spots, and various arts and cultures around the world. It's divided into nine areas: the World Square; Asian, Oceania, European, Africa, and American Quarters; Recreation Centre of Modern Science and Technology; World Sculptures Gallery; and the International Street. Altogether, it includes 118 scenic spots, including a model of the Eiffel Tower. An evening "Night Carnival" consists of colorful national dances and folk festivals around the world.

ACCOMMODATIONS

Many people commute to Shenzhen from hotels in Hong Kong or Guangzhou. However, a day trip may mean you'll miss out on the two fabulous cultural performances (Shenzhen Splendid Ethnic Costume Show Troupe and the China Folk Culture Carnival Parade) at the China Folk Culture Village which start at 7:30pm and 8:30pm respectively. It's worth staying overnight just to see these performances.

If you plan to stay over in Shenzhen, you'll find several business hotels in the city of Shenzhen (Shangri-la Hotel being the best) and a few hotels in OCT Shenzhen. If your major purpose in coming here is to visit the theme parks, then you should stay at one of the conveniently located hotels at OCT Shenzhen. The most conveniently located hotel is the four-star **Shenzhen Bay Hotel**. It's located right on the water next to the three theme parks. Across the street is the **Sea View Hotel**.

RESTAURANTS

There's not much to recommend for restaurants in OCT Shenzhen. You'll find lots of places to eat in the various theme parks as well as in the hotels. However, you should try the main restaurant on the grounds of the China Folk Culture Village park. Serving very unique and historic food from all over China, this popular restaurant is a great place to dine just before attending the two evening cultural shows on the grounds of this park. Since the first show starts at 7:30pm (Shenzhen Splendid China Ethnic Costume Show Troupe), you may want to begin dining around 5:30pm or 6:00pm.

ENTERTAINMENT

OCT Shenzhen offers two evening cultural performances that are "must see" events in Shenzhen as well as China. They are spectacular, rivaling some of the best that Disney World and Las Vegas have to offer. Since both are scheduled back-to-back at the Splendid China theme park, be sure to get tickets to both events. Since the final performance is not over until 10pm, you probably will want to stay over in Shenzhen rather than commute to Hong Kong or Guangzhou.

❑ **Shenzhen Splendid China Ethnic Costume Show Troupe:** Performing since 1992, 30 female performers from such ethnic groups as Han, Mongol, Tibetan, Hi, Bai, Tujia, and Uygal put on a spectacular performance (singing and dancing) in the air-conditioned Central Theater. While most of this Las Vegas-style show is a dramatic presentation, this hour-long extravaganza is very professionally produced. The models could hold their own on any catwalk in the world; the costumes are breathtaking and overall presentation is first-class. Starts at 7:30pm and lasts one hour.

❑ **China Folk Culture Carnival Parade:** Held outdoors and involving nearly 500 performers, this combination folklorical and carnival is an impressive show involving lots of action, lights, flash, and noise. A visual feast that may leave you exhausted at the end of the evening. While not as professional and classy as the 7:30pm ethnic costume show, it nonetheless is one of the most spectacular nonstop shows of its kind. Begins at 8:30pm and lasts about one hour.

ADDITIONAL PLEASURES

As Shenzhen develops as a major resort destination, it also offers several additional things to see and do. Its many tourist attractions continue to expand. Among these include:

❑ **Sea World Entertainment Center:** Housed in the retired French ocean liner Ming Hua and anchored in Shekou, this maritime entertainment center includes nine floors with 120 suites and several restaurants serving Chinese and French dishes. Also includes a pub, dance hall, shopping arcade, and the China Folk Culture Exhibition Center.

❑ **Golf Courses:** Shenzhen has two 18-hole golf courses, the Shenzhen Golf Club and the Bao Ri Golf Tourist Limited Company.

❑ **Safari Park:** This 120 hectare park on the banks of Xili Lake houses 3,000 animals of 150 species from around the world.

❑ **Honey Lake Country Club:** A relatively large resort, it consists of seven hotel blocks and an amusement park offering more than 70 rides.

HONG KONG AND GREATER CHINA IN YOUR FUTURE

Once you're in Shenzhen or Guangzhou, Hong Kong is just an hour or two away. Now part of China, but with special economic and administrative status, Hong Kong retains its reputation as one of the world's greatest shopping centers as well as one of its most expensive cities. Boasting fabulous hotels, restaurants, entertainment, and sightseeing opportunities—unlike any you will encounter in Greater China—high-rise, beautifully harbored, and fast-paced Hong Kong is an in-your-face city. It's simply electric. If you've never been to Hong Kong before, you'll be amazed at this place. If you're returning after a lengthy absence, you'll be fascinated by the many changes. But one thing has not changed about Hong Kong—it's all about money, making it, spending it, and making more. Best of all, its many treasures and pleasures are conveniently located within close proximity to one another given the relatively compact nature of this city.

If you're interested in pursuing the treasures and pleasures of Hong Kong, see our companion volume, *The Treasures and Pleasures of Hong Kong: Best of the Best*. While this is unquestionably an expensive city, it's also one of the most thrilling places to visit. For in visiting Hong Kong, you will complete the circle that encompasses both the old and new China. As Hong

Kong increasingly becomes a part of Greater China in the years ahead, we expect the many places we visited in China to become more like Hong Kong than vise versa. China's 21st century should prove to be much more than *"socialism with Chinese characteristics."* If Hong Kong has anything to say about it—and it most certainly will—the New China in the coming decade will most likely be *"capitalism with a Chinese face"* and it will probably be a Hong Kong variety of capitalism with closer connections to Los Angeles, New York City, and Washington, DC than to Tokyo, Paris, or London. China will most likely become the economic giant it envisions being. Best of all for travelers, China will continue to offer some fabulous treasures and pleasures but within a more convenient setting. In this new decade, tourism should truly come of age in China. Not surprising, you'll probably want to return to see an even newer China that offers the best of the best in travel treasures and pleasures. In the meantime, don't forget to visit Hong Kong.

Index

BEIJING

CHONGQING &
YANGTZE RIVER

GUANGZHOU

SHANGHAI

SHENZHEN AND HONG KONG

XI'AN

The Authors

W inston Churchill put it best—*"My needs are very simple—I simply want the best of everything."* Indeed, his attitude on life is well and alive amongst many of today's sophisticated travelers. With limited time and careful budgeting, many travelers seek both quality and value as they search for the best of the best.

Ron and Caryl Krannich, Ph.Ds, discovered this fact of travel life 15 years ago when they were living and working in Thailand as consultants with the Office of Prime Minister. Former university professors and specialists on Southeast Asia, they discovered what they really loved to do—shop for quality arts, antiques, and home decorative items—was not well represented in most travel guides that primarily focused on sightseeing, hotels, and restaurants. While some travel guides included a small section on shopping, they only listed types of products and names and addresses of shops, many of which were of questionable quality. And budget guides simply avoided quality shopping altogether.

The Krannichs knew there was much more to travel than what was represented in most travel guides. Avid collectors of Thai, Burmese, Indonesian, and South Pacific arts, antiques, and home decorative items, the Krannichs learned long ago that one of the best ways to experience another culture and meet its talented artists and craftspeople was by shopping for local products. Not only would they learn a great deal about the culture and society, they also acquired some wonderful products, met many interesting and talented individuals, and helped support local arts and crafts.

But they quickly learned shopping in Asia was very different from shopping in North America and Europe. In the West, merchants nicely display items, identify prices, and periodically run sales. At the same time, shoppers in the West can easily do comparative shopping, watch for sales, and trust quality and delivery; they even have consumer protection! Americans and Europeans in Asia face a shopping culture based on different principles. Like a fish out of water, they make many mistakes: don't know how to bargain, fail to communicate effectively with tailors, avoid purchasing large items because they don't understand shipping, and are frequent victims of scams and rip-offs. To shop a country right, travelers need to know how to find quality products, bargain for the best prices, avoid scams, and ship their purchases with ease. What they most need is a combination travel and how-to book that focuses on the best of the best.

In 1987 the Krannichs inaugurated their first shopping guide to Asia—*Shopping in Exotic Places*—which covered Hong Kong, South Korea, Thailand, Indonesia, and Singapore. Receiving rave reviews from leading travel publications and professionals, the book quickly found an enthusiastic audience amongst other avid travelers and shoppers. It broke new ground as a combination travel and how-to book. No longer would shopping be confined to just naming products and identifying names and addresses of shops. It also included advice on how to pack for a shopping trip (take two suitcases, one filled with bubble-wrap), comparative shopping, bargaining skills, and communicating with tailors. Shopping was serious stuff requiring serious treatment of the subject by individuals who understood what they were doing. The Krannichs subsequently expanded the series to include separate volumes on Hong Kong, Thailand, Indonesia, Singapore and Malaysia, Australia and Papua New Guinea, the South Pacific, and the Caribbean.

Beginning in 1996, the series took on a new look as well as an expanded focus. Known as the Impact Guides and appropriately titled *The Treasures and Pleasures . . . Best of the Best*, new editions covered Hong Kong, Thailand, Indonesia, Singapore, Malaysia, Paris and the French Riviera, and the Caribbean. In 1997 and 1998 new volumes appeared on Italy, Australia, China, and India. While the primary focus remains shopping for quality products, the books also include useful information on the best hotels, restaurants, and sightseeing. As the authors note, *"Our readers are discerning travelers who seek the best of the best. They are looking for a very special travel experience which is not well represented in other travel guides."*

The Krannichs passion for traveling and shopping is well represented in their home which is uniquely designed around their Asian and South Pacific art collections. *"We're fortunate in being able to create a living environment which pulls together so many wonderful travel memories and quality products,"* say the Krannichs. *"We learned long ago to seek out quality products and buy the best we could afford at the time. Quality lasts and is appreciated for years to come. Many of our readers share our passion for quality shopping abroad."* Their books also are popular with designers, antique dealers, and importers who use them for sourcing products and suppliers.

While the Impact Guides keep the Krannichs busy traveling to exotic places, their travel series is an avocation rather than a vocation. The Krannichs also are noted authors of more than 30 career books, some of which deal with how to find international and travel jobs. The Krannichs also operate one of the world's largest career resource centers. Their works are available in most bookstores or through the publisher's online bookstore: *www.impactpublications.com*

If you have any questions or comments for the authors, please direct them to the publisher:

Drs. Ron and Caryl Krannich
IMPACT PUBLICATIONS
9104-N Manassas Drive
Manassas Park, VA 20111-5211
Fax 703-335-9486
E-mail: *krannich@impactpublications.com*

More Treasures
and Pleasures

The following "Impact Guides" can be ordered directly from the publisher. Complete the following form (or list the titles), include your name and address, enclose payment, and send your order to:

IMPACT PUBLICATIONS
9104-N Manassas Drive
Manassas Park, VA 20111-5211 (USA)
Tel. 703/361-7300 or Fax 703/335-9486
E-mail: *china@impactpublications.com*

All prices are in U.S. dollars. Orders from individuals should be prepaid by check, moneyorder, or Visa, MasterCard, or American Express number. If your order must be shipped outside the U.S., please include an additional US$1.50 per title for surface mail or the appropriate air mail rate for books weighting 24 ounces each. We accept telephone orders (credit cards). Orders are shipped within 48 hours. For information on the authors and on our travel resources, visit our site on the Internet's World Wide Web: *www.impactpublications.com*

Qty.	TITLES	Price	TOTAL
__	Treasures and Pleasures of Australia	$15.95	_____
__	Treasures and Pleasures of the Caribbean	$16.95	_____
__	Treasures and Pleasures of China	$14.95	_____
__	Treasures and Pleasures of Hong Kong	$14.95	_____
__	Treasures and Pleasures of India	$14.95	_____

___ Treasures and Pleasures of Indonesia $14.95 _____
___ Treasures and Pleasures of Italy $14.95 _____
___ Treasures and Pleasures of Paris
    and the French Riviera $14.95 _____
___ Treasures and Pleasures of Singapore
    and Malaysia $14.95 _____
___ Treasures and Pleasures of Thailand $14.95 _____

               SUBTOTAL ------------- $ _____

- Virginia residents add 4.5% sales tax $ _____

- Shipping/handling ($5.00 for the first
  title and $1.50 for each additional book) $ _____

- Additional amount if shipping outside U.S. $ _____

         TOTAL ENCLOSED ---------- $ _____

SHIP TO:

Name _____

Address _____

_____

_____

PAYMENT METHOD:

❏ I enclose check/moneyorder for $ _____
   made payable to IMPACT PUBLICATIONS.

❏ Please charge $ _____ to my credit card:

❏ Visa ❏ MasterCard ❏ American Express ❏ Discover

Card # _____

Expiration date: _____/_____

Signature _____